LUCID WAKING

LUCID WAKING

MINDFULNESS AND THE SPIRITUAL POTENTIAL OF HUMANITY

GEORG FEUERSTEIN

Inner Traditions International
Rochester, Vermont

Inner Traditions International
One Park Street
Rochester, Vermont 05767
www.gotoit.com

Library of Congress Cataloging-in-Publication Data
Feuerstein, Georg.
    Lucid waking : mindfulness and the spiritual potential of humanity /
Georg Feuerstein.
        p.   cm.
    Includes bibliographical references and index.
    ISBN 0-89281-613-9 (alk. paper)
    1. Life.   2. Conduct of life.   I. Title.
    BD435.F48 1997   97-7875
    291.4'4—dc21   CIP

Printed and bound in the United States

10 9 8 7 6 5 4 3 2 1

Type design and layout by Peri Champine
This book was typeset in Life Roman

Distributed to the book trade in Canada by Publishers Group West
(PGW), Toronto, Ontario

Distributed to the book trade in the United Kingdom by Deep Books,
London

Distributed to the book trade in Australia by Millennium Books,
Newtown, N. S. W.

Distributed to the book trade in New Zealand by Tandem Press,
Auckland

Distributed to the book trade in South Africa by Alternative Books,
Ferndale

In Memory of Willis Harman (1917–1997), whose mind probed the possibilities of the future and whose heart embraced everyone in the now.

For all fellow travelers
on the path of lucid waking

Structures of Consciousness
Holy Madness
Sacred Paths
Wholeness or Transcendence?
The Philosophy of Classical Yoga
The Yoga-Sūtra of Patañjali
Introduction to the Bhagavad-Gita
Living Yoga (with Stephan Bodian)
Shambhala Encyclopedia of Yoga
Shambhala Guide to Yoga
Sacred Sexuality
Spirituality by the Numbers
In Search of the Cradle of Civilization
    (with Subhash Kak and David Frawley)

CONTENTS

AND YET . . .

We have built bridges across rivers and nations,
leveled unwholesome differences as well as cities,
eased the pain of millions and caused
unspeakable suffering to many more.

We have reached beyond the void separating
our planet from other planets,
our star from the next,
our galaxy from the rim of the universe,
but seldom have we filled the void
that yawns in our own hearts.

We have traveled in our thoughts
beyond the confines of the body,
even beyond the mind itself,
and yet have largely failed to visit
our neighbor in need of compassion.

We have created masterpieces of literature
and art of exceeding beauty,
but in sculpting our own destiny
have shown neither aesthetic judgment
nor much wisdom.

We have spread our seed liberally
over the entire surface of our planet
and are poised to spill out into space;
yet we do not recognize the barrenness
that saps our strength,
eroding our noblest ideals
and loftiest aspirations.

We hail ourselves as the greatest species
ever to spring from the cauldron of evolution,
claiming dominion over all other forms of life,
while we refuse to hear the plaintive song
of the legions of fellow creatures
who share land, air, and water with us.

We are unchallenged masters
at hurling our senses outward,
at grasping, holding, incorporating;
yet we lack mastery over ourselves.

And yet and yet,
concealed in us is a sublime depth
we sense only dimly
but, when revealed, raises us
to undreamt heights
beyond all petty notions
of who we are.

That depth is our unblemished future.

There are some who are awake even while asleep, and then there are those who, apparently awake, are deeply asleep.

Lalla

PREFACE

"Life's but a walking shadow," wrote the immortal bard in *Macbeth*, "a poor player/That struts and frets his hour upon the stage/And then is heard no more: it is a tale/Told by an idiot, full of sound and fury,/Signifying nothing." The Spanish dramatist Calderón, who composed his comedy *La Vida es Sueño* nineteen years after Shakespeare's death, called life a dream. Two hundred years later, the American poet Henry Wadsworth Longfellow qualified this further when he spoke of life as an "empty dream." Whether the dream of life is empty or not, we seem to be very much caught up in it. We move around in the waking state like shadow figures—not quite awake and yet not completely asleep.

Ever since the late 1960s, through the efforts of dream researchers like Patricia Garfield, Celia Green, Ann Faraday, and especially Stephen LaBerge, we have been hearing a great deal about lucid dreaming.[1] This is the ability to be consciously aware in the dream state, thereby allowing us to control and direct it creatively. Lucid dreaming is actually one of the arcane arts of antiquity, and, as is the case with many other modern discoveries, we are merely rediscovering knowledge that has been lost for a time. Many, if not most, of us have knowingly or unknowingly experienced lucid dreaming. However, as a systematic discipline it remains the province of a minuscule minority of Western enthusiasts and Eastern spiritual adepts.

The fact is that almost all of us still find it difficult to be fully aware in the waking state, never mind the sleeping state. Most of us sleepwalk through life. As psychologist Charles Tart observed:

> Each of us is in a profound trance, consensus consciousness, a
> state of partly suspended animation, of stupor, of inability to
> function at our maximum level. Automatized and conditioned
> patterns of perception, thinking, feeling, and behaving domi-
> nate our lives. For too much of life, we are like the evolved
> crane/sorter: we appear to be intelligent and conscious, but it
> is all automatized programs. Many of these automatized and
> conditioned patterns may have been adaptive once upon a time,
> but they don't work well anymore: indeed, they may destroy us.
> We live in and contribute to mass insanity.[2]

Waking up from the dream that we call the waking state is the
goal of all the great spiritual traditions of the world. Thus, the spiritual title *buddha* literally means someone who is "awake," who has
awakened from what Tart calls the "consensus trance" of ordinary
life. Such spiritual awakening is traditionally known as enlightenment or illumination. It is the condition of suprawakeful awareness
that is continuous throughout all states of consciousness—waking,
dreaming, and even deep sleep.

Enlightenment begins with lucid waking, or intensified atten-
tiveness or mindfulness in the waking state—a quality that still continues to elude most of us. It calls for a deliberate act of will, a
metanoia, by which we consciously relate to life in a new way. This
is universally experienced as a most difficult challenge. And yet,
clearly, if even a single individual has awakened from the dream of
life—and this is what all major spiritual traditions emphatically
affirm—then such waking is possible for our species as a whole. For
if one person can wake up, we all can!

However active and apparently fulfilling our lives may be, as
long as we are caught up in the dream of waking life, we merely
passively endure our destiny. In contrast, to put it somewhat dra-
matically, even if we never moved a muscle but were in full possession of conscious awareness, we would be masters of our destiny.
For destiny rules where there is unconsciousness or semiconscious-
ness. Freedom, on the other hand, is the fruit of undiminished,

pristine awareness. The cultivation or recovery of such awareness is the ultimate purpose of the philosophical life—the thoughtful life of spiritual self-transformation. And therein lies the great promise of humankind.

Some would have us believe that the world is utterly doomed. No doubt they have their reasons for thinking so, and there are indeed many telltale signs of impending planetwide disaster—not the least of which include overpopulation; increasing pollution of land, air, and water; exhaustion of earth's natural resources; and virulent epidemics. However, the unjaundiced eye also perceives many hopeful signs, notably the growing awareness and accompanying sense of urgency that we are heading toward collapse and must learn to cooperate globally to prevent it. While I do not believe that we have seen the worst yet, I also have a deep conviction that we will not only survive the crisis looming ahead of us but emerge wiser and stronger as a result. This view is also shared by most of the 145 contributors to *Voices on the Threshold of Tomorrow,* edited by my wife, Trisha Lamb Feuerstein, and me.

Lucid Waking: Mindfulness and the Spiritual Potential of Humanity is a statement of my unshakable faith in the great potential and future of the human species. It consists of seventeen essays, all of which in some way give witness to the enduring vitality of humankind and to the ever-present possibility within each of us to meet the challenges of existence sanely, creatively, courageously— that is, *philosophically:* wide awake and mindful of our ever-present spiritual nature.

The opening chapter, "In Praise of the Philosophical Life," is my vote for the necessity and beauty of philosophy—in the sense not of arid academic theorizing but of life-giving love of wisdom. Without such philosophy, or passionate reason and spiritual lucidity applied to the business of living, we are undeserving of the self-bestowed title of *Homo sapiens.* The unexamined life, observed the wise Socrates, is not worth living—at least not for human beings, who have a potential far exceeding that of a rock, maple tree, cockroach, or even chimpanzee. Our nervous system is designed for a responsiveness to life that is, at least as far as we presently know, quite unparalleled in nature (on earth). It is the task of philosophy to give meaningful direction to that responsiveness. Philosophy, as understood here, is the theory and practice of lucid waking.

Chapter 2, "The Seminal Question: Who Am I?" goes straight to the heart of the philosophical life: the nature of our humanness. We all have our own answer to the question "Who am I?" Even if we cannot or do not choose to articulate our answer in words, we nevertheless express it indirectly through our behavior. Asking questions is an integral part of being human; finding valid answers to the most important of them is essential to our survival as a species and to our growth as individuals.

Chapter 3, "The Challenge of Embodiment," is based on the premise that for philosophy to be viable it must take the human body fully into account. Academic philosophizing all too frequently ignores the fact that we are flesh-and-blood beings, not merely rational computers. We breathe and feel, and most of our intentional life revolves around our embodiment. If we acknowledge this properly, we will not fall into the metaphysical error of extreme gnosticism, which looks upon the body as little more than the grave of the soul. Moreover, far from being an obstacle to our ultimate awakening, or enlightenment, the body is the only solid ground from which we can hope to fulfill our highest destiny. In fact, enlightenment is the enlightenment of the whole body: the body that is not confined to one particular cellular organism but includes all forms.

But what is the soul that psychology denies and the spiritual traditions extol? This question is pondered from a historical perspective in Chapter 4, "The Changing Fortunes of the Soul." In particular, I show how, after an all-too-protracted interlude of soul-destroying scientific materialism, we are returning to a deeper self-understanding, which includes the notion of the soul. As our quest for more satisfying answers to the Big Questions becomes more penetrating and unencumbered by conventional ideologies, we find that the classic spiritual traditions and their metaphysical cornucopia are not as remote and implausible as they once seemed. The language of soul is keenly pertinent in the context of lucid waking because it addresses realities that our science-worshiping Western culture has long tended to ignore.

Chapter 5, "Who or What Is the Spirit?" offers a historical overview of the traditional concept of Spirit, which, like the concept of soul, has made a comeback outside the confines of traditional religiosity. But often a fog of misconception hangs around it, blocking our approach to the Spirit as an actuality. The Spirit—or Self or consciousness—is the fulcrum of philosophical inquiry. How we relate to it, or avoid relating to it, defines the remainder of our cosmology and our attitude toward life. This is basically a matter of our imagination, the mind's most potent force for determining our future in decisive ways. Like the language of soul, the language of Spirit offers a useful conceptual platform for considering the actualities of lucid waking.

Chapter 6, "The Power of Imagination," examines the psychological capacity that underlies the wide spectrum of human creativity and, in fact, looms large in the background of our entire civilizational enterprise. Imagination was celebrated prior to the rise of scientific materialism, which demeaned it to the status of unproductive and even dangerous fancy. However, after the collapse of behaviorism and with the gradual reemergence of the idea of consciousness beyond the twitchings of the human nervous system, the concept of imagination made a comeback in both intellectual and popular circles. It is invoked in the arts, the healing arts, and even the hard sciences. Einstein epitomized this change of attitude when he wrote "Imagination is more important than knowledge." Richard Tarnas wrote:

> It is only when the human mind actively brings forth from within itself the full powers of a disciplined imagination and saturates its empirical observation with archetypal insight that the deeper reality of the world emerges.[3]

Lucid waking, in a sense, is the application of disciplined imagination to our daily life. Depending on our imagination, we either enhance or diminish our lucidity or wakefulness and thus either enhance or diminish ourselves.[4]

Chapter 7, "Right View," continues the consideration of the preceding chapter by bringing the focus firmly back to the individual.

It deals with the important question of the life-shaping impact of our vision of life, affirming the need for personal spiritual and philosophical practice with its inevitable moral consequences.

In Chapter 8, "Intuition: The Other Way of Knowing," I ask how, in practical terms, we can catch up with the new understanding that is emerging in our Western culture and recover our spiritual authenticity. Here I examine the hidden means of knowledge, intuition, by which we come to understand not only life but also the spiritual dimension in ways more direct and instantaneous than rational knowledge.

Chapter 9, "Creativity: Self-Actualization and Transcendence," considers the godlike power of creativity and how in the exercise of our creative impulses we can transcend the limiting gravitational pull of our ego-personality and gain happiness and freedom.

This consideration leads straight into the subject of Chapter 10, "Higher Consciousness." This often-used phrase has a variety of connotations; here I try to disentangle them and provide a sensible accounting of the nature of higher consciousness.

Chapter 11, "The Art of Self-Understanding and Self-Transformation," looks at the three fundamental phrases of the philosophical life, or a life lived with the dignity of *Homo sapiens sapiens:* the doubly wise human. All life is change, but voluntary, conscious change presumes a certain measure of self-knowledge or self-understanding. Once we have grasped something about what makes us tick, about both our sunny and our dark sides, we can go on to make the changes we feel are necessary to develop our innate potential more fully—in other words, to become whole. This inevitably involves going beyond our psychological status quo. That is, we must cultivate the art of self-transcendence, which is another way of saying we must engage spiritual life. The sweet fruit of the exacting discipline of self-observation, self-understanding, self-transcendence (to the point of ultimate spiritual enlightenment), and never-ending self-transformation is our presence in the world as benign agents of illumination, leading all other beings to their own realization of happiness and freedom.

Chapter 12, "The Shadow of Enlightenment," shows how our human complexity manifests itself even at the highest levels of spiritual attainment. Where there is light, there is shadow. While we can elevate ourselves above the obscurity of egocentric life, we cannot entirely escape the limitations inherent in physical existence. So long as there is a physical body, there is also a certain personality, marking us as imperfect. Without it, life would be entirely drab, but its persistence after enlightenment is a fact to be reckoned with by those who are prone to turn enlightened beings into paragons of perfection. Even enlightenment must be scrutinized by the mature philosophical mind, enriched by first-hand experience of the spiritual dimension of existence.

Chapter 13, "Freedom, Destiny, and the Quantum Reality" looks at the wondrous interplay between body and Spirit and how we are essentially free even in the midst of all the constraints of physical embodiment. For the enlightened being, personality is as little destiny as is biology. Or, more precisely, personality is not ultimately decisive but a mere sport of nature, which is moment by moment transcended in enlightenment. This opening (Martin Heidegger's "clearing in the forest"), realized fully in the state of enlightenment, is always with us. Freedom is our essential condition. This fundamental truth is unexpectedly reflected in the uncertainty principle of quantum theory. The philosophical implications of quantum theory are vast, and many thinkers, both inside and outside of physics, have marveled at the parallels existing between quantum theory and Eastern metaphysical thought. In particular, the fundamental quantum-theoretical notion of the interconnectedness of all things has been seen as a confirmation of age-old ideas about the universe as a holon: a comprehensive organic whole.

In Chapter 14, "The Quest for Wholeness," I reflect on the current preoccupation with wholeness and our tendency to make an ideology out of it rather than use the idea of wholeness as a guide to actual moral and spiritual transformation. Thus, despite all the attention on wholeness, we as individuals and as a social collective have so far remained fragmented. Yet, simultaneously, there is a detectable evolutionary thrust toward an integrative type of consciousness.

In Chapter 15, "The New Age: Regression or Possibility?," I put to the test the notion of a New Age, which some proclaim as expressing the emergent consciousness and others debunk as mere pop ideology founded on no more than wishful thinking and mass hysteria. In this connection, I also look at the power of imagination when focused on the threshold of 2000 A.D. Chronologically, the year 2000 is a comparatively arbitrary marker; yet, psychologically and therefore also sociologically, it is acquiring increasing significance—possibly even a significance that will prove decisive for the future of our species. I have coined the phrase "millennium effect" to describe this curious phenomenon.

The emergent consciousness is the subject of Chapter 16, "Toward Integral Consciousness." Here I introduce a broader historical framework for the philosophical consideration of human nature, basing my consideration on the epochal work of the Swiss cultural philosopher and poet Jean Gebser. His account of the evolution of human consciousness in four distinct mutations—from the archaic to the magic, mythic, and mental-rational consciousness—is one of the most helpful models for understanding the growth not only of human culture but of human individuals as well. Long before the New Age movement, Gebser, who conceived his life's work in the early 1930s, pointed out promising signs of a newly crystallizing consciousness modality, which he called the "arational-aperspectival-integral consciousness." How must we understand this new consciousness in regard to the perennial task of actualizing the Spirit?

The concluding chapter, "Remembering the Future," is intended as a reminder that while the past pushes us from behind, the future pulls us from ahead. Our potential is so great because, paradoxically, at the deepest or highest level of our being we have never left the destination toward which we picture ourselves traveling. The detour of our personal and collective history is of course never wasted because it brings us, in increments and seldom in a linear fashion, to the gradual realization of this fundamental fact. The challenge is always to live more and more out of the certainty, or faith, that our destination is an inalienable part of ourselves, regardless of the length or difficulty of our journey. We must not sink romantic taproots into the past or lose ourselves in the frenzy of the present moment, nor yet idealistically project ourselves ahead into a future that is still unfurling itself. All three attitudes are basically failures. The needful art is to keep step with the present, fully aware that we are both expressing and continuously remaking the past, as well as allowing the future to manifest. Thus we will fulfill the promise of *Homo sapiens sapiens*, the being endowed with superlative wisdom.

The greatest challenge arising from our immense potential as a species is the embodiment of the Spirit. This is not only a lifelong task for each individual but an enduring obligation for humankind collectively. There may never be a golden age on earth, but we must constantly strive for its creation *within our own psyche*. In this way we not only give extraordinary meaning to our ordinary individual existence but also ennoble our species and contribute to the upliftment of all life on this planet.

Ja! Diesem Sinne bin ich ganz ergeben, .
Das ist der Weisheit letzter Schluss:
Nur der verdient sich Freiheit wie das Leben,
Das täglich sie erobern muss.[5]

Yes! I utterly subscribe to this conviction,
which is the pinnacle of wisdom:
Only he earns freedom and life
who conquers them each day anew.
                                                —Goethe

ACKNOWLEDGMENTS

I owe thanks to several friends and colleagues who have made room in their busy schedules for reading and commenting on various versions of the manuscript: Allan Combs, Richard Heinberg, Subhash Kak, John Nelson, and Ken Wilber. I have benefited from all their feedback and have incorporated as many of their suggestions as proved feasible—my heartfelt gratitude to each of them not only for their practical help but also for their generous moral support. I also thank my wife, Trisha, for going over the manuscript with her customary thoroughness. She has a detective's fine-honed sense for locating missing characters and questionable elements. I am grateful to the acquisitions editor, Jon Graham, for seeing the promise of this work, to my publisher, Ehud Sperling, for adopting it into his program, and to Rowan Jacobsen for managing the whole project so expertly and making several valuable editorial suggestions that helped improve the book.

1

IN PRAISE OF THE PHILOSOPHICAL LIFE

THE SOCRATIC LEGACY

My philosophical odyssey started when I was about fourteen years old and began to read the great German thinkers—Kant, Hegel, Leibniz, Schopenhauer, and Nietzsche. Everybody seemed to be in awe of Kant, and so I cut my philosophical teeth on his three critiques. I am not sure how much I really understood of Kant's work, but I remember being impressed enough to write an essay on the philosopher of Königsberg. I memorized his famous categorical imperative and can still recite it in mantralike fashion in the original German. It did not take me long to figure out that thoughtful people were apparently so awed by Kant because his abstract system proved largely incomprehensible to them. After the initial excitement of discovering a philosopher who seemingly had pushed reason to its upper limit and furnished neat definitions for everything worth defining, I realized that I did not feel at all sustained by Kant's explanations. They seemed disconnected from the world I lived in. Immersing myself into his world of ideas was like confining myself to the hygienic air of an oxygen tent—safely removed from life-threatening bacteria and viruses but also from the life-giving rays of the sun.

I experienced the same sense of disappointment with Hegel and Leibniz. Not so with Schopenhauer and Nietzsche, who embodied a different, more vital quality of philosophizing. However, I found Nietzsche somewhat too wild and exaggerated, though felt perfectly comfortable with Schopenhauer, who created for me an exciting link between Western philosophy and the Eastern wisdom traditions that I had just discovered.

I also delved into Plato and quickly recognized in Socrates a truly great human being and a rare philosophical and spiritual genius, though I couldn't help wondering which were the teachings of Socrates and which were Plato's. But before I could appreciate Socrates' philosophy more fully, I was magnetically drawn into the wonderland of Indian metaphysics and spirituality. Only many years later, after a long and enlivening voyage through Hinduism and Buddhism, did my interest in Socrates and other Greek philosophers return.

I have come to regard Socrates as the Greek counterpart to the Upanishadic sages of India and as the principal Western exemplar of the individual who pursues the philosophical life with vigor and unwavering commitment. It was he who, at his trial in 399 B.C., reminded his contemporaries that the unexamined life is not worth living. Charges of impiety and the corruption of young men had been brought against him, and his accusers, notably Meletos, called for the death penalty. To satisfy existing law, Socrates was asked to propose an alternative penalty. At the end of an eloquent speech that should have convinced everyone of his perfect innocence, he suggested, no doubt tongue in cheek, a nominal fine of one mina of silver, which translates into a hundred dollars or so. The 501 citizens composing the court voted for the death sentence. After hearing the judgment, Socrates again addressed the assembled court, accepting the sentence with perfect equanimity and even a sense of humor. Such was his moral fortitude and nobility of soul that he assured everyone he bore no anger toward either his accusers or his judges. He concluded his speech with the words: "And now it is time to go, I to die, and you to live; but which of us goes to a better thing is unknown to all but God."[1] We know from Plato that Socrates drank his cup of hemlock bravely, even consoling those of his friends who burst into tears at the philosopher's imminent demise.

The story of Socrates best illustrates the nature of philosophy and the philosophical life. As is well known, our English word *philosophy* stems from the Greek word *philosophia*, meaning "love of wisdom." Thus, philosophy in its original form was not mere critical analysis or intellectual speculation, but a matter of love, or *philia*. The ancient Greeks made a distinction between *philia, eros*, and *agape*. Much has been written about these three modes of loving, and I will refer the reader only to Alan Soble's fine anthology, which contains numerous bibliographic references for further study.[2]

Briefly, the word *eros* in the sense of "love" or "desire" made its first appearance in Homer's epics. But as a philosophical idea it goes straight back to the Platonic dialogues, notably the *Symposium*. Here it stands for the cosmic principle of attraction on all levels of existence. Specifically, Plato looked upon *eros* as the essential power that draws us to the supreme ideal of beauty, while he saw beauty as the bridge between the material realm and the perfect and eternal world of ideals. *Eros*, according to Plato, is always love of beauty, whether it is expressed as the sexual passion between lovers or as the pure desire for universal beauty.

The Greek word *agape* belongs to the early Christian tradition, and it originally denoted the utterly unselfish, eternally self-giving love of the Divine, the Creator-God, for creation, especially human beings. This connotation was extended to the pure love between men and women, mirroring the divine love. The early Christians attempted to make this pure, blessing love the bedrock of all other forms of affection, attraction, and desire.

For the Greeks, *philia* meant something like "fondness," "liking," or even "friendship." Aristotle, Plato's star pupil, devoted the eighth and ninth books of his famous *Nichomachean Ethics* to an exposition of the ideal of *philia*. "Perfect friendship," he wrote, "is the friendship of men who are good, and alike in virtue; for they wish each other well in the same way owing to their inherent goodness."[3] It is this *philia* kind of love that draws philosophers to the pursuit of wisdom *(sophia)*. In return, wisdom grants them a friendship that is infinitely rich, helping them to realize truth, goodness, and beauty.

Wisdom is truth in action, goodness in action, beauty in action, and not least love in action. It is a form of knowing that engenders truth, goodness, beauty, and love. Such knowing is never a matter of mere learning or even mere experience. It is a precious distillate of knowledge and experience created in the higher mind, which the ancient Greeks called *nous* and the Hindu philosophers named *buddhi.* The latter term stems from the Sanskrit verbal root *budh,* meaning "to be awake," which also underlies the word *buddha,* or "enlightened one," and *bodhi,* or "enlightenment." Wisdom, then, is lucid understanding, and as such is the single most important factor in a life dedicated to lucid waking.

The philosophical life is the steady application of wisdom to even the most banal events and tasks of everyday existence. Paul Brunton, whom I value as one of the few true sages of the twentieth century, had this to say:

> The basis of philosophic living is simply this: the higher self feels nothing but the good, the true, and the beautiful; we are its projections and are to become its reflections. Why then should we not, here and now, discipline ourselves until we also feel only the same?[4]

Brunton also wrote:

> Genuine philosophy is a living force actively at work in molding the character and modifying the destiny of its votaries.[5]

> The philosophic ideal is not merely an intellectual one, but also a mystical one, not merely practical, but also emotional. It develops harmonies and balances all these different qualities.[6]

The philosophical, spiritual, or lucid-wakeful life is not abstract but highly participatory. It is what the Polish-American philosopher Henryk Skolimowski calls the "yoga of participation," as opposed to the "yoga of objectivity" practiced by means of the so-called scientific method—a procedure artificially separating the observer from the observed.[7]

LUCID WAKING VERSUS PHARMOCOLOGICAL MYSTICISM

The philosophical life, which is the Socratic way of life, opens the doors of understanding. These doors are more important than the doors of perception, of which Aldous Huxley wrote in his small but explosive book of the same title. He was referring to the possibility, and need for, expanding our perceptual input in order to burst through the granite walls of our consensus reality. To break down his own doors of perception, he took mescaline and succeeded in deconstructing his familiar universe, at least temporarily, and was totally enamored of what he then perceived.

Sadly, he even belittled Plato, "poor fellow," for having been quite unable to experience the world around him with such vivid intensity. But, I believe, Huxley got it all wrong. He mistook a sensory experience, however magnificent, for the eternal formless reality that Plato called Being and that some seven centuries later the Buddhist teacher Nagarjuna called Voidness *(shunyata)*.

LSD apostles Timothy Leary and Richard Alpert (now Ram Dass, fully reformed), as well as Terence McKenna (who enthuses about dimethyltryptamine, or DMT, and ayahuasca) have committed the same error. McKenna in particular is today the single most vociferous advocate for pharmacological mysticism, in which he places great apocalyptic hope. In his book *The Archaic Revival*, he writes:

> Of all the techniques used by the shaman to induce ecstasy and visionary voyaging—fasting, prolonged drumming, breath control, and stressful ordeals—I now feel confident that the use of hallucinogenic plants is the most effective, dependable, and powerful.[8]

This is fine as far as it goes, but ecstasies and visions do not amount to understanding or wisdom. Fishing for support, McKenna makes the audacious and quite unsubstantiated claim in his book that in India "almost all sadhus, all yogis, are inveterate hash smokers and/or users of datura."[9] No question, there are ascetics and yogis who are fond of psychedelics of one kind or another, but they are typically uneducated and have very little in common with the high road of Yoga. It is true that even such a classic scripture as Patanjali's *Yoga-Sutra* lists herbs (*aushadhi,* herbal concoctions) as a means of attaining certain paranormal powers. But nowhere does this Sanskrit text state that higher realizations, never mind ultimate enlightenment, can be gained surreptitiously by means of consciousness-altering substances.[10] Indeed, scriptures like the *Yoga-Shikha-Upanishad* distinguish between artificial and nonartificial powers, emphasizing that only the latter, which arise naturally from one's persistent spiritual practice, are truly potent, enduring, and also acceptable to the Lord *(ishvara).*

In an attempt to explain his inability to win support for his lopsided worldview among his intellectual peers, McKenna significantly makes the following admission:

> Metaphorically, DMT is like an intellectual black hole in that once one knows about it, it is very hard for others to understand what one is talking about. One cannot be heard. The more one is able to articulate what it is, the less others are able to understand.[11]

With an admission such as this, McKenna's simultaneous claim that "the social consequence of the psychedelic experience is clear thinking"[12] leaves one wondering. While mystical states of consciousness, whether drug-induced or evoked through spiritual practices, certainly can expand one's cognitive horizon in a flash, they do not in themselves generate understanding. If they did, we would have a legion of sages braving today's rush-hour traffic, for the same men and women who, in the late 1960s and 1970s, were regularly high on LSD and other psychedelics are now (mostly) middle-aged upright or even uptight citizens. And judging from their own children, many of whom are simply adrift, these ex-hippies do not particularly demonstrate the power of wisdom in their lives.

Looking back on the hippie period, I marvel that I should have been left quite so unmoved by it. In fact, I never felt tempted to experiment with psychedelic drugs, though I was surrounded by fellow students who ingested every kind of mind-altering compound.

For the most part, they were too stoned to realize that I was not participating in their psychochemical ritualism. Or else they cultivated the fine art of "live and let live." I instinctively knew that no substance in this world could yield the one thing I was after: lucid understanding through real inner growth.

It was not until 1992 that, partly out of curiosity and partly to make a point to a drug-addicted friend, I took MDMA ("Ecstasy"). It took about twenty minutes for the effects of the drug to kick in. Right away I spontaneously moved into a witnessing stance. I was intrigued by the reactions in my nervous system, observing carefully the unfolding of the chemical's impact on my body-mind. Later I just sat back, relaxed, and enjoyed the considerable pleasure of the buzz. At one point, my hands grew cold and cramped, and then I suddenly felt violently nauseated. Throughout that experience, my friend was an unobtrusive guide, reassuring and assisting when necessary.

When I was able to communicate verbally with my friend again, I told him that I was clearly aware of the difference between true bliss, as I had come to experience it in meditation, and the happiness of the drug-induced state of mind. This shook him up noticeably. After a few more hours of watching me sit silently, my friend, who possibly had hoped for a more outward demonstration of the drug's effect, got bored and retired. I slipped in and out of the meditative state all night long and found myself utterly exhausted the next morning.

By the afternoon my energies had picked up again, though I was still periodically drawn into deep mental absorption. That night, when the drug still had not worn off and I could not sleep, I started to experiment a bit with my internal environment and got myself into a paranoid state and—by applying every shred of clarity I could muster—out of it.

I had taken a fairly hefty dose of the drug, and my nervous system, primed by years of meditation and drug-free existence (I hardly ever take even an aspirin), reacted correspondingly. Many of the effects on me were so exaggerated that they resembled those of LSD, and at one time I even suspected that my friend had played a trick on me—which was, however, not the case. I continued to have

perceptual hallucinations for a couple of weeks, which I found partly entertaining and partly annoying. But the drug proved a dry well
as far as wisdom was concerned. Sure enough, it was a fascinating
experience, showing the close relationship between brain chemistry
and conditional consciousness, but it offered little more. Once the
novelty of sensory hallucinations wore off, I went about the business of understanding this experience.

Psychedelic drugs undoubtedly open the doors to the mind's
panopticon, but what we see in the mental mirrors are mere dis-
tortions of reality, not reality itself. Is the experience of a simu-
lacrum, a caricature of reality, worth the risk of possible damage to
the brain and nervous system, heart attack, psychosis, or addiction?
Every person must answer this question for him- or herself. Some
people seem to have been shaken out of their complacency by consciousness-altering drugs, but how many of them have since slipped
back into philistinism? Is it not true that few have been able to
wrest genuine life-transforming insights from their psychedelic
experience? Drugs are downright unphilosophical![13]

THE SUPREME VALUE OF WISDOM

Philosophy is not about experience, high or low, but about understanding, awareness, and lucidity. There are no shortcuts to reality
or to authentic existence, which must be won by the hard work of
personal actualization. An aspirin tablet can remove a headache, but
it cannot eliminate the cause behind the symptom. Psychedelic
drugs can remove the barricades in our mind and nervous system
that prevent us from experiencing all perceivable objects at once.
They can give us a transient feeling of happiness and can even throw
a prepared individual into a state of formless existence. But they
cannot permanently remove the cause of our psychological insularity and suffering. In traditional metaphysical terms, they are incapable of disabling, once and for all, the mechanism of self-contrac-
tion that is responsible for our self-experience as finite beings.
Pharmocological mysticism is not a substitute for spiritual discipline
and the gradual transmutation of our most deep-seated karmic patterns that stand in the way of enlightenment and genuine happiness.

By contrast, philosophy as understood here has the specific task of effecting such a transmutation and illumination of our being. Although everyone is in principle capable of the philosophical life, not everyone is ready to assume responsibility for it. Traditionally, philosophy has been reserved for the few, which is not an elitist point of view but a fact of life. Moreover, as the twelfth-century Jewish philosopher Maimonides explained in his *Guide for the Perplexed* (I:34), those who have a penchant for the philosophical life must first be tempered in the fire of ordinary life. Without emotional and intellectual maturity, the prized philosopher's stone escapes us. In other words, we must partake of a measure of wisdom before we can travel the high road of wisdom to full enlightenment. The discipline of life prepares us for the far more difficult, if sweet, discipline of philosophy.

The fruits of the philosophical life are manifold, and we begin to reap them the very moment we take the first step on the path of self-transcendence and self-transformation. As Paul Brunton remarked:

> One of the first fruits of philosophy is perhaps the balanced understanding which it yields. In no other way can men arrive at so truthful, so fair, and so just a view of life, or indeed of anything upon which they place their thinking mind. And this splendid result could not come about if the philosophic quest did not bring the whole man of thought and feeling, of intuition and will, into activity in a harmonious and well-integrated way.[14]

Wisdom inspires and empowers disciples of philosophy not only to reflect upon life with sagacious tranquility but also to behave thoughtfully, harmoniously, and compassionately. Harmony, expressed in the ancient Greek idea of the golden mean, is essential to the mature, philosophical life. In his book *The Conquest of Happiness*, philosopher-mathematician and Nobel laureate Bertrand Russell made these highly relevant remarks:

> The golden mean is an uninteresting doctrine, and I can remember when I was young rejecting it with scorn and indignation,

since in those days it was heroic extremes that I admired. Truth, however, is not always interesting, and many things are believed because they are interesting although, in fact, there is little other evidence in their favor. The golden mean is a case in point: it may be an uninteresting doctrine, but in a very great many matters it is a true one.[15]

Wisdom will not increase our IQ, but it will bring the power of integrity to our intelligence. As Brunton observed:

The acquirement of spiritual wisdom does not necessarily prevent the disciple from making worldly mistakes; but because it develops the qualities which will prevent them, and because it takes to heart the lessons of experience, humbly and receptively, it does reduce the frequency of those mistakes.[16]

Thus wisdom reshapes our life and transforms our character, slowly purifying us in the alchemical crucible of finite experience until, as the great German philosopher-mystic Meister Eckehart would say, we have become void of ourselves. As Helena Petrovna Blavatsky, the widely underappreciated founder of the Theosophical Society, observed in her magnum opus:

The true philosopher, the student of the Esoteric Wisdom, entirely loses sight of personalities, dogmatic beliefs and special religions.[17]

The idiom of self-voiding, or ego-transcendence, is another way of articulating the task of philosophy: to realize the void, the ultimate zero, which, paradoxically, is the Plenum. Philosophy is holistic, and it fulfills itself in the actualization of the Whole, the mighty transrational Reality outshining conditional existence. Philosophical understanding, or wisdom, is liberating gnosis. It helps us recover our true identity and cross the threshold from the finite to the Infinite, and then it helps us cross the same threshold back into the finite without loss of the Infinite. Lucid waking is the fully participatory life.

2

THE SEMINAL QUESTION: WHO AM I?

BIG QUESTIONS, BIG ANSWERS

What is the human being? Every culture and every age has its own answer or answers. The question has vast ramifications encompassing all of life and the entire spectrum of philosophical and religious reflection. For instance, "What is the human being?" implies "What are the basic constituents of the human being" (anatomy, physiology, biochemistry, physics), "Whence does humanity come?" (paleontology), "How has humanity progressed through the ages?" (history, archaeology), "Whither does humanity go?" (anthropology, futurology), "What is the relationship between the human being and the world?" (deep ecology), "How does the human being interact with others of its kind?" (sociology, economy), "What makes a human being tick?" (psychology), "What can go wrong with a human being?" (medicine, psychiatry, psychotherapy), "Are human beings capable of transcendence?" (metapsychology), "Is there a course of action appropriate for human beings?" (ethics), "Is there any meaning to existence?" (philosophy), "What is the relationship between the human being and the ultimate Reality?" (metaphysics), and so on.

Thus, "What is the human being?" is the key existential question, and how we answer it involves a more or less comprehensive or a more or less articulated anthropology, cosmology, or metaphysics. "A lopsided definition of man," notes Henryk Skolimowski, "leads to innumerable consequences, some of which—later—surprise us with their savage outcomes."[1]

Clearly, our human destiny is bound up with the destiny of the world we live in and with reality as a whole. As intelligent, meaning-seeking organisms, we straddle the material universe and, in our religious and spiritual aspirations, even seek to reach beyond the manifest cosmos.

In asking "What is the human being?" I do not mean to pose a merely abstract or, worse, rhetorical question. Rather, the question holds profound personal significance for all of us. It implies "Who am I?" or "Where do I stand in the midst of the complexity of human life and of life itself?" We endeavor to make sense of our existence, the world around us, and the transcendental "spaces" beyond us primarily to find answers that give meaning to our individual life. Only secondarily do we speculate on behalf of our species. In this sense, all the Big Questions are highly personal questions.

The search for meaning is endemic to our human species, as it is presumably characteristic of all intelligent life in this vast universe. Intelligence, in fact, can be defined as the capacity to ask questions. Rudyard Kipling wrote the following witty poem, which states this human quality well:

> I keep six honest serving-men
> (They taught me all I knew):
> Their names are What and Why and When
> And How and Where and Who.

Victor Frankl, the founder of logotherapy, rightly observed that while we are motivated to realize happiness, we ought not pursue it directly.[2] Rather, happiness manifests itself spontaneously when we find meaning in our life, in other words, when we have found our own answers to the Big Questions. Carl Gustav Jung emphasized that we cannot recover meaning and be truly healed unless we regain a deeply religious—that is, spiritual—outlook. Those who find themselves in an existential vacuum sooner or later develop physical illness, which is the outer manifestation of their inner "dis-ease."

But to pose questions means to look for answers, and our answers are almost as varied as the individuals in our numerous species. One of the labels pinned on humanity is that of *homo quaerens,* the questioning being. But we might as easily call ourselves *homo respondens,* the answering being, because we have little tolerance for unanswered questions and will restlessly seek for answers.

On her deathbed, Gertrude Stein asked, "What is the answer?" When no one in the room responded, she asked, "Then what is the question?" Let us recall here the famous ancient riddle of the Sphinx in Greek mythology to which only Oedipus gave the correct answer. The riddle was "What is it that has one voice and yet becomes four-footed, two-footed, and then three-footed?" The answer is the human being, who crawls on all fours as an infant, walks upright on two feet as an adult, and leans on a cane in old age. What the riddle of the Sphinx captures is the fact that we are a riddle to ourselves, yet have the solution within us.

As is well known, some of the most creative intellectual innovations have been the direct product of an unexpected, original question—a question that typically contains the hidden nucleus of a surprise answer. Thus, Charles Darwin was curious about the variations in certain plants and animals in South America and wondered about their origins. He pondered this subject for five years, all the while assiduously gathering information to fertilize his imagination. His ruminations led him to formulate the theory of natural selection.

Nearly a century later, in 1953, Francis Crick and James Watson announced the result of their contemplations on the question of how inheritance works. They had departed from the then popular grooves of scientific imagination, approached their subject matter obliquely, and received expected results. They formulated the double-helix model of deoxyribonucleic acid: DNA.

Also in the 1950s, researchers began to speculate about chemical evolution preceding biological evolution. Harold Urey's and Stanley Miller's experiments (which are a form of questioning) showed that organic life could have arisen out of a soup made from ammonia, carbon, and water, suitably potentized by electrical discharges.

Darwin's theory of evolution and its Neodarwinian derivatives have been shown to be problematic, as they cannot account for all the known facts and are even contradicted by some. Thus, questioning continues in this area of investigation, and microbiologists are formulating new and perhaps more satisfactory answers.

Questions act like fertilizer on the mental level. They help answers to sprout and grow. Our civilization has handed down to us some veritable questions—the Big Questions. These are powerful memes. The term *meme* was coined by zoologist Richard Dawkins and explained in his widely read book *The Selfish Gene* as "a unit of cultural transmission, or a unit of *imitation*."[3] A meme can be an idea, a tune, an archetypal image, a catch phrase, a writing style, and so on. Vehicles of memes are musical records, picture galleries, books, libraries, languages, tools, gadgets, buildings, and not least entire cosmologies or ideologies.

Civilization has handed down to us not only Big Questions but also Big Answers—the various traditional belief systems, which are potent meme carriers. In bygone ages, tradition was all-powerful, and only the most intelligent members of the tribe dared question (quietly, in the privacy of their own minds) the transmitted knowledge, which was held sacred. Today, however, many people are at odds with the tradition into which they were born, and so they must find their own answers by posing the Big Questions for themselves. If our personal answers resonate with the answers of any given tradition, we can make that tradition our intellectual, emotional, and sociocultural home. But if the two sets of answers do not match sufficiently, it would be best to tread our own lonely path. I am not sure which takes greater courage and staying power: to make one's home in a tradition with which one is not in agreement on important points or to be one's own light and tradition.

The Trappist monk and popular author Thomas Merton suffered the intense struggle of someone who obviously had an enormously creative mind, strong personality, and quite independent answers and yet chose to remain within the fold of the Catholic tradition. In more recent years, the personal tug-of-war between the Vatican and Matthew Fox, the leading proponent of creation spirituality, has become public knowledge. Fox wants to belong but at the same time does not wish to abandon his own views and refuses to be silenced. By contrast, the well-known British novelist and encyclopedist H. G. Wells demonstrated the difficulty of a life lived in separation from the religious environment in which he was brought up, struggling with his "apostasy" all his life. His inner struggle culminated in the book *Crux Ansata*, written toward the end of his life. This work is an all-out attack on the Roman Catholic Church. In a subsequent interview for the *London Literary Guide*, Wells reiterated his condemnation of the church, saying that "it stands for everything most hostile to the mental emancipation and stimulation of mankind."[4]

There is little support for those who try to make it on their own. A person must have incredible inner resources to go the solitary route. But some people seem destined to walk this particular razor's edge to wisdom. As long as the philosophical life flourishes, it does not matter what form it takes.

Those who do not ask themselves existential questions are either fully enlightened or asleep. The Russian spiritual teacher George Ivanovich Gurdjieff, who drew much public attention in the years preceding and following World War II, particularly espoused this metaphor of sleep—a metaphor to which most gnostics are partial. He remarked:

Contemporary man is born asleep, lives asleep and dies asleep. And what *knowledge* could a sleeping man have? If you think about it and at the same time remember that sleep is the chief feature of our being, you will soon understand that if man wishes to obtain knowledge, he should first of all think about *how to awaken himself*, that is about *how to change* his being.[5]

As psychologist Charles Tart, who is an avid student of Gurdjieff's teachings, put it: ordinary individuals are asleep in a consensus trance.[6] They do not "remember" themselves; that is, they are not continuously aware of their existence but instead become "lost" in thought, action, or simple daydreaming. They muddle along, perhaps occasionally surfacing for a few fleeting moments of lucidity. Even those who seriously ponder existential questions succumb to such dulling of awareness throughout the course of the day, but at least they seek to pierce the veil of forgetfulness by their philosophical activity. Mindfulness is crucial to the philosophical life. Without it, understanding remains merely on the intellectual level but cannot touch us at the core of our being. It is in the context of mindfulness—the cultivation of lucid self-awareness—that the philosopher creates meaning out of the overabundance of human experience.

There is no *necessary* meaning to the universe itself or to reality as such. That is not to say that the world is absolutely meaningless, for the world includes human beings, who are makers or finders of meaning. But we must recognize meaning as an intelligent creation, a conscious act of relating apparently disparate factors so as to generate the intellectual and emotional conviction that the nexus or order we have thus created is inherently appropriate and good. Therefore, it is ultimately always the human being who stands at the event horizon of all those networks of meaning. In some cases, such as humanism, the human being stands unashamedly both at the event horizon and in the center. For this reason, the exact meanings we create are crucially important, for they can enhance our life or diminish and even destroy it.

The most profound experience of meaningfulness coincides with the recovery of our true identity as incarnate spiritual beings. It is then that we are made whole. The American physicist David Bohm saw this with great clarity:

> When life as a whole is harmonious, we don't have to ask for an ultimate meaning, for then life itself *is* this meaning. And if it isn't, we have to find the reason, by looking into life as a whole, which includes the source of the stream and the basic roots of consciousness and the thought process. If we do this, we will generally find that a lack of meaning in life has its root in sustained and pervasive incoherence in our thoughts, in our feelings, and in how we live, along with a self-deceptive defense

of the whole process against evidence that it has serious faults.

We could say that life as a whole is grounded in the matter of the universe and also in some subtle level that we could call *spirit*, which literally means "breath" or "wind." We have to reach this total ground to be able to live a life that *is* its own meaning. If we take less than this sort of overall cosmic approach, the meaning we find will ultimately prove not to be a viable meaning but one that will sooner or later break down into incoherence.[7]

BEYOND REDUCTIONISM

The question "What is a human being?" is integral to the human phenomenon as a whole and therefore cannot fruitfully be answered from a single perspective, such as physics, biochemistry, biology, anthropology, sociology, economics, psychology, or metaphysics. Otherwise we end up with the kind of reductionism that merely yields different forms of ideological totalitarianism. Thus, the human being is not merely a conglomeration of matter, or a chain of chemical reactions, or a gene-driven organismic machine, or an animal that plays, or *Homo economicus*, or a political animal, or a self-conscious creature, or even merely the Spirit. All reductionistic answers are partial and inherently deficient. They are failed attempts at understanding human nature.

However, there is another side to this problem. In the final analysis, *all* human answers are partial and to that extent reductionistic. We never have the total view. Hence, as mentioned earlier, each culture or age has its own answer(s) to the Big Questions. The historical reason for this lies in the different life experience, stock of knowledge, and intellectual capacity, as well as visionary ability, of the cultural leaders who express the overall mood of their cultural environment, or what Suzanne Langer calls its feeling, while at the same time elaborating the common knowledge framework.[8]

Today we encounter a unique situation: in our pluralistic and increasingly global civilization, many such answers are in circulation. Most of them are demonstrably deficient, deriving from one or another type of reductionistic (usually scientistic) orientation. Some of these answers are more widely held than others, which does not necessarily speak for their validity. Most importantly, not a single answer or response could be pointed to as a possible candidate for species-wide acceptance. There is no common unifying central image that would cement all the constituent parts—now highly fragmented—of our troubled human world. If there were one, it would be an ideological magnet that most thinking individuals, however distraught by the lack of harmony and shared meaning, would vigorously resist. A shared answer or response to life must grow out of life itself and not merely be superimposed on it by some elitist organization or social body.

To be sure, the current lack of a shared answer or answers to the Big Questions is more a symptom than the cause of our civilizational malaise. Consequently, attempts to restore to our civilization a commonly accepted answer or guiding image are doomed to fail as long as they ignore the fact that the root cause of our problems does not lie in the intellectual realm but in the spiritual dimension—that is, in our living relationship to Reality, or Spirit, which is the ultimate context of all of life.

We do not need another totalitarian worldview or "ism" but a shared *praxis* growing out of fundamental insights into the nature of human existence, as they have been expressed in the *philosophia perennis*. Such a *praxis* would simply be a nonideological response to the undeniable fact that as human beings we have the capacity for body-transcending and mind-transcending realization. This self-transcending ability is to be understood as a psychospiritual and somatic process of intelligent *presencing*, that is, mindfulness in whatever state of consciousness we may be experiencing.

I suggested earlier that intelligent life and questioning go hand in hand. It should now have become clear that I do not wish to define the human being exclusively as the "question-posing animal." As human beings we do more than ask questions and fabricate answers to them. We also transcend the whole question-and-answer game in the "thunderous silence" of being present as that which does not appear to be confined to sensations, emotions, or thoughts. If anything, the Big Questions and our answers to them pertain to the realm of paradox, because in order to make a rounded response, we are obliged to transcend the questions and our possible answers and hence the entire mood of questioning and knowing.

Yet, also paradoxically, we need to contemplate the Big Questions so that we may, like Alice, step through the looking-glass of our own mind and recapture the tremendous humor of the eternal silence that underlies all existence. We need to ask questions and find answers, for our answers will furnish us with incipient self-understanding and world-understanding—two forms of intellectual and intuitive comprehension that can serve as the foundation for the dawning of gnosis: revelations of naked Reality. Love of wisdom (philosophy) guides us to gnosis. Yet, it is not the philosophical activity in itself that fulfills our deepest yearning for Reality. Rather, it is wisdom that provides fulfillment, because it is coessential with Reality. The ultimate wisdom is silence itself. In his perceptive book *Fingers Pointing Toward the Sacred,* artist Frederick Franck recounts his conversation with Michiko Kimura, a young Japanese student of Zen. She made a speculative comment that because it bears much truth is worth relating. Michiko remarked that possibly questions like "Who am I?" can never be expressed in words. "The true answer," she stated, "is perhaps nothing more than the awareness of having the capacity to ask this question and it is this capacity that reveals my humanness."[9]

At the same time, of course, we desire coherent intellectual frameworks to communicate our realized presence, the eternal silence, to others. That communication is as essential to our humanness as our realization of the mind-transcending presence. Being and becoming, silence and knowledge, eternity and finitude, realization and actualization together make up our distinctly human existence. As long as we are human, we ought to treasure this life-giving polarity in our nature, and attend to both aspects with equal care. For to deny one aspect in favor of the other is to cripple ourselves and deny life the opportunity to express itself fully in and through us.

3

THE CHALLENGE OF EMBODIMENT

HEALING THE SPLIT

Who am I? We cannot adequately answer this question, which epitomizes lucid waking, without reference to the body. Those who have done so have effectively maneuvered themselves into the impasse of spiritual idealism. On the other side, those who have equated the I with the body are guilty of the complementary fallacy of misplaced concreteness, or materialism. We are creatures of time and space, but not only! The difficulty is that many people behave as if the body exhausted their identity, and yet few of them feel at ease with the embodied state. "Can't live with it and can't live without it" fittingly describes their attitude.

When we are born we have no notion of our body. Obviously, we can feel our arms and legs, sense our stomach when it is empty or full, and feel discomfort or ease, but we have no concept of being an embodied individual. This awareness dawns on us only gradually. During the first six years of our life, our body image by and large includes only what we ourselves can see of the body. The invisible parts, like the spinal column and internal organs, are integrated into our body image only in subsequent years, as our self-awareness increases.

In fact, the body image of many people never attains completion. Those parts that are associated with emotional trauma—often the reproductive organs—are excluded from integration into the body image. They remain invisible out of shame, guilt, or fear. Also, because modern society places a premium on intellectual competence and does not encourage kinesthetic experience, the development of an integrated body image is arrested in many people. They are at odds with their physical existence. Psychiatrist Rollo May commented as follows:

> It is a curious fact that most adults have so lost physical awareness that they are unable to tell how their leg feels if you should ask them, or their ankle, or their middle finger or any other part of the body. . . . As a result of several centuries of suppressing the body into an inanimate machine, subordinated to the purposes of modern industrialism, people are proud of paying no attention to the body. They treat it as an object for manipulation, as though it were a truck to be driven till it runs out of gas.[1]

This neurotic attitude, as May further observed, is vividly apparent in our passive relationship to illness. We wait for doctors to cure our diseases and are generally unwilling to consider the causes of our illnesses or even to make changes in lifestyle to assist the healing process or prevent future similar difficulties. Although we say "I am sick," we really mean specifically the body, not realizing that disease is an imbalance of the whole person and that the physical symptoms are merely the outermost manifestation of that overall imbalance.

Likewise in our sexual life, we dissociate from the body, turning the lover into an object of desire and "performing" intercourse with the predictability of a machine. We regard ourselves as operators of the body as if it were a car or a crane.

This objectification of the body, together with a poor body image, presumably explains why almost all cultures endorse or prescribe various ways of altering the body. For the most part, the overt purpose of such alterations is to beautify the body. The hidden reason, however, is to conceal its natural state.

We decorate and modify our body to conform to certain canons of aesthetics—from grooming our hair and removing unwanted body hair to applying perfumes, painting finger and toe nails, and brushing and whitening our teeth; from applying lipstick, rouge, shadows, lotions, and deodorants to engraving tattoos on trunk, arms, legs, and face; from inserting jewelry into our earlobes, nose, lips, and other body parts to artificially elongating labia and neck (as do the women of certain African tribes); from surgically reducing or enlarging breasts to changing the anatomical structure of the feet (as in Chinese footbinding or, less obvious, in the Western fashion of wearing high-heeled shoes). People now undergo liposuction to reduce body fat and other forms of cosmetic surgery to look younger or more appealing. They consume diet pills for weight loss, go jogging, and frequent (as I do) the gym to attain fitness and strength.

In the name of religion or society, we have also since ancient times inflicted on our fellow humans a variety of mutilations, notably circumcision, clitoridectomy, and (among the Australian Aborigines) subincision. Circumcision is still widely practiced around the world either for religious or for questionable medical reasons, while the horrible and painful practice of clitoridectomy continues to be inflicted on women in various African countries.

Who can tell what people will do when bionic implants become affordable and when genetic research has progressed far enough to give those who clamor for it gills, webbed fingers and toes, a back-up heart, and other nonhuman characteristics?

Despite this overt obsession with our physical nature, we are alienated from the body. This alienation is epitomized in Jean-Paul Sartre's feeling of nausea when contemplating his own body and human existence in general. We objectify the body through these various means, as if it were a thing separate from us. We conceal the body's "dirty" or "ugly" aspects, especially urine, feces, saliva, menstrual blood, and perspiration. We do not like to be reminded that the body is a living organism. We go into shock when we see ourselves ooze blood or lymphatic liquid. We are afraid of pain, pampered by modern medicine with its battery of analgesics and its fine art of anesthesia. We are especially afraid of death and conceal its reality by giving our dead—euphemistically called "the dearly departed"—a thorough cosmetic makeover before we face them one last time in the mortal flesh.

We split the mind from the body, and yet the body is a faithful image of our inner life. In his book *Bodymind*, Ken Dychtwald describes how John Pierrakos, a master practitioner of bioenergetics, gave a completely accurate description of Dychtwald's inner attitudes merely by scrutinizing his naked body. "He was reading my life from my body," noted Dychtwald, "as an archaeologist might read Egyptian history from its hieroglyphics."[2] In a certain sense, the body is the crystallization of our past psychological activity. In turn, the body feeds back into the mind, and the two are mirror images of one another. Body and mind are really *body-mind*, an organic unity (like space-time) that dissolves into its two constituent parts only at death.

The radical scission between body and mind has historical roots, which go back to the seventeenth-century French philosopher and mathematician René Descartes. His book *Discours de la méthode* (Discourse on Method) is one of the cornerstones of modern thought. Autobiographical in tone, this work is a succinct treatment of Cartesianism. While spending a leisurely day in a warm, stove-heated room in a German house, Descartes, then aged twenty-three, was struck by how many opinions he held in his mind and how little he could actually be completely certain of. It took another nine years for him to begin the deliberate deconstruction of his opinions, which by then had grown considerably through his extensive studies and thinking. He compared his task to the demolition of an old building, and he boldly proceeded with it. Descartes felt that of all the ideas in his head, only one held absolute certainty for him: *Cogito ergo sum*, "I think, therefore I am." He explained:

I concluded that I was a substance whose whole essence or nature consists in thinking, and whose existence depends neither on its location in space nor on any material thing. Thus the self, or rather the soul, by which I am what I am, is entirely distinct from the body, is indeed easier to know than the body, and would not cease to be what it is, even if there were no body.[3]

From there, Descartes went on to reconstruct the objective
world and God. In retrospect, it is easy to say how, despite his best
intentions, he fooled himself into logically deducing precisely those
metaphysical ideas that had been important to him beforehand. In
my mid-teens, after reading an introductory book on philosophy, I
frustrated myself with endeavoring a Cartesian-type house-cleaning
of my mental library. The only certainty I was able to find was that
there is awareness, which is aware of itself, and that this awareness
also seems to include patterned perceptions called objects. I never
got beyond this rudimentary realization, feeling dismayed that all
my ideas were acquired from other minds through the medium of
language and that even my most original ideas were only more or
less creative combinations of these handed-down notions. There
vanished the possibility of an academic career in philosophy for me.

In venturing forth beyond this initial sense of awareness *(cogito ergo sum)*, Descartes showed great daring and optimism but perhaps also great foolishness. Compared with the sophisticated analyses of the philosopher-sages of India, his arguments come across
almost as fumbling. Be that as it may, the Cartesian method canon-
ized the split between being and consciousness—a split on which
our modern civilization's worst ills have been blamed.

Descartes ripped the mind, or pure thinking substance, from
the body, which he felt could not yield certainty of knowledge. He
distrusted the information gathered from the senses and, true to a
mathematician's love of abstraction, took refuge only in the mind.
He did not extend his analysis to that feeling of certainty itself, and
a later crop of philosophers tried, inconclusively, to correct this
shortcoming. To Descartes the body was a machine. The relationship between the body and the mind (or "soul") was, for him, a pre-
carious one. For how could an immaterial substance interact with a
piece of matter extended in space? He invoked the pineal gland as
the vital conduit between these two incompatible entities, thereby
raising more questions than he answered.

Surprisingly, it was Immanuel Kant who rejected the Cartesian
dualism in his *Critique of Pure Reason*. According to him, substance is not an actual object or entity but a category of experience.
Therefore, there can be no question of the "substance" of mind

being isolated from the "substance" called body. Kant thus prepared the ground for later generations of philosophers, who approached the body-mind problem from a novel, phenomenological perspective: philosophers like Edmund Husserl, Maurice Merleau-Ponty, Gabriel Marcel, and the existentialist Jean-Paul Sartre. More recently, the American philosopher Drew Leder has contributed significantly to this philosophical debate.

Leder, a professor at Loyola College in Maryland who also has a medical doctorate, is concerned with the "lived body": what in German is called *Leib* as opposed to *Körper* (from Latin *corpus*). In his book *The Absent Body*, he writes:

> Human experience is incarnated. I receive the surrounding world through my eyes, my ears, my hands. The structure of my perceptual organs shapes that which I apprehend. . . . From the most visceral of cravings to the loftiest of artistic achievements, the body plays its formative role.
>
> Yet this bodily presence is of a highly paradoxical nature. While in one sense the body is the most abiding and inescapable presence in our lives, it is also essentially characterized by absence. That is, one's own body is rarely the thematic object of experience. When reading a book or lost in thought, my own bodily state may be the farthest thing from my awareness.[4]

As Leder illustrates, the body tends to "disappear" in many other circumstances throughout our daily life. We pay no attention to it so long as it functions properly, but we become acutely aware of our somatic dimension whenever its smooth functioning is interrupted by physical and emotional discomfort, pain, physical threat, or social factors such as exposure to body-intense experiences involving the birth, injury, sickness, or death of others.

The lived body is the wholesome counterpart to the absent body that characterizes our modern way of life. In Leder's words:

> This body's roots reach down into the soil of an organismic vitality where the conscious mind cannot follow. Its branches

spread throughout the universe. When I gaze upon the stars, or
the face of another, or the symbols of divinity, I transgress my
limits. Through the lived body I open to the world. This body
is not then simply a mass of matter or an obstructive force. It is
a way in which we, as part of the universe, mirror the universe.[5]

Here we encounter the archaic idea of the body being a micro-
cosmic replica of the macrocosm. Leder, who has a Neoconfucian
spiritual background, comes out in favor of spiritual teachings that
help us cultivate the "one body" as it is experienced in the ecstatic
state. Ecstasy demonstrates the validity of those moral teachings
that recommend transcendence of the separative ego and commu-
nion with the universe. On the other hand, compassion and selfless
service are the fruits of the truth revealed in ecstasy. As he states:

In the ecstasy that comes upon us in the woods, we feel the
leaping beyond constriction, the spaciousness of our extended
body. We register our flesh-and-blood chiasm [intersection]
with the world.[6]

Then Leder asks, "Can we open to the one-body experience just
as much in a parking lot as in the woods?" That indeed is the
question.

THE BODY OF GLORY

Beyond this unitive experience lies an even greater spiritual adventure, marking the fulfillment of lucid waking. This is hinted at in
the traditional notion of the transubstantiated body or the "body of
glory," as it is called in the Christian mystical tradition. This expression goes back to the apostle Paul's letter to the Philippians (3:21),
though its underlying idea is much older and is not confined to
Christianity. The apostolic missive contains this statement:

He [Jesus the Christ] will transform the body of our humiliation
[i.e., the fleshly body] so that it may conform to the body of his
glory.

Here the "body of glory" specifically refers to the luminous resurrection body of Jesus of Nazareth, as witnessed by his disciples. According to the apostle Mark, Jesus appeared first to Mary Magdalene, and when she reported the good news to the other disciples, they did not believe her. Then he appeared to two more disciples, but again their excited report fell on deaf ears. Finally, Jesus manifested himself to the eleven principal disciples while they were at supper, and he reprimanded them for their lack of faith. St. John provided the additional detail that on this memorable occasion St. Thomas was not present, and when he was told of Jesus' appearance he too did not believe. He remarked to his fellow disciples that he would be convinced only if he could put his own fingers on Jesus' wounds. Eight days later, Thomas had just this opportunity, when Jesus himself invited the doubting apostle to touch the wounds in his hands and his side. Apparently Jesus manifested himself in such a way that the marks of his crucifixion were visible. However, he had been raised beyond all suffering and mortality.

The apostle Paul promises in 1 Corinthians 15:44 that those who are resurrected in Christ similarly come to enjoy an immortal spiritual body. He makes a distinction between the "natural body" *(soma psychikon)* with which a person is born and the "spiritual body" *(soma pneumatikon)* that is the fruit of a person's spiritual labors. In the same epistle (15:58), Paul states:

> Therefore, my beloved, be steadfast, immovable, always excelling in the work of the Lord, because you know that in the Lord your labor is not in vain.

Jesus attained his body of glory as a result of his divinely inspired life on earth, and his disciples—those who take upon themselves the spiritual discipline taught by him—likewise acquire a luminous, immortal body in the moment of their own resurrection.

Why "body of glory"? In the Old Testament, the Hebrew word for *glory* is *kabod*, which stands for weightiness, notably the weight of a person's esteem or honor but also the Divine's potent radiance. Thus, the divine epiphany appearing to Moses in the form of a burning bush on Mount Horeb or in the bright cloud that guided the Hebrews through the wilderness to the promised land are instances of this glory.

In the New Testament, the Greek word for *glory* is *doxa*, which is used 167 times in the gospels, with no fewer than 57 occurrences in St. Paul's writings. Outside the New Testament literature, *doxa* generally means "view" or "opinion." However, the early Christian writers understood it primarily as "glory" or "radiance," though in some places in the gospels the Greek term also connotes "honor" or "reputation." The Greek verb *doxazo* means "to glorify" and in this sense is used, for instance, in Paul's epistles. Thus, we find that in the Old and the New Testaments, "glory" is traditionally related to radiance or luminosity, especially the eternal splendor of God made manifest in specific sacred moments.

A most profound connection between Jesus and God's glory is made in the apostle John's gospel. From it we learn that on the night before his crucifixion, Jesus prayed that in his death the heavenly Father might glorify him and that he might glorify the Father, and also that the glory might be passed on to Jesus' disciples.

The Christian sacrament of baptism can be viewed as planting the seed for the body of glory. Interestingly, some of the church fathers, notably Justin, spoke of baptism as "illumination" (*photismos* in Greek). In doing so, they based themselves on Paul's epistle to the Hebrews (6:4) where those who have tasted the "heavenly gift" and have shared the Holy Spirit are spoken of as being "illumined" (*photistentas*).

The Holy Spirit itself has traditionally been depicted as a flame above the head of those whom it blessed with its presence. And saintly folk were believed to be able to see the luminous resurrection body of Jesus the Christ, as had the apostles themselves. Great saints, furthermore, were thought to radiate light from their physical body—a belief that is found in many spiritual traditions. When at prayer, the Egyptian Christian monk Abba Joseph is said to have filled his cell with light "like a fire." The Russian Orthodox saint Seraphim of Sarov is remembered to have been so luminous on occasions that his disciples were unable to look at him.

The Christian gnostic teaching of the body of glory is not merely a fascinating doctrine to be believed or dismissed but is anchored in actual spiritual realization of an advanced degree. This is borne out by the fact that analogous teachings are prominent in Hinduism, Buddhism, Taoism, and other spiritual traditions. They acknowledge the existence of immortal adepts who can materialize and dematerialize at will. Thus, the Hindus and Buddhists know of eighty-four *maha-siddhas* ("great accomplishers"), and the Taoists speak of eight immortals. These are the true alchemists, for they have completely refashioned themselves, transmuting the base metal of the ordinary, confused mind into the gold of pure mind. As the Bulgarian adept Omraam Mikhael Aivanhov observed in his characteristically straightforward language:

> An initiate uses all the subtlest, purest, most divine elements from within himself in the construction of this body. Every time he experiences a sublimely poetic moment of adoration or sacrifice, he uses it as material with which to build up this body, just as he would model a statue. . . . [H]e uses all the materials gleaned from the higher realms during his meditations and contemplations. All these sublime emotions serve to form that body, making it gradually so radiant and powerful that it is even capable of carrying his physical body away to distant places. And, at this point, he is invulnerable; nothing can harm him any longer. He has reached his secret refuge on high; he has become immortal.[7]

Alchemical self-purification is the means to the literal enlightenment of the body. This self-purification is at the heart of every spiritual path. It consists in the gradual obliteration of all those factors that freeze the unimaginable energies of reality into the standing wave of what we know as the human body-mind. Through ever more uncompromising dedication to the radical transformation of every aspect of our existence, we progressively transcend the narrow destiny of ordinary life, ascend to the spiritual dimension, and from there descend again, allowing our true nature, or the spirit, to work the miracle of supertransformation in us. This work of alchemical self-purification begins and ends in the body. It necessarily begins in the physical body and ends in the universal Body, which is a body of infinite light. According to social scientist and visionary Duane Elgin,

If we don't use this physical body and world to discover our capacity for self-luminous knowing, when we die we may look out from our subtle body of light and awareness and not recognize our refined existence. If we use our time in this precious body and physical world to come to self-referencing awareness, we anchor the gift of eternity in direct knowing. We can then evolve through the ever more subtle realms of the Meta-universe without forgetting ourselves.[8]

In his magnificent book *The Future of the Body*, a comprehensive survey of the available information about the body-mind's extraordinary capacities, Michael Murphy makes this statement:

That we can creatively alter our muscles, organs, cells, and molecular processes is clearly established. Given that fact, we can wonder about the limits of self-induced bodily change. May our bodies accommodate alterations beyond those presently mapped by medical science? Since new abilities among our animal ancestors were in many instances made possible by alterations of their bodies, we can suppose that analogous changes—developed through practice rather than natural selection—might accompany and support a lasting realization of metanormal capacities. . . . Metanormal restructuring of the body, in short, might involve atomic or molecular reformations that would eventually change the look, feel, and capacities of tissues and cells.[9]

In light of traditional teachings about what Murphy calls our metanormal embodiment, we must admit that we as individuals and as a species have barely begun our evolutionary journey. The great realizations of the celebrated adepts of Christianity, Hinduism, Buddhism, Taoism, Sufism, and other spiritual traditions testify not only to their genius but also to our own immense potential. Having fulfilled the highest human potential, they mirror our own bright future, or at least our own possibility.

4

THE CHANGING FORTUNES OF THE SOUL

A GENERATION WITHOUT SOUL

For centuries, the concept of the soul meant something to people. It was among their most meaning-charged symbols, exciting them intellectually and sustaining them emotionally. In other words, *soul* referred to a reality that had great potency in their lives. Theirs was an ensouled universe. Then, toward the conclusion of the nineteenth century, the concept and the term began to fall into disuse among the more educated men and women of the West. They had come under the spell of philosophical positivism and empirical, behaviorist psychology. This was the last wave in what historian Morris Berman called the "disenchantment of the world." He wrote:

> The story of the modern epoch, at least on the level of mind, is one of progressive disenchantment. From the sixteenth century on, mind has been progressively expunged from the phenomenal world. At least in theory, the reference points for all scientific explanations are matter and motion—what historians of science refer to as the "mechanical philosophy."[1]

Since 1912, when J. B. Watson launched the movement, behaviorism has been trying hard to establish psychology as a "mechanistic" science on a par with physics and chemistry, as if the human psyche could be sliced, spliced, and quantified. In the process, behaviorists ended up striking the term *soul* from their vocabulary, roundly dismissing the traditional ideas underlying it. Behaviorism has been characterized as a psychology without psyche. This is analogous to a body drained of all blood, which would make it a corpse. In other words, behaviorism bluntly refuses to ask the Big Questions and rules out any answers that would satisfy the soul thirsting for wisdom.

I remember conversations in my student days with unhappy soul-seekers who had perchance signed up for courses in psychology and were baffled by the stale crumbs doled out to them in lectures and seminars. This unfortunate situation has remained intact at most universities—those factories of superficial learning.

Perhaps emboldened by the earlier philosophical debunking of the concept of God, behaviorists dismissed the idea of soul as an unverifiable metaphysical belief that is inherently meaningless and serves no useful purpose. This dismissal was merely the tip of a massive iceberg of behaviorist deconstruction (some would say destruction). Behaviorists in fact rejected all "mentalistic" notions, such as "mind," "consciousness," and "introspection." They insisted on explaining everything in terms of stimulus–response and habit formation. Whatever fell outside these explanatory categories was of questionable reality and hence worthy of rejection, if not contempt.

In discarding all these notions, especially that of the soul, behaviorism impoverished not only psychological language but thought and culture as well. Had those psychologists enjoyed the metaphysical sensitivity and perceptual range of our ancestors, or of the so-called primitives of our own time, they would never have maneuvered themselves into the cul-de-sac of reductionism and determinism. For, as has become clear from extensive anthropological studies among the world's preindustrial communities, tribal people live close not only to the heartbeat of Nature but also to the eternal verities that are the domain of spirituality and metaphysics.

The Swiss scholar Jean Gebser pointed out that in all probability, early humanity's perceptual spectrum was different from ours.[2] Our ancestors saw more than we do. Like some yogis and mystics, they were able to perceive the psyche as a living radiance, an "aura" interpenetrating and surrounding the human body. In other words, unlike modern experts in psychology, they experienced directly what they professed to know. In fairness, it must be said that our ancestors also saw less than we do, for our modern cognitive environment—what Pierre Teilhard de Chardin called the "noosphere"[3]—is distinctly more complex, affording us understanding undreamed of by our forebears.

In contrast to yogis, mystics, and shamans, behaviorists with their passionate commitment to the golden calf (or Trojan horse) of "objectivity" absurdly tabooed even such an everyday experience as consciousness. Yet, this did not prevent them from proffering behaviorism as a general philosophy of life, as if we could live humanly (that is, meaningfully) without consciousness. However, we who are witnessing the demise of the mechanistic paradigm are apt to look at behaviorist philosophy as little more than a bandage on the open wounds caused by the destruction of traditional religion and spirituality.

Without question, behaviorism has merit when it comes to the study of physiological responses and conditioning at the most primitive level of psychological functioning. However, as a more general approach to the study of the complex dynamics of our inner life, it has proved to be far too denuded. A friend of mind, who is a professor of psychology, commented that I am flogging a dead horse here and that today's real culprit is reductive cognitive science. Behaviorism may well be a minority viewpoint at American universities nowadays, but it is still thriving in other parts of the world, which have not yet caught up with developments during the past twenty years. Surprisingly, India is one of the countries that is still haunted by the ghost of behaviorism, as it is haunted by the equally nonviable ghost of Marxism. As for cognitive science, which focuses on the automaticities of the mind, it contains little that could be construed as evidence of the emerging integral consciousness.

Be that as it may, in America and Europe, behaviorism historically provoked much criticism and, in due course, gave rise to the inevitable countermovement. Thus, ever since the 1960s, the term *consciousness* has been restored to a modicum of respectability in psychology. This is partly due to developments in the hard sciences (especially quantum physics, which has caused more philosophically minded physicists to fret over the interaction between the observer and the observed). And partly it is the outcome of the popular and scientific fascination with psychoactive, or mind-altering, drugs during the counterculture days of the 1960s and 1970s. More than anything, psychedelics drove home the absurdity of the academic denial of consciousness. They induced altered states of something that supposedly did not exist.

Most recently, the language of soul has resurfaced. Writers like Larry Dossey, Gary Zukav, June Singer, Sandra Ingerman, Michael Grosso, Aminah Raheem, William Barrett, and Marilyn Chapin Massey have unabashedly made use of the term *soul*.[4] We even see *soul* in the title of books on politics and economics. Writing still in the heyday of behaviorism, C. G. Jung antedated by six whole decades the present wave of "soul" pioneers with his influential work *Modern Man in Search of a Soul*.[5]

Given the unflattering modern history of the concept and term *soul*, it is surprising that recent authors do not reflect more extensively on their usage of this term. This lack of reflection evokes the wrong notion that the word is quite unambiguous. Even if we agree that it is appropriate to reinstate the term, this does not automatically mean we can deploy it with the requisite clarity.

THE MEANING OF SOUL

What, then, is the soul? First of all, we may note—the behaviorist ban on the word notwithstanding—the word *soul* has had a rather persistent life in popular discourse. Thus, we have expressions like "a good old soul," "to have no soul" (no sensitivity, feeling), "a soul-destroying job," "a soulful gaze," "soul mate," "the heart and soul of the party," "a troubled soul," "soulless writing," "soul-stirring music."

As is obvious from these various idiomatic usages, *soul* refers by and large to the emotional or feeling aspect of our being. A common synonym for it, consequently, is *heart*. However, some of the above expressions suggest something more: soul as essence. This comes closest to the traditional religious or spiritual connotations of the concept. The essence of a thing is its life, and this is exactly the etymological meaning of *soul* and its equivalent in diverse languages.

The word *soul* stems from the Old English *sawol* and is related to the Anglo-Saxon *sawel* or *sawl*, the Icelandic *sala* or *sal*, the Danish *sioel*, the Swedish *själ*, the Gothic *saiwala*, and the German *Seele*. The word is also possibly a distant cousin of the Sanskrit term *sara*. All these Indo-European terms connote something like "essential quality" or "immaterial power substance."

In other languages, notably Greek, Latin, and Hebrew, the equivalents for the English word *soul* typically mean "life" or "breath." Thus, Hebrew *nephesh* and Arabic *nafs* both denote "life." The onomatopoeic Hebrew word *ruah*, the Greek terms *psyche* and *pneuma*, and the Latin word *anima* all signify "breath" in their original meaning. This primal connotation is also contained in the Latin word *spiritus* (our "spirit") and the Sanskrit term *atman* (commonly rendered as "Self"). In his book *The Origins of European Thought*, R. B. Onians shows that our modern notion of the soul is derived from an early European cultural matrix, which included the Egyptian, Babylonian, Hebrew, Celtic, Slavic, Germanic, Indian, and other Indo-European peoples.[6]

The association of the soul with breath and life unquestionably derives from empirical observation, for upon death, when a person draws his or her last breath, the soul is severed from the physical body. The soul is the animating principle that keeps the body's fire lit, whereas the body on its own is as inert as a rock—or nearly so.

To be sure, in so-called primitive thought, there is nothing that is not ensouled, and even a seemingly lifeless stone is filled with life, or soul. Anthropologists speak of this archaic way of viewing reality as animism, often ignoring the fact that this is not merely a belief but primarily an immediate experience for the tribal peoples they are studying. Besides, some version of animism seems to be implicit in quantum mechanics, which is perhaps the most advanced product of the theoretical imagination of modern times. According to some interpretations of quantum reality, each and every particle in the world possesses a degree of consciousness.[7] This theory, also known as panpsychism, has been ably represented by the German biologist Bernhard Rensch, who speaks of the "protophenomenal" nature of molecules and atoms.[8]

According to E. B. Tylor, one of the pioneers of anthropology, premodern humanity arrived at the belief in a soul by observing the phenomena of dreams as well as the influence of the breath upon life and death.[9] However, there is a whole range of other soul-affirming experiences to which tribal people had and still have ready access, not the least of which is the ecstatic state achieved through various tribal rituals such as prolonged drumming and dancing. In these states the immaterial essence of a person is experienced as leaving the body.

Even modern humanity is no stranger to out-of-body experiences, though more often than not they are the result of traumas, such as accidents or operations, rather than the deliberate product of trance-inducing ceremonies. The parapsychological literature includes numerous reported cases of this type, which make for fascinating reading.[10]

Moreover, there is a widespread traditional belief that clairvoyants—individuals who have the inherited or acquired ability to see beyond the ordinary spectrum of vibration—can actually see the soul, which they describe as a more tenuous double *(Doppelgänger)* of the physical body. There is a rich anecdotal literature on this subject. A friend of mine, who is an advanced practitioner of Tibetan Buddhism, told me that several years ago while conducting one of his weekly healing circles he saw a spirit—the husband of one of his students—enter the room. At first, my friend thought that the man had unconsciously projected his consciousness to be with them. Then he sensed that something more serious was going on. Unbeknownst to everyone at the time of the gathering, this man apparently had fallen asleep at the steering wheel of his car, was thrown out of the car, and was run over by a truck. He was killed instantly. The victim's spirit was not yet aware that he had just died when he visited the healing circle. Through long training, my friend has been able to extend his vision beyond the range of the normal, and seeing spirits is nothing out of the ordinary for him.

Undoubtedly, there were similarly gifted individuals among our tribal ancestors who evolved the notion of the soul. Indeed, there is every indication that people in communities living closer to nature are more psychic than the average denizen of our modern urban jungle. We live so much in a state of outward-directedness and stress that we seldom slow down long enough to perceive anything but the coarsest forms of existence. Many people do not even remember their dreams, which shows the degree to which the psychic dimension is shut down.

While the idea of a soul can be found in almost all cultures— even Buddhism has a version of this belief—each culture offers its own interpretative variations of what appears to be a universal, or near-universal, experience. Only among the educated population of our own time have skepticism and nihilism gained such prominence that the soul no longer instills awe and wonder, but rather a degree of discomfiture. Many people find it awkward to talk about the soul, just as they find it embarrassing to mention God other than in the exercise of profanities. However, as noted above, there are signs of a renaissance in the spiritual worldview, in which these metaphysical intangibles assume their proper place.

THE PRINCIPLE OF IMMORTALITY

The experience of the soul as the life-infusing principle of the body led in due course to a momentous insight, which was destined to dominate the thought of most cultures on earth. This is the understanding that the soul is not only nonphysical but also not subject to any of the laws governing the physical realm. In particular, the soul was understood to transcend not only material space but the flow of time. The belief (or inner certainty) arose that the soul survives the demise of the physical body. It came to be viewed as the indestructible, immortal principle of the human being.

Very likely, this belief was originally based on subjective, clair-voyant experiences: the shaman or religious specialist saw the soul exit the body of the dying individual and then continue on in the spiritual realms. Or the shaman witnessed an ancestral soul visiting the tribe during an important celebration, or he or she saw a particular soul entering the womb of a pregnant woman. This is probably also the source of the associated belief, quite widespread in tribal societies, of reincarnation. If souls can be seen departing from a dying body and entering a fetus, then it is plausible that the same soul might come to inhabit another body—body after body.

This possibility may have occurred already to the Neanderthals, because they buried their dead very carefully, complete with weapons, perhaps to encourage them to move on in their postmortem journey in the spirit realms and simultaneously to discourage them from returning to the corpse and causing trouble for the living. Thousands of years later, the Egyptians and, independently, the Tibetans developed a formal ritual of transition for their dead. These rituals are designed to maintain continuity of awareness throughout the death process. The Tibetan *Bardo Thödol* and the Egyptian *Book of the Dead* are guidebooks for the departing soul.

In his commentary to the German version of W. Y. Evans-Wentz's translation of the *Bardo Thödol*, C. G. Jung made this acerbic but to-the-point remark:

> Whenever the Westerner hears the word "psychological," it always sounds to him like "*only* psychological." For him the "soul" is something pitifully small, unworthy, personal, subjective, and a lot more besides. He therefore prefers to use the word "mind" instead, though he likes to pretend at the same time that a statement which may in fact be very subjective indeed is made by the "mind," naturally by the "Universal Mind," or even—at a pinch—by the "Absolute" itself. This rather ridiculous presumption is probably a compensation for the regrettable smallness of the soul.[11]

It appears that the process of reincarnation—fitting a soul to a new body—is spontaneous and, according to most traditions, beyond the control of the individual. The great traditions of Hinduism, Buddhism, and Jainism invoke a special universal law of moral causation to explain the movement of the soul from one embodiment to the next. According to this teaching, the post-mortem life of the soul is governed by the karma of the individual. The Sanskrit word *karma* (or *karman*) literally means "action." It is intended to epitomize the fact that all our actions have consequences. As St. Paul wrote to the Galatians: "Whatsoever a man soweth, that shall he also reap." In the words of Pythagoras, as recorded in the *Protreptics* of Iamblichus:

> As we live through soul, it must be said that by the virtue of this we live well . . . We should betake ourselves to virtue as to an inviolable temple, in order that we may not be exposed to any ignoble insolence of soul with respect to our communion with, and continuance in life.[12]

The reason for Pythagoras' concern about living a virtuous life was quite simply that whereas sin defiles the soul, virtue uplifts it. And the quality of a soul determines the quality of its life circumstances, its destiny.

As the sages of India made clear, action also includes our thoughts and intentions. Thus, karma is a manifestation of the moral consequences deriving from the totality of an individual's self-expression in life. Karma is thought to determine the quality and length of the afterlife as well as the quality and type of body with which the soul becomes associated. The new body, in turn, determines to some extent the quality and type of life of the reincarnated soul. When asked about the purpose of this cycle of embodiment and disembodiment, the sages of India replied that it is to mature spiritually, to discover that embodiment is unnecessary, and to learn that a person's true being is aspatial, atemporal, and formless. The Hindu sages spoke of the *atman*, the soul beyond the psyche, as that ultimate principle residing eternally outside the cosmos.

Gautama the Buddha, who formulated his own distinct path of self-transformation, refused to speculate about the ultimate reality. He specifically rejected the popular notion of an eternal soul that migrates from body to body until it voluntarily abandons all forms of embodiment upon illumination. Yet, even the Buddha described nirvana—the desirable state of "extinction" of the individual soul—as "the *realm* where there is neither earth nor water, neither fire nor air . . . no coming or going, no duration or destruction, or origination . . . without support, without continuance, without condition . . . the end of suffering." He also preached the value of virtue as the means of ensuring better conditions for one's future embodiment. But for him the karmic process was not one of a soul wandering from body to body but of conditions effecting conditions effecting conditions, until the whole nexus is broken at the moment of enlightenment. For the Buddha, the soul of one incarnation was neither identical to the soul of the preceding incarnation nor wholly different from it—a rather sophisticated understanding of the rebirth process.

The archaic teaching of a migration of souls may have entered the Greek civilization, where it was known as metempsychosis, through the esoteric traditions of Orphism and Pythagoreanism. Pythagoras, the Leonardo da Vinci of antiquity, studied in Babylonia, Chaldea, and Egypt. We also know that some Hindu sages visited Athens, impressing the Greeks with their wisdom and astonishing miracle-working. According to Diogenes Laertius, Pythagoras remembered several of his past lives. Thus, he believed that in a previous birth he had been Aethalides, the son of Hermes, who was subsequently reincarnated as Euphorbus, then as Hermotimus, and then as the fisherman Pyrrhus of Delos. It was Hermes who granted Pythagoras—in his incarnation as Aethalides—the gift of remembering the route of his transmigrating soul.

Among other things, Pythagoras reportedly taught that human souls can reincarnate in animal bodies, with the convenient exception of those few animal species enumerated by him as appropriate for sacrificial rites. Perhaps this explains the story told by Iamblichus in which Pythagoras instructed an ox not to eat beans, which were a taboo food among the Pythagoreans, after which the intelligent animal is said to have curbed its appetite for the fruit of leguminous plants (establishing the ox as inappropriate for sacrifice).

Pythagoreanism was extremely influential and was particularly formative in the evolution of Plato's philosophy. Its ideas later merged with Neoplatonism, originating some time in the first century B.C., which in turn influenced Christian theology. For instance, the belief in transmigration was an integral part of some early Christian communities, notably the followers of the Alexandrian teacher Origen, the most prolific of the church fathers. However, this teaching was explicitly anathematized by the church. Origen himself was condemned as a heretic by the Second Council of Constantinople in 553 A.D.

Yet, there are statements even in the New Testament suggesting that Jesus himself believed in the repeated return of souls. In a well-known biblical passage in the gospel of Matthew (16:13), Jesus asks his disciples: "Whom do men say that I, the Son of man, am? And they said, 'Some say that thou art John the Baptist; some, Elias; and others, Jeremias, or one of the prophets.'" Both the question and the answer would be nonsensical without reference to rebirth, which was apparently a widely held belief among the Jews, who, like the Tibetans, were always looking for the reincarnations of their great spiritual teachers. It is a curious and regrettable twist of fate that the church voted early on to outlaw this powerful teaching. Perhaps the ecclesiastic leaders felt that it would undermine the sense of urgency that they tried to instill in the faithful. For, if we are born again and again, what reason is there to take up the spiritual life now?

The prospect of multiple lives does not at all reduce the significance of the present life, which is an opportunity to disrupt the cycle of incarnation. But to become motivated to make the all-out spiritual effort necessary to break free from the conditional world in the form of the consensus trance, a person must first be overwhelmed by the suffering that is the fruit of all incarnations and be attracted to the ideal of liberation or, in Christian terms, the kingdom of God. And that is always a matter of spiritual ripening.

THE ARCHITECTURE OF THE SOUL

If we moderns are confused about the nature of the soul, it is because this inherited concept has had a rather checkered history. Christian theologians have bequeathed to us a variety of interpretations, leaving us to do the job of disentangling and making sense of them.

It was Plato, and before him Pythagoras, who taught that the soul is tripartite, and this schema is prevalent in Christian theological works. The soul's three aspects, or what Plato called energies, are the rational aspect, which is located in the head; the irascible aspect, which is associated with the heart and is the source of action and movement; and the appetitive or concupiscible aspect, which is the source of the grosser passions and instincts, disappearing upon physical extinction. The diversity of human personalities is explained by the different mixes of these three components of the psyche.

In the Homeric poems, *psyche* still means "life" and "departed life," or existence as a ghost. The identification of the psyche with conscious life was probably introduced by the Ionian philosophers, and its identification with higher mental life was first made, in Greece, by Socrates. In his *Phaedo,* Plato observed that only the rational part of the soul—the *nous*—is immortal. This was also the view of Aristotle. As is evident from the *Timaeus,* Plato furthermore believed in a world soul as the source of cosmic order and harmony, which seems to have been the view of many Presocratics as well.

For Plato, the soul was like a substance separate from the body, while for Aristotle, who did not share his teacher's mystical bent, it was a form of the living body. Aristotle, who is considered to be the father of Western psychology, proffered two working definitions in his *Peri Psyches* ("On the Psyche"). He called the psyche "the entelechy, or first form of an organized body which has potential life," and he also wrote, "The soul is that by which we live, feel, or perceive, move and understand."

Next, Aristotle distinguished a nutritive or vegetative aspect of the soul (by which plants and animals grow and reproduce), a sensitive aspect (causing sensation and feeling), a motive aspect (causing locomotion), an appetitive aspect (the source of desire and will), and a rational or reasonable aspect, as the seat of reason and intellect. Only the human being possesses all these faculties, or "energies," of the soul. The medieval scholastics, who built their theology on the foundations of Aristotle's "heathen" philosophy, reverted to a tripartite model of the psyche, dropping the motive and appetitive aspects.

Plotinus' concept of the soul combined the Homeric notion of it as life force that leaves the body at death with the Pythagorean and Orphic notion that it is a spiritual entity descended (fallen) from the heavenly domain into the physical realm and capable of returning to its higher origins. According to Plotinus, who was a true animist, the psyche extends from rocks to God. At its highest expression, the psyche is the suprapersonal *nous* and is thus individual as well as cosmic. He considered the *nous* to be one step below God. At times Plotinus distinguished the *nous* from the *psyche*, arguing that the former belongs to a higher level of hierarchic existence.

In this sense, *nous* corresponds not so much with *atman*, the transcendental Self of the Vedanta philosophers and sages, than with *buddhi*, the faculty of wisdom believed to be the highest aspect of the human personality according to Hindu metaphysics. It is by means of this higher intelligence that we may discover the luminous transcendental Self. In the *Katha-Upanishad*, an ancient Sanskrit work on Vedantic Yoga, the following striking metaphor is found: The body is the chariot; the senses are the unruly horses; the lower mind *(manas)* is the reins; the higher mind *(buddhi)* is the charioteer; and the Self is the chariot master. This image suggests a hierarchy of interlinking psychic faculties. We must appreciate that it took thousands of years to arrive at this integrated model of the soul.

A similar effort is represented by the Upanishadic teaching of the five "sheaths" *(kosha)* of the soul. Thus, according to the *Taittiriya-Upanishad*, which is well over three thousand years old, there are five levels of human functioning:

1. *anna-maya-kosha* — sheath composed of food (i.e., the physical body)
2. *prana-maya-kosha* — sheath composed of breath (also known as the "etheric double" or "plasma body")
3. *mano-maya-kosha* — sheath composed of mind (i.e., the lower mental functions)
4. *vijnana-maya-kosha* — sheath composed of intelligence (i.e., the higher mental functions of discernment and wisdom)

5. *ananda-maya-kosha*   sheath composed of bliss (i.e., that
                           aspect of the personality structure which
                           is revealed in states of ecstasy)

These sheaths, or bodies, are coverings around the immortal soul, the transcendental Self, which is everlasting awareness without object. The practical spirituality of Yoga is geared toward "piercing" these casings until the Self shines forth in its original splendor. This realization is considered ultimate enlightenment, or liberation, which cannot be lost. Piercing the sheaths means not to identify with them as if they were the transcendental Self. But this disidentification must be preceded by the conscious experience of each casing (or vibrational field) in meditation. It is not a mere intellectual act.

We know from our day-to-day experience on the physical level how easy it is to fuse with our material body to the point where we mistakenly identify with it. This error is just as easily committed on more subtle levels of existence, as encountered in meditation and ecstatic states. Each form of bodily identification is also a form of bondage, which brings with it its own experience of suffering. Even at the level of the blissful sheath, exclusive identification with bliss is ultimately limiting and hence a form of suffering. Only Self-identification—that is, realization of the supraconscious Self, or Spirit, as our true nature—is liberating.

Today the idea that the psyche is a multistory building is found almost everywhere in the esoteric or occult literature. Most of these doctrines on multiple "subtle bodies" derive directly or indirectly from Hindu metaphysics, often by way of Theosophy. The most comprehensive compilation of such teachings is J. J. Poortman's four-volume work *Vehicles of Consciousness*, published in 1978.[13] Also an important work is G. R. S. Mead's *The Doctrine of the Subtle Body in Western Tradition*, another theosophical publication, which was first issued in 1919.[14] It should be noted here that a great deal of soul lore in various cultures is more speculative than experiential, and the massive evidence available—consisting of both first-hand accounts and theoretical elaborations—awaits its Einstein to be properly appraised and organized into a general theory of soul.

The notion that the psyche comprises more than one level of existence has exerted a lasting influence even on more conservative strands of modern thought. Sigmund Freud, for instance, divided the psyche into three parts: unconscious, preconscious, and conscious. In his pioneering work on psychoanalytic dream interpretation, Freud quoted Carl Du Prel with approval:

> The problem: what is the psyche, manifestly requires a preliminary examination as to whether consciousness and psyche are identical. But it is just this preliminary question which is answered in the negative by the dream, which shows that the concept of the psyche extends beyond that of consciousness, much as the gravitational force of a star extends beyond its sphere of luminosity.[15]

Thus, whereas the thinkers of antiquity were eager to prove the soul to embrace a higher dimension—*nous* or *buddhi*—Freud and his disciples were anxious to drive home the fact that the soul also has its nether regions. Today, transpersonal psychology strives to integrate these two orientations: the higher or transpersonal mind and the largely disowned "shadow" of the psyche.

In her book *Soul Return*, transpersonal psychologist Aminah Raheem notes, "I have found that the person develops from the soul center outward, in progressive personality layers that form around it."[16] She goes on to say:

> Ideally, these two forces—soul and personality—would be integrated and aligned in common purpose, with the personality acting as a vehicle through which the soul might fully manifest its purpose and destiny.

Statements like this illustrate that psychology has come full circle. It is no longer merely verbal knowledge *(logos)* about the psyche but an incipient wisdom teaching that guides people to the discovery of the spiritual reaches of existence. It is again—at least for some of its practitioners—the Socratic *therapeia* of the soul, assisting us in our endeavor to practice lucid waking. What Socrates was hoping for, and what transpersonal psychologists are aiming at, is to recover the wholeness of the soul. Socrates, who was not merely a philosophically minded intellectual but a great mystic and visionary, taught that the soul, as the immortal principle, must be tended to and strengthened in us, and that this is the proper task of human life lived with lucid awareness, or mindfulness.

To conclude with a fitting observation by C. G. Jung, who pushed the envelope of psychology to its limits and prepared the ground for today's transpersonal psychology:

The psyche is the world's pivot: not only is it the one great condition for the existence of a world at all, it is also an intervention in the existing natural order, and no one can say with certainty where this intervention will finally end.[17]

5

WHO OR WHAT IS THE SPIRIT?

THE BREATH OF THE SPIRIT

As a child I was very confused about the notion of the Holy Spirit, then still called the Holy Ghost. I could not figure out why the apostles upon whose heads the Holy Spirit had descended in the shape of a flame did not catch fire. (They did so figuratively, of course.) Nor did I comprehend how at times the Holy Spirit could manifest as a beautiful dove. I enjoyed the imagery, but it made no sense to me at all. In my teens I jettisoned this and most of the other Christian (Protestant) beliefs I had inherited from my parents, and I wrote an essay in which I challenged myself with heart-searching questions about the existence of God. Had I then known St. Augustine's motto *credo ut intelligam* ("I believe in order to understand"), I would most certainly have rejected it as irrational. I would have had even less sympathy for Tertullian's *credo quia absurdum est* ("I believe because it is absurd"). I was very eager to construct a satisfying rational framework for myself, and mere belief in some doctrine or other was no longer possible for me.

An uncle, who until then had been very supportive of me, misunderstood entirely the intent of my essay and reprimanded me for allowing my philosophical quest to slip into atheism. He obviously found my radical questions too threatening. I was gesturing toward agnosticism rather than atheism: We could not know anything about a divinity that was, by definition, beyond the comprehension of the mind. Inexplicably, my uncle, who was otherwise a reasonable man, refused to listen to me further on this topic, so I was unable to clear up the misunderstanding. I wanted to tell him that even though I could not intellectually substantiate the existence of God (especially not a divine father figure), in my heart I very much carried a sense of certainty—as distinct from doctrinal belief— about the existence of a spiritual dimension of being.

This dilemma of intuiting the Spirit but finding no intellectual justification for this inner certainty stayed with me for many years. I think that many people who have become aware of the limitation of mere belief are in the same situation. They sense that there is something over and above material existence, but they have no intellectual clarity about this fundamental intuition. In the absence of a philosophical passion that pushes them to inquire into the nature of knowledge, belief, and intuition, they remain metaphysically disoriented.

My philosophical thinking underwent a crucial transition when I encountered the claim of mysticism that Spirit can in some way be experienced or, more accurately, realized. This realization was one of essential identification with the Spirit, which is not an object but our innermost subjective core. I was able to immediately accept the validity of this claim. It simply corresponded to my own intuition, and I also had no reason to doubt the testimony of so many individuals from diverse cultures and eras. To realize the Spirit, rather than think around it, became a *leitmotif* in my life. After my encounter with India's mystical traditions, which speak of *brahman, atman, purusha,* or *dharmakaya,* I mostly discontinued using the noun *Spirit,* though the reality for which it stands has remained a constant personal and philosophical concern of mine.

Like the concept of soul, that of Spirit has had a checkered evolution. This is reflected in the dictionary definition of the term. Thus, *Random House Webster's College Dictionary* lists twenty-four connotations, the most important of which are:

1. life principle
2. soul
3. consciousness, mind, intellect, intelligence
4. will, motivating principle
5. ghost or supernatural being (e.g., an angel)
6. essential style, as in the German zeitgeist (spirit of the times)

Because of its various prosaic applications (notably in the sense of "alcohol"), we use the word *Spirit* more liberally than *soul* in everyday speech. However, our understanding of the term's metaphysical import is just as opaque as in the case of the term *soul*. When we return to the roots, as discussed in the previous chapter, we enter into a whole different domain of world experience, namely that of myth and symbolic analogy.

Let us begin this historical bird's-eye view with the Hebrew heritage, which is the foundation upon which Christianity was erected. The Old Testament uses the term *ruah* to denote Spirit. This word literally means "wind" and is often used in this sense in the Bible. By extension, it can also refer to the "wind" in the human being, that is, the breath. Both wind and breath are invisible forces that are yet detectable by their effects: The wind causes branches to sway and leaves to swirl, or even whole trees to be uprooted; the breath can extinguish the flame of a candle or, in mouth-to-mouth resuscitation, rekindle life in another person. For the ancient Hebrews, the imperceptible power of wind and breath was a convincing metaphor for the Spirit, which is also invisible but which lights up a person's eyes and animates the body.

In Genesis 1:2 we find a first union of the natural and the theological connotation of *ruah*. Here God's breath/Spirit is described, in archetypal mythological terms, as hovering over the primordial waters. The Spirit of Yahweh is his divine creative power or will or name (since name and power are equivalent in archaic thought). This idea was subsequently taken up in Proverbs 8:22, where God is said to have possessed wisdom (Hebrew *hokma;* Greek *sophia*) before he launched the world. Wisdom is portrayed as a female ("Lady Wisdom"). This whole notion forms a striking parallel to the Hindu metaphysical idea of *shakti*, the creative potency of the Divine. Some biblical scholars have suggested that possibly Lady Wisdom represents a more sophisticated version. of an ancient Hebrew Goddess, who was Yahweh's divine partner. This idea is central to the Kabbalistic teaching of the Shekinah. In later thought, in any case, God is explicitly stated to be singular, and therefore his (feminine) Spirit must not be thought different from him. In like fashion, *shakti* (the transcendental feminine power) is one with *shiva* (the transcendental male essence).

Turning to the New Testament, we find that St. Paul in his first epistle to the Corinthians (1:24) equated the Christ with "the power of God and the wisdom of God." The "wisdom" tradition became more prominent with the church fathers. Many of them continued Paul's christological equation, but some—notably the second-century bishop Irenaeus, famous for his book *Against Heresies*—identified wisdom with the Holy Spirit. Others, like St. John, preferred the theological idiom of the divine Word *(logos)*, which has the long-established authority of Genesis (1.3: "Let there be light") itself. Given these multiple lines of interpretation, we need not be surprised at the resulting terminological confusion, leading to endless theological gyrations then and now.

Perhaps the most valuable insight to emerge from the entire history of Christian thought is that the divine Spirit somehow inheres in each human being, expressing itself as "our" individual Spirit. Among the sages of India the same recognition formed the bedrock of a fabulous variety of philosophical positions. On the basis of their extensive mystical practice, the Indian thinkers pursued the equation "divine Spirit = human Spirit" with a vigor unmatched in any other intellectual or spiritual tradition. Happily, I discovered their wisdom teachings early in life, and they helped me to fill the void left by my break with Christianity at the age of fourteen. For outside the fold of a religious tradition, Spirit is nonexistent in our highly secularized culture. As the renowned Protestant theologian Paul Tillich remarked:

> One of the unfortunate consequences of the intellectualization of man's spiritual life was that the word "Spirit" was lost and

replaced by "mind" and "intellect", and that the element of vitality which is present in "Spirit" was separated and interpreted as
an independent biological force. Man was divided into a blood-
less intellect and a meaningless vitality. The middle ground
between them, the spiritual soul in which vitality and intention-
ality are united, was dropped. At the end of this development it
was easy for a reductive naturalism to derive self-affirmation and
courage from a merely biological vitality. But in man nothing is
"merely biological" as nothing is "merely spiritual". Every cell of
his body participates in his freedom and spirituality, and every
act of his spiritual creativity is nourished by his vital dynamics.[1]

THE HINDU PERSPECTIVE

Had I encountered Tillich's work in my youth I might conceivably
have explored Christianity more. As it was, I found myself resonat-
ing very naturally with India's spirituality, first through the prism of
the cognate traditions of Yoga, Samkhya, and Vedanta, and then
through the prism of Buddhism and Jainism as well as the archaic
spirituality of the Rig-Veda, which continues to intrigue and inspire
me. The Rig-Veda, which is now held to be an excellent candidate
for being the oldest extant scripture in the world, is a collection of
1,028 hymns composed in an early form of Sanskrit.[2] Many of the
hymns are crafted in a sophisticated poetic-mythological language
and hint at mystical knowledge of a high order. They are the philosophical foundation of the later Upanishads, those "Himalayas of
the soul," as one translator praised these texts.

It is in the Upanishads, the oldest of which date back to the
beginning of the second millennium B.C., that we find the first clear
articulations of the mystical teaching of all-identity. According to
this teaching there is only one transcendental reality, called *brahman* ("that which is vast"), which is beyond "name and form"
(nama-rupa) and is inconceivable. That singularity underlying the
manifest universe is perfectly identical with the core, ground, apex,
or ultimate depth of the human being, which is called *atman*
("self"). This identity is the pivot of Vedanta, the most prominent

metaphysical tradition within Hinduism. In the Yoga tradition, we find the same idea in the concept of *purusha*. The etymology of this term is uncertain—it may mean something like "he who rests in the city [of the body]"—but its metaphysical meaning is clear: It refers to the "nonlocal" transcendental Spirit. There are differences between the Vedantic idea of *atman* and the yogic notion of *purusha*, but they are irrelevant to the present discussion.

What is relevant, however, is the fact that *atman* originally meant "breath." Thus, in the Rig-Veda (X.16.3), we find the line *suryam cakshuh gacchatu vatam atma,* "May the eye go to the Sun, the breath *(atma = atman)* to the wind." In the famous hymn of creation (Rig-Veda X.129), we are told that prior to creation the One "breathed breathlessly" *(anid avatam).* The cosmos is, as it were, an exhalation of that singularity—a concept that some three thousand years later was reiterated by Plotinus, perhaps the greatest mystic philosopher of European antiquity.

Another significant fact about *atman* is that it is the eternal subject beyond the human ego. At best, the ego is a distortion of the *atman*; at worst, it is the *atman's* enemy. The Upanishadic sages, like the Vedic seers before them, invested their lives in realizing that ultimate singularity, the eternal Spirit, behind the world of multiplicity (and duplicity), or beyond the Platonic cave of shadows.

Each religious or spiritual tradition has its own definition of Spirit, but this is not the place for a comparative study, which would require a book of its own. The fundamentally important fact is that with the notable exception of Hinayana Buddhism, all the major spiritual traditions of the world have one or more terms denoting what in the Christian tradition is called Spirit. Without wishing to preclude the validity of other explanations, my own explanation of Spirit leans heavily on the idealist metaphysics of Advaita Vedanta and Mahayana Buddhism. For me, then, *Spirit* is the ultimate reality (the only reality there is) as viewed from the perspective of the individual. This perspective contains a cognitive distortion that makes the singular reality appear to be unique to each person, which it is not. So long as we understand that there is only one Spirit and not many Spirits (as in Samkhya philosophy), there is no danger in using the term *Spirit.* Bearing this stricture in mind, I suggest further that Spirit is translocal (transcending space-time, yet not being apart from it as a separate entity), supraconscious (not merely unconscious but also not conscious in the sense of implying a distinction between subject and object), transpersonal (not merely impersonal but also not personal), and supremely blissful (not merely the absence of suffering but also not happiness resulting from a conditional cause).

Furthermore, since this singular Spirit is the only reality (all else being either a misrepresentation of it or a hallucination), it must necessarily be our true nature. If it is our true nature, then we are at present caught in a dream (or a nightmare) in which we mistakenly identify with the images we create out of our own accord. Also, if it is our true nature and we are at present dreaming, we have the intrinsic capacity to spontaneously remember ourselves. In other words, we are fully capable of self-realization. This is, in fact, the fundamental message of all spiritual traditions.

When understood in the deepest possible way, the well-known maxim of the Delphic oracle—*gnothi se auton*, "know yourself"— means exactly this: Know yourself (your Self) as the only reality that is. The corresponding version in Sanskrit is *atmanam viddhi*, suggesting both "know yourself" and "know *the* Self," the Self being none other than the transcendental Spirit.

Self-knowledge leading to actual self-realization is the essence of spiritual life, that is, a life governed by principles that make self-realization possible. To make it plain, spiritual life is not simply about self-improvement, personal growth, visions, ecstasies, occult powers, energies, channeling, biofeedback, or crystals. Spiritual life is not even merely moral life dedicated to goodness and the conquest of evil. Something far more radical is intended: the transcendence of good and evil through the transcendence of the ego-personality in the context of lucid waking, or mindfulness.

LIVING THE SPIRIT

Here I want to emphasize the fact that spiritual life is always embodied life. This implies that it must bring the transcendental unity of the Spirit down to earth. That is to say, spiritual life is about living from the viewpoint of the Spirit, which is the same in everyone and everything. Translated into moral terms, this means cultivating unqualified compassion, friendliness, generosity, patience, and all the other great virtues found, for instance, in the *bodhisattva*. In Mahayana Buddhism, *bodhisattvas* are those who have understood the essential unity, or coessentiality, of all beings and who, on the basis of this wisdom, swap themselves with others. They behave as if there were no distinction between themselves and others, heaping upon others only good in every possible way. In this manner, they pile up merit (or favorable energy) for themselves, which they then dedicate to the welfare of others. They keep nothing for themselves, and even their core aspiration to attain enlightenment has the unselfish motive of increasing their capacity to help other beings. Their only desire is to bring about the enlightenment of all beings. This resolution and approach to life is known as the mind of enlightenment *(bodhicitta)*.

In his *Bodhicaryavatara* ("Entering the Way of Enlightenment"), the eighth-century Buddhist teacher Shantideva extols the *bodhisattva* ideal as follows:[3]

Goodness *(shubha)* is always weak, whereas the power of evil is great and most terrifying. By what goodness is that evil conquered if not by the mind of enlightenment *(bodhicitta)*? (I.6)

Reflecting for many eons, the master sages realized this mind of enlightenment to be good. In this way, joy growing from joy spills over into the immeasurable mass of people. (I.7)

The mind of enlightenment must not ever be abandoned by those wishing to escape the hundreds of sorrows of existence, by those wishing to remove the suffering of others, and by those wishing to enjoy the many hundreds of joys. (I.8)

From the moment one dedicates one's mind, with unwavering attention, to deliverance from the endless dispositions *(dhatu)* of beings . . . (I.18)

. . . from that moment on, despite repeated sleep and inattention, streams of merit flow continuously, like the sky. (I.19)

Over and over again the *bodhisattva* brings about the fulfillment of all happiness for those who are afflicted and hankering for happiness, and cuts off all their afflictions. (I.29)

He[4] also destroys their delusion. Where else is there goodness *(sadhu)* equal to his? Where else is there such friendship, or where else is there such virtue? (I.30)

I rejoice at the release of beings from the suffering of conditional existence *(samsara),* and I rejoice at their Bodhisattvahood and Buddhahood. (III.2)

I am medicine for the sick. May I be their physician and their nurse until there is no recurrence of sickness. (III.7)

Having dedicated myself to the happiness of all embodied beings, may they strike me! May they revile me! May they cover me constantly with dirt! (III.13)

May they play with my body, laugh at or toy with me! Having given my body to them, why should I be concerned? (III.13)

May those who denounce, mock, or injure me, as well as all others, share in enlightenment! (III.16)

May I be a protector for those without protection, a guide for travelers [on the path], a boat, a bridge, a passage for those desiring the farther shore. (III.17)

This mind of enlightenment has arisen in me somehow just as a blind man might find a jewel in a heap of dirt. (III.27)

This elixir has arisen to eliminate death in the world. It is the imperishable treasure removing the world's poverty. (III.28)

It is the supreme medicine for removing the world's sickness, and it is a restful tree for a world weary of wandering in [conditional] states of existence. (III.29)

In Christian terms, *bodhisattvas* are always in the divine presence, and all their deeds are inspired by the spirit of *agape* (selfless love) and *caritas* (selfless charity). Their spiritual heroism knows no bounds, and they willingly forego entrance into transcendental Buddhahood so that they may, in the course of countless eons, guide all other beings to peace, joy, harmony, and the fulfillment of the highest human destiny. *Bodhisattvas* always seek to bring out the best in others, reminding them of their own intrinsic Buddha nature and exhorting them to practice lucid waking. William James, as he did so often, hit the mark when he observed:

> The saints, existing in this way, may, with their extravagances of human tenderness, be prophetic. Nay, innumerable times they have proved themselves prophetic. Treating those whom they met, in spite of the past, in spite of all appearances, as worthy, they have stimulated them to *be* worthy, miraculously transformed them by their radiant example and by the challenge of their expectations.
>
> From this point of view we may admit the human charity which we find in all saints, and the great excess of it which we find in some saints, to be a genuinely creative social force, tending to make real a degree of virtue which it alone is ready to assume as possible. The saints are authors, *auctores*, increasers, of goodness.[5]

If we are suspicious of such nobility it is only because our contemporary civilization is driven by a maniacal disregard for the spiritual potential of our species. The mass media celebrate the false heroism of crime and sports, wealth and power, and other similar "newsworthy" products of a culture of pleasure-seekers ever in search of entertainment but oblivious to joy, wisdom, kindness, and love. Those who recognize this unfortunate state of affairs can do nothing better than to embody the values of the *bodhisattva,* the Buddhist saint, in all their personal relationships, whether at home or at work. Only if a sufficient number of men and women live from the viewpoint of true philosophy, as explained in the opening chapter, can there be significant change for the better in our ailing society. In fact, the survival of the human race may well depend on this.

6

THE POWER OF IMAGINATION

IN PRAISE OF IMAGINATION

Imagination is to the mind what the breath is to the body. Without imagination, we would be condemned to live a purely instinctive life. We would still be walking about naked, ignorant of fire, and constantly foraging for food. We would not even have the wits to construct simple shelters to protect ourselves from the elements.

Without imagination, we would never have uttered the first word, never mind grammatical sentences. Nor would we have discovered the healing properties of plants. We would be utterly oblivious to the fact that by grinding rocks and plants we could create colorful pigments with which to paint our bodies and decorate our dwellings. There would be no cave art, Byzantine icons, Chinese landscape paintings, or da Vinci's *Last Supper* and *Mona Lisa*; no Boticelli's *Birth of Venus,* Michelangelo's *Last Judgment,* Dürer's woodcuts, Rembrandt's portraits; no *Sunflowers* by van Gogh, no *Guernica* by Picasso, and no Disney art.

We would have no Stonehenge, pyramids, Chinese Wall, coliseum of Rome, Taj Mahal, or cathedral of Notre Dame; no Eiffel Tower, Empire State Building, or Golden Gate Bridge. Nor would there be a Venus of Willendorf, Sphinx, mask of Tutankhamun, Venus de Milo, Michelangelo's *David*, or Rodin's *Thinker*.

Without imagination, we would be bereft of all writing and literature—from the Vedas of India to the Sumerian clay tablets and Egyptian hieroglyphic inscriptions; to the Pali Canon, Tao Te Ching, *Iliad* and *Odyssey*, Bible, Koran, Kabbalah, Mexican Popol Vuh, and *Aesop's Fables*; to the writings of Plato, Aristotle, Euripides, St. Augustine, Thomas Aquinas, Dante, Shakespeare, Chaucer, Dickens, Tolstoy, Dostoevsky, Goethe, Thoreau, Emerson, Whitman, Joyce, Sartre, the Brontë sisters, and Gertrude Stein.

We would also have no ethnic drumming, Gregorian chants, Bach cantatas, or Handel oratorios; no symphonies by Beethoven, Tchaikovsky, or Mozart; no piano concertos by Chopin, operas by Wagner, waltzes by Strauss, operettas by Gilbert and Sullivan, ballets by Stravinsky; and no folk songs, jazz, Beatles' songs, or "Star-Spangled Banner."

Without imagination, there would certainly be no wheeled vehicles, electric light bulbs, microwave ovens, refrigerators, radios, televisions, telephones, fax machines, computers, motor cars, boats, airplanes, spacecraft, particle accelerators, radio telescopes, or the myriad other technological inventions that characterize modern life, for good or for bad.

In the absence of imagination, we would neither care for the sick and elderly nor bury our dead. We would lack all social sensitivity and compassion. We would have no thought of the great beyond and would never contemplate our existence. There would be no philosophy, psychology, politics (some might consider this a blessing); and no history, linguistics, mathematics, or any of the natural sciences. Without imagination, a life of lucid waking would be utterly impossible.

IMAGINING IMAGINATION: THE TWO WESTERN TRADITIONS

Imagination, then, is fundamental to human life. It is the motor behind society and culture, and it undergirds our individual existence. But what is imagination? There is no agreed-on definition. The word is currently used in at least four different ways to denote:

1. The ability to form mental images of things that are not presently experienced ("I can still see my late husband's face very clearly") or have never been experienced ("I am picturing a fire-breathing green dragon"), and the actual process of doing so.
2. The ability to understand and cherish the creative work of others, as when we admire a child's drawing or appreciate the beauty in a mathematical formula.
3. An actual idea or image held in the mind (mostly poetic usage).
4. A fanciful notion, guesswork.

In Western philosophy, many thinkers—taking their cue from Plato—opted for the fourth definition and started a whole lineage of suspicion against imagination. Plato appears to have equated imagination with conjecture and guessing, which are the opposite of certain knowledge, which he was mostly concerned with. Perceptible objects, insisted Plato, could never give us true knowledge, because they are subject to constant change. Only the immutable essence of a thing could yield real knowledge. For this, Plato taught, we must look at the essential properties that similar objects have in common. This was exactly the task of philosophy as he envisioned it.

Plato also maintained that poetry, which only mimics the great eternal ideas or forms, cannot reveal true knowledge of the essence of things and therefore is vastly inferior to philosophy. Therefore, all that the poet accomplishes is to muddle up emotion with reason. In fact, in his famous *Republic*, Plato goes so far as to suggest that imitative poets should be banned from the ideal state because they pervert the truth. This view has proven very influential and long-lived in Western thought, because it happened to coincide with the traditional Christian attitude toward imagination.

Thus, the seventeenth-century French philosopher and mathematical genius Blaise Pascal, a man of the utmost imaginative ability, settled for the Platonic (fourth) option and dismissed imagination as the "mistress of error and of falsehood." Pascal's appraisal was perhaps unduly influenced by his reading of the Bible, which states that "the imagination of man's heart is evil from his youth" (Genesis 8:21).

But such a negative interpretation hardly does justice to the power of human imagination, which can flow both toward the good and toward the bad. Throughout human history, imagination has been responsible for countless benign accomplishments and genuine acts of heroism and also for untold destruction and misery. The same imagination that has discovered anesthetics, penicillin, antihistamines, acupuncture, and homeopathy also has invented gun powder, nuclear weapons, biological warfare, forms of torture, and the electric chair. In the words of the British poet Percy Bysshe Shelley, imagination can be "the great instrument of moral good"— but only if we harness it properly.

Pascal himself demonstrated imagination at its best when he invented the calculating machine and the hydraulic press and when he advanced mathematics by his theory of probability and by his contribution to differential calculus. Moreover, his *Pensées* are a lasting tribute to the human imagination in its literary and philosophical expression.

Aristotle, Plato's genius pupil, took a stance quite different from that of his teacher. He saw in imagination a pervasive mental ability to form images out of sense impressions (corresponding to the first definition listed above). He thus placed imagination between sensation and reason. Many subsequent thinkers followed Aristotle's lead, notably the seventeenth-century British philosopher Thomas Hobbes and the German philosopher Immanuel Kant, who lived a century later. Hobbes, who was overly fond of mechanistic explanations, considered imagination to be "nothing but decaying sense." As he saw it, our experience of the objective world begets memory, which in turn leads to judgment and fancy. It is fancy—or fantasy—that gives birth to poetry and the other arts. While he did not at all dismiss poetry—he himself prepared a verse translation of the *Iliad* and the *Odyssey* at the age of eighty-six!— he did deem it necessary to control imagination by means of reason.

Kant, whose *Critique of Pure Reason* is a masterwork of the abstract imagination that ushered in a new era in philosophy, characterized imagination as a "blind but indispensable function of the soul, without which we should have no knowledge whatsoever, but of which we are scarcely ever conscious."[1] He ascribed two related roles to imagination. First, imagination completes the input from the senses. Thus, when we look at a house, we actually see only a part of it because we cannot see around to the back of it, nor can we see its bottom. Yet, our imagination constructs for us a complete image of the house. In fact, this constant mental construction work allows us to navigate reasonably well and safely in our environment. Kant gave the technical name of reproductive imagination to this particular function of the mind (or "soul," as he would say). Second, imagination combines all our varied mental representations or images of the world into a unified whole. He called this function productive (i.e., creative) imagination. Without it, our experience would be utterly disjointed and meaningless. Genius, according to Kant, arises from the combination of imagination and reason. He also noted that whereas imagination employed in the service of knowledge is subject to certain restraints, artistic imagination is untrammeled, or free.

Kant's theory of imagination never achieved popularity outside the circle of professional philosophers. Literary minds were more inspired by Samuel Taylor Coleridge's theory of imagination. He contrasted genuine imagination from fancy, "a mode of Memory emancipated from the order of time and place." Like Kant, he differentiated between two types of imagination: primary imagination (corresponding to Kant's productive imagination), which synthesizes all perception, and secondary imagination, which is the source of artistic creativity. In his work *Biographia Literaria,* Coleridge explained that secondary imagination "dissolves, diffuses, dissipates, in order to re-create." Its purpose is to unify through idealization. He placed the truth-revealing capacity of artistic creativity (imagination) above the creativity (imagination) exercised in the sciences, mathematics, or philosophy. In this he turned upside down the widely held opinion of earlier European thinkers, who considered the arts inferior to the sciences and reason.

Coleridge was true to the spirit of romanticism. Similarly, in his *System of Transcendental Idealism,* Johann Gottlieb Fichte praised art as the consummation of philosophy. And Novalis stated, "Poetry is what is absolutely and genuinely real."

Then along came the British philosophical psychologist Gilbert Ryle, who dismissed the universally held idea that imagination was all of a piece. Instead, he insisted that what we mean by imagination is not a singular mental faculty but a composite of several internal processes: imaging, supposition, fancy, pretense, impersonation, and so on. His radical view was that the idea of mental imagery is completely redundant. This idea appeals to those who like to dismantle everything and are suspicious of all attempts at synthesis.

While imagination may run afoul of reality, this mismatch could signal an advantage rather than a loss. This was Jean-Paul Sartre's position. In his acclaimed book *The Psychology of Imagination,* he proposed the view that through imagination we realize the intrinsic freedom of consciousness. This notion is central to Sartre's existentialist philosophy.

Philosophical thinking about imagination is incredibly complex. What is for certain is that neither the Platonic nor the Aristotelian lineage of interpreting imagination is entirely adequate. Hence, a handful of contemporary philosophers, notably the German philosopher Hans Georg Gadamer, are struggling to achieve a better understanding of this mysterious mental faculty. And so the philosophical enterprise, itself a product of imagination, continues as it has for thousands of years.

IMAGERY AND IMAGINATION

How should we understand the nature of imagination? The word itself is derived from the Latin term *imago,* meaning "picture," which is of course also the source of the English word *image.* While an image can be either external or internal, imagination stands for mental picturing or the psychological process of imaging. We do not perceive the world as it is in its raw state. Rather, because of the way we are built, we must translate our sensory perceptions into mental representations so that they can become data for our consciousness. This representation is a matter of forming images.

The Würzburg school of psychology, relying on introspective analysis alone, maintained that there is such a thing as imageless thought. But Edward Bradford Titchener and his teacher Wilhelm Wundt, the nineteenth-century founder of modern experimental psychology, thought otherwise. After 1920, their structural psychology, which also relied on introspection and had too narrow a compass, was replaced by functionalism and behaviorism in America and by gestalt psychology in Germany.

Mental images are not merely visual. As psychologist P. McKeller explained in his book *Experience and Behavior*, there also are images involving hearing, motion, touch, taste, smell, pain, and temperature.[2] The visual image is the most common (97 percent), followed closely by the auditory image (93 percent). The least common are pain-related images (54 percent) and temperature-related images (43 percent). Therefore, it is not surprising that methods of enhancing mental imagery focus on visual images. But we would also profit from making more conscious use of auditory images (the sounds of Beethoven's Pastoral Symphony, church bells, or the rustling of leaves from a gentle breeze).

The mental process of imaging comprises both actual imagery in the mind and imagelike thoughts or ideas that are not exactly seen on the inner screen but are still somehow felt to be present and may sprout into visual imagery at any point. For instance, when we think about the president of the United States, we have an overall feeling image, a total gestalt, of him. We associate distinct physical characteristics and emotional qualities with him, and we could probably describe him well enough to produce a good likeness for a "wanted" poster. Some of us have the additional ability to close our eyes and conjure up a reasonably faithful mental snapshot of him.

This ability to retain visual images with great vividness, distinctiveness, and wealth of detail is known as eidetic imaging or photographic memory. It is common in young children but quite rare in adults. One man who had developed this form of imagination to a superlative degree was Nikola Tesla, one of the unsung scientific heroes at the turn of the century. His contribution to the field of electricity was extraordinary. As Willis Harman noted in *Higher Creativity*:

"Nikola Tesla" is hardly a household name. Yet if it weren't for Tesla's discoveries and inventions, the typical industrial-era household would scarcely be what it is today. If you were to remove all traces of Tesla's major contributions from your home, you would have to eliminate the electrical power grid that your wall socket taps into to feed your appliances. You would also have to eliminate many of the appliances, starting with your television and radio, as well as fluorescent and neon lighting.[3]

Tesla was apparently capable of such vivid visualization, or internal imaging, that he could test his electrical machines without having to build or even draw them. He allowed them to run in his imagination, checked in with them regularly, and determined the wear and tear after so many hours of purely imaginary running. He improved his hypothetical machines by making the appropriate adjustments in his mental imagery. When he was satisfied that an invention was running at optimal performance, he would finally set about building it. His mental simulations invariably proved accurate.

We can witness the same kind of astonishing visualization in some meditation masters of the Tibetan Buddhist tradition, who are able to construct complex and extraordinarily vivid inner images of various deities and their divine environments. It is said of some of these practitioners that they can see the white in the eyes of these internally constructed representations of gods and goddesses from the Tibetan pantheon. Also, they are able to maintain these visualizations for hours at a time, during which they move deeper and deeper into the mysterious multilevel world of consciousness.

Other Tibetan yogis are able to create so much body heat through visualization that they can sit naked at the top of Himalayan mountain peaks and dry wet cloths on their bare skin, melting the snow around them to boot. Since this extraordinary accomplishment has been captured on film, we know that this is not mere legend or wishful thinking. Few of us are capable of such feats, however, and therefore I focus here on the first type of imagination, the kind that allows us to combine existing ideas so that we may create novel ideas.

In his *Essay sur l'imagination créatrice,* published in 1900, the French psychologist T. Ribot distinguished between three levels of imagination corresponding to three developmental stages in individual psychological growth:

1. *Imagination ébauchée* ("rough imagination"), which covers dreams, fleeting images, fancies, vague hopes.
2. *Imagination fixée* ("fixed imagination"), which comprises myths, abstract theories, and artistic creativity.
3. *Imagination objectivée* ("objective imagination"), which is the practical imagination involved in invention.

Ribot valued the objective, practical imagination the highest. He would no doubt have found an ally for his opinion in most of today's technophiles. However, the form of imagination that is most common is the first type, and especially the imagination of dreaming. It is here that our imagination is predictably unleashed and demonstrates its tremendous versatility. We do not have to be great philosophers or novelists to exercise this form of imagination, either, but merely have to learn to pay attention to this natural wellspring of mental creativity.

THE IMAGINATIVE WORLD OF DREAMS

Our imagination unhooks from its conventional mooring when we take certain psychedelic drugs, such as LSD. Then our experienced world turns upside down and inside out. Tables can walk, curtains can twist themselves into humanoid shapes, colors become associated with specific sounds. This places us in the kind of looking-glass world that Lewis Carrol portrayed so vividly in *Alice's Adventures in Wonderland* (1865).

Fortunately, we do not need to ingest potentially or actually harmful drugs to free our imagination. In the drowsy state just prior to falling asleep, we can tap into the pictorial potential of the mind. When we close our eyes and allow our mind to drift off into sleep, we can see what psychologists call hypnagogic imagery. The word *hypnagogic* is derived from the Greek words *hypnos,* meaning "sleep," and *agogeus,* meaning "conductor." This type of imagery is described as hallucinatory or quasihallucinatory and occupies the territory between wakefulness and sleep. In the third century A.D., the Syrian Neoplatonic philosopher Iamblichus noted that just before we wake from sleep we sometimes can hear voices or see "a bright and tranquil light shine." According to some researchers, one-third of the adult population experiences hypnagogic imagery, and the incidence is expectedly much higher in children. Most adults are scarcely aware of this phenomenon, just as we tend not to remember our dreams and sometimes think that we have not had any or never dream. Hypnagogic imagery includes abstract designs, concrete objects, natural scenery, familiar and unfamiliar people, and also fantastic creatures.

I remember spontaneously exploring presleep imagery in my early teens. I was curious about the luminous, constantly changing, and ever-mysterious patterns I was seeing, and wanted to know whether I could consciously influence them. I vaguely recall that my conclusion was negative. I had more luck with actual dream imagery, which on occasion seemed to yield moderately to my conscious intent. It is almost as though the hypnagogic images are like steam boiling off from the brain. Hence, some researchers have concluded that such images do not strictly belong to the realm of human imagination. But the hypnagogic state can certainly be cultivated through biofeedback training and utilized for imaginative and creative work as well as for therapeutic purposes.

When we enter rapid eye-movement (REM) or paradoxical sleep—better known as dreaming—we are at the level of full-fledged imagination. It is difficult to retain an observer consciousness in dream sleep, but it can be done. In fact, this is an actual yogic practice—known as Dream Yoga—in the Tibetan tradition of Vajrayana Buddhism. As the Buddhist teacher Tarthang Tulku observed:

> Dreams are a reservoir of knowledge and experience, yet they are often overlooked as a vehicle for exploring reality. In the dream state our bodies are at rest, yet we see and hear, move about, and are even able to learn. When we make good use of the dream state, it is almost as if our lives were doubled.[4]

The art of conscious dreaming is gradually being learned anew by Western scientists, who speak of lucid dreaming. According to Stephen LaBerge, who pioneered this kind of research, lucid dreaming is "the union of two separate elements, dreaming and consciousness." In his best-selling book *Lucid Dreaming,* he mentions how he himself used the imaginative power of lucid dreaming to recast his doctoral dissertation.[5] In a subsequent book, *Exploring the World of Lucid Dreaming,* he provides numerous practical methods for coaxing the mind into the paradoxical state of remaining awake while falling asleep and for exploiting that state to enhance creativity. "Dreams," he writes, "can be a fabulous source of creativity."[6] He explains creativity as "the use of the imagination to produce some new thing, from a work of art to a homework paper."[7]

As long ago as 1867, H. de Saint-Denys wrote a book entitled *Dreams and How to Guide Them* and in it reported his own experiments with hypnagogic vision and lucid or conscious dreaming. In the year 1619, Descartes inadvertently made what he called his greatest discovery—the unity of the human sciences—in a series of three dreams punctuated by wakefulness. While dreaming he suddenly became aware of the dream and even interpreted it before reentering the full waking state.

But lucid dreaming has a deeper significance than its usefulness for creativity. It demonstrates that lucid waking can be extended beyond the waking state to other states of consciousness. Enlightenment is ultimate wakefulness in *all* states of consciousness.

For thousands of years, the creative power of dreams has been recognized and put to practical use. Literature and the arts would be barren without the rich imaginative world of dreams. This world was rediscovered and shaped into a therapeutic tool by Sigmund Freud, whose *Interpretation of Dreams* (1900) still makes for fascinating reading. Imagination is rampant in our dreams and often contains significant messages to us, if only we care to notice them.

Dream interpretation itself is an imaginative task. The many popular cookbooks for do-it-yourself dream interpretation are an insult to the wonderful imagination that is responsible for the creation of dreams. Carl Gustav Jung acknowledged this when he said:

The interpretation of dreams and symbols demands intelligence. It cannot be turned into a mechanical system and then crammed into unimaginative brains. It demands both an increasing knowledge of the dreamer's individuality and an increasing self-awareness on the part of the interpreter. . . . Even a man of high intellect can go badly astray for lack of intuition or feeling.[8]

Jung, who more than anyone of his time understood the role of imagination in our lives, developed a therapeutic technique that uses imagination to great advantage and that has similarity to certain Eastern contemplative practices. His "active imagination" is a technique that allows one to access the potent images of the psyche. The first stage of this method, which is similar to conscious dreaming, consists in observing, without censorship, whatever imagery the unconscious may produce in any given moment or in response to a particular thought or mood one wishes to explore. Fixing one's attention on the arising image will make the image change, creating new images that must be carefully noted. Ideally, they should be recorded in writing or expressed artistically in drawings, paintings, sculpture, or even dance. At the second stage of this process, one must begin to evaluate, that is, give meaning and significance to the imagery spawned by the psyche. In this way, consciousness and the unconscious can be integrated, bringing wholeness to the personality. Jung likened this achievement to a waterfall connecting above and below.

THE HEALING POWER OF IMAGINATION

Today, avant-garde physicians enlist the help of imagination in the battle against disease. One of the first to use imagination in this way was O. Carl Simonton, director of the Simonton Cancer Center in Fort Worth, Texas. Simonton and his wife Stephanie asked their patients to visualize their cancer cells being attacked by white knights or angels, or being destroyed by rats.[9] The positive results obtained from these visualizations have puzzled and upset many of their more conservative colleagues.

Beverly Hills psychotherapist William Fezler has developed a whole system of visualizations, which he gives to his patients under hypnosis, again with excellent results. In his book *Creative Imagery,* Fezler writes:

> You possess the power of imagination. It's only a matter of developing this power. Many people complain to me that they have "lousy" imaginations. The fact is they haven't learned to use their brain's right side properly.[10]

Fezler explains the mechanism underlying imagination and visualization in this way:

> You perceive "reality" in much the same way you do a picture on a television screen. The TV picture is composed of thousands of tiny "bits," or dots, which combined give you the total image. Sounds, tastes, smells, and tactile feelings are also the result of a combination of thousands of "bits" involving wave frequencies, chemical configurations, and electromagnetic patterns.
>   You can recall the bits in the same design and order that you received them or you can replay them in new combinations. . . . The power of your imagination and imagery is a function of your ability to retrieve those recorded sensory bits. All imagery involves your recall of sensory bits once recorded in your cortex. The more bits you are able to recall the more vivid your image will be.[11]

And, it seems, the clearer the mental image the more effect it has on one's body chemistry, physiology, and even behavior. The best proof for the power of imagination is the so-called placebo effect. Physician Martin L. Rossman reported in his book *Healing Yourself* the following well-known medical experiment conducted in 1961.[12] In those days, patients suffering from chest pains (angina pectoris) had a relatively minor artery in the chest tied off to feed more blood through the arteries supplying the heart muscle. Many but not all experienced good improvement of their physical condition. In the experiment, patients were duly anesthetized and a small surgical incision was made, but the wound was immediately sewn up again without any other procedure being done. Remarkably, they experienced the same relief from chest pain as the patients who underwent the actual operation!

But internal imagery not only has the power to evaporate cancer cells, improve blood circulation, lower blood pressure, stop addictions, erase undesirable memories, and eradicate a poor self-image, but can also kill a person. This is illustrated by the true story of a patient who experienced a complete remission of his cancer after being given a new "miracle" drug. He remained symptom-free until he read in the papers that the drug did not work after all. He died of cancer a short time thereafter. This power of imagination in the healing process is epitomized in the title of Kenneth Pelletier's well-known book *Mind as Healer, Mind as Slayer.*

"I became aware," writes Jungian analyst Albert Kreinheder in his book *Body and Soul,* "that every pain, every illness, every symptom has a psychological content that goes with it. This is the symbolic part. This is the way our imagination perceives the illness or the symptom."[13] He mentions perceiving his arthritis pain as "a kind of demon or god who desired intimacy with me." As he talked to his pain, his body was filled with a warmth. "The experience was of a being, an intelligence, not merely an energy. There was also the knowledge that it was aware that I was aware of it. It was like a stream of divine love caressing my crippled body."[14]

When we focus on the symbolic aspect of an illness or symptom, we look at the prodigious power of imagination at work within us. This also is our portal to well-being and happiness. As Kreinheder concluded, "imagination is real."

THE DISCIPLINING OF IMAGINATION

In the nineteenth century, the British social critic John Ruskin saw in imagination "the open sesame of a huge and endless cave, with an inexhaustible treasure of pure gold scattered in it." Albert Einstein shared this view when he admitted that "imagination is more important than knowledge." Because of the tremendous power of imagination, we must understand and assume responsibility for it. Lucid waking is disciplined imagination.

As the story of human civilization amply shows, we exercise imagination all too easily in the wrong way, causing ourselves and others harm and impeding the creation of a truly humanitarian society. It was none other than the French emperor Napoleon Bonaparte who exclaimed, "The human race is governed by its imagination." We remember well the temper of Napoleon's imagination!

Mary Shelley's story of Victor Frankenstein, who created a monstrosity that killed his bride and his best friend, illustrates what can happen when we allow imagination to run wild without considering the possible consequences. Some writers have seen in Robert Oppenheimer's involvement in the creation of the first atomic bomb a chilling contemporary real-life parallel to the Frankenstein myth. To his horror, in 1945 he had to witness the holocaust at Hiroshima, which was unprecedented in human history. He and his colleagues at Los Alamos intended conclusively to end the war but merely succeeded in proliferating the nuclear madness and in killing and horribly maiming—in a split-second flash—some 130,000 men, women, and children, which led Oppenheimer to confess that "the physicists have known sin."

Unbridled imagination can be seen at work in schizophrenia. I once gave a ride to a hitchhiker who turned out to be a harmless schizophrenic. In the course of a ten-minute ride his mind produced more fascinating and entertaining ideas than I had heard in all the academic discussions I had ever participated in. But they were all weirdly disjointed and totally out of context. In a way, the schizophrenics' imagination is their hell. Both madness and genius stem from imagination. As Shakespeare wrote in his well-loved comedy *A Midsummer-Night's Dream* (Act V):

> *The lunatic, the lover, and the poet*
> *Are of imagination all compact: . . .*
> *Such tricks hath strong imagination,*
> *That, if it would but apprehend some joy,*

It comprehends some bringer of that joy;
Or in the night, imagining some fear,
How easy is a bush supposed a bear!

Thus, our mental images are far from being passive residents in our mind. They actively influence us. The more vital an image is, the greater will be its impact on our body, mind, and behavior. It matters little whether that image is anchored in reality or is derived purely from fantasy. If we strongly believe in an image, or idea, we derive strength and courage from it. When the Dalai Lama was asked why he chooses to be optimistic about life, he replied that it made him feel good. Of course, we may assume that there is a lot more to his answer, though it makes perfect sense, simple as it is.

The positive influence of visualization on physical and emotional health and healing is increasingly recognized. So is the role of imagination and visualization in sports. Michael Murphy (cofounder of the Esalen Institute) and Rhea A. White (founder of the Exceptional Human Experience Network) collaborated on a fascinating book entitled *In the Zone: Transcendent Experience in Sports.*[15] It documents the secret weapon of many athletes capable of peak performance, namely, visualization. For instance, Lee Evans, four-hundred-meter Olympic champion and world record holder, visualized over and over again every step of his four hundred meters in his practice for the 1968 Olympics. Olympic hurdle champion David Hemery also rehearsed his race in his mind and in his dreams, not merely in his training sessions.

Champion boxer Rocky Marciano lived in seclusion for up to three months prior to a major fight. He lived and breathed only for the upcoming championship, always picturing his opponent before him and focusing on the decisive opening second of the bout. Quarterback Fran Tarkenton ran whole blocks of plays in his head prior to a game. Bodybuilder Arnold Schwarzenegger sculpted his exceptional physique in accordance with his precise mental imagery. Numerous other extraordinary examples are given in Murphy's and White's book.

There are also less spectacular but still significant illustrations of the impact of mental images on our daily lives. For instance, if we create and nurture the image that we can accomplish a certain task or achieve a certain goal, we will certainly be more likely to do so than without the assistance of our positive visualizations. Ever since Emmet Fox's *Power Through Constructive Thinking* was published in 1932, a whole spate of books has tried to teach us the art of "positive thinking," which is really the art of constructive imagination.

The potency of imagination and images can be seen very readily in the metaphors we use in everyday speech. A perfect example is how we think of arguments as a form of war. Thus, we say, "You can't seriously *defend* this position," "He *attacked* and absolutely *demolished* their argument," or "Your criticism is *right on target*." Arguments, like wars, are "won" or "lost." More than that, our imagery, or metaphors, can even shape our body language. We angrily jut out our chins or puff up our chests like roosters. When an argument gets out of hand, the metaphor of war can easily translate itself into actual acts of aggression.

Another good example of how a mental image can manifest itself in powerful metaphoric language, which then influences our behavior (often negatively), is the widespread notion of time as money. Thus, we say, "Don't *waste* my time," "I can't *spend* time on this right now," "They *invested* a great deal of time in this project," "He is living on *borrowed* time."

The reality we live in is the web of our ideas *about* reality. We occupy a metaphoric space, a "virtual reality" of our own making. This is a really important point to grasp, not just in an abstract way but at the gut level. It is a very sobering realization! Once we are— and oblige ourselves to remain—aware of this fact, we can begin to see the formidable power our ideas have over us and others. Then we can also start to be more responsible for them. In particular, we can stop the habit of using negative metaphors that merely hurt and disempower others and are like time bombs waiting to explode in our faces. For example, we can curb harmful expressions like "He's a good-for-nothing fellow," "She's just a dumb blonde," "They're absolute weirdos," and so on.

Language is one of imagination's most potent products. It can be a soothing balm or a destructive tool. Therefore we are challenged to use language with true creativity to be a benign influence in the world.

When ideas congeal into rigid belief systems we call them ideologies. Their power is enormous. Ideologies like Marxism, capitalism, or Christian fundamentalism become powerful by triggering
over and over again the same images in people's minds until they
completely invade their imaginations. In the end, no one can conceive of any alternatives to the status quo, confusing the glittering
ideological imagery in their minds with reality. Analyze the speech
of any politician and you will see this principle in action.
Advertising works in the same nefarious way.

How do we escape the baneful influence of ideologies? The
only way is by becoming more aware of the significance of imagination in our lives and by tapping into our personal font of images.
We must develop faith in our own creative potential and draw from
it to shape our own life.

To put it differently, we must learn to become a little bit more
like the geniuses of our species, who are by definition very independent spirits. Geniuses are those who are endowed with creative
imagination to a superlative degree. They feel compelled to fashion
the world in their own image rather than have the world mold
them. They have tremendous faith in their own creative process.
They are the true revolutionaries.

Most of us are neither geniuses nor schizophrenics. However,
we all have tremendous creative and imaginative abilities—more
than we sometimes admit to ourselves. We only need to unlock our
innate capacity for imagination. Let us not forget Thomas Alva
Edison's famous words, "Genius is 1 percent inspiration and 99
percent perspiration." Edison also remarked, "Imagination is not a
talent of some men but is the health of every man."

THE SPIRITUAL IMAGINATION

It is clear by now that imagination governs our lives and shapes our
destinies. Depending to a considerable degree on our guiding
images, we become either mayor of a local city or president of an
entire nation; employee or entrepreneur; criminal or saint.
Throughout the ages, there have always been those who feel that
the highest purpose to which we can put our imagination is to

realize our spiritual destiny. These are the God-seekers, adepts, mystics, and shamans of all cultures and eras. They believe that only when we have discovered our true Self, or Spirit, which lies beyond the ego-personality, can we live sensibly and compassionately in this world.

The great thirteenth-century mystic Meister Eckehart explained in one of his German sermons how the psyche, or soul, possesses a rich store of images. But these images separate the human being from the Divine. Even the image of God as the Trinity is limiting, and only when the soul turns away from all imagery can it discover the formless Divine, which is pure Being. In his own words:

> You should love God mindlessly, that is, in such a way that your soul is mindless and stripped of all mentality. For, as long as it has images, it has something mediating. As long as it has something mediating, it has neither unity nor simplicity. As long as it has no simplicity, it cannot love God rightly. For to love rightly depends on unanimity. Therefore the soul should be devoid of mind, should exist mindlessly. For if you love God as God or spirit or person or image—all this must be removed. "How, then, should I love him?" You should love him as a non-God, a non-spirit, a non-person, a non-image, but rather as the unalloyed, pure, lucid One apart from all duality. And in this One we should be eternally immersed from Something to Nothing. May God help us. Amen.[16]

The transcendence of all imagery: what a remarkable insight! Eckehart, who held a high office in the Christian church, moved on dangerous ground with his daring theological formulations. By contrast, his counterparts in India never suffered such clerical restraints. Since the time of the Rig-Veda, which goes back to the third millennium B.C., they have been able to speak and write freely of the unimaginable, unthinkable One.

Imagination played a huge role in the work and thought of another remarkable German mystic, Jacob Böhme (1575–1624), who was a shoemaker by trade.[17] He understood imagination as the will of God, the cosmogonic urge and power that led to the picturing and creation of the universe. He spoke of it as "divine magic." In itself, the Divine is an imageless "eternal naught" *(ewiges Nichts)*, which was also Eckehart's view (and experience). God's imagination is at work on all levels of cosmic existence— from the most subtle levels to the gross physical level. Everything that can possibly be experienced is woven by the spell of the divine magic *(imago magia)*, and for Böhme, this imaginal power is both the "mother" and the "daughter" of the Holy Trinity. In other words, imagination is both creative cause and created result.

Because imagination is not merely present at the highest level of cosmic existence, the level of the Creator, it can be used constructively as well as destructively. Imagination is not only the eye that reveals eternity but also the mirror in which the finite self can see and become enamored of its own image. Thus, the perversion of imagination caused Lucifer's steep fall from his angelic state of being and likewise drove Adam out of paradise. True to the deeply optimistic spirit of all mystical traditions, Böhme taught that we are not condemned forever but can save our souls through the right use of imagination.

If in our imagination we can turn away from the Divine, the realm of light, and toward the relative darkness of the material world, we can also imaginatively reconnect with the Divine and thereby recover the lost paradise within ourselves. When we turn our imagination upon the ultimate Reality, we actually participate in it. We are always immersed in it, of course, but through our imagination we build a conscious bridge between ourselves and the Divine and thus become active participants in the divine play. In a metaphor reminiscent of certain Upanishadic passages, Böhme spoke of "eating" God. By "eating" or imbibing the Divine, we become of like nature to it. Thus, he understood imagination as the transformative power of faith by which we can identify with the Divine, or ultimate Reality. This magical function of imagination underlies all spiritual work, for it is only by placing ourselves outside our present circumstance and into the spiritual or transcendental plane that we can grow into its "image."

It would be possible to write an entire history of mysticism from the perspective of imagination and its transcendence in the highest states of ecstatic elevation, and India would figure prominently in such an account. As India's branch of humanity realized long ago, the mind, or imagination, is the rope by which we can climb to the topmost plateau of our own psyche, beyond the clouds of ignorance. But once we have reached that plateau and get ready for the final ascent to the sunlit peak, the *sanctum sanctorum*, we must leave our rope and climbing gear (body and mind) behind. Writing in *Re-Vision* journal, the American psychiatrist Gerald Epstein noted:

> It is my contention that without the presence of the dimension of imagination in human existence, one cannot grasp the presence of the holy—that which is transcendent and immanent. The holy is related to the wholeness of experience and cannot be comprehended by a process that fragments. The holy is an experience, not a logical proposition. Many people who open their imagination experience some connection with holiness, and somehow . . . there is an organic connection between holy and healing. Imagination is the catalyst.[18]

We are healed when we are made holy, when we have reconnected *(religare)* with the Spirit. Health, wholeness, and holiness are merely different words for the same state of being, which is beyond comprehension. But, as I have stated before, after our ascent to the peak of existence, we must descend again into the valley of ordinary life, bringing with us the gifts of truth, beauty, and goodness. Henceforth we are empowered to live out of the fullness and the emptiness of that ultimate singularity we may call "Spirit," "transcendental Self," "divine spark," "*atman*," or "Being-Consciousness." Now that our own human destiny has fulfilled itself, we can dedicate the least exercise of our will, or imagination, to the ultimate happiness of all others. Therein lies our own joy.

7

RIGHT VIEW

THE REALITY OF THE INVISIBLE

"Seeing is believing." This popular adage, which typically characterizes a materialistic attitude, has its useful applications. However, it is at best a half truth. A more important truth is epitomized in the reverse statement, "believing is seeing." For, as I elaborated in the previous chapter, our images or preconceptions greatly define our perceptions, and they often do so in matters that are most significant. For instance, if we believe that the end of the world is near, we will squeeze every life experience, every fact and factoid, into this belief. Consequently we will behave as if the world were coming to an end. At the turn of the first millennium, Christians everywhere sold or gave away their estates and personal belongings and went into the hills to prepare for the Second Coming. Their rash actions caused considerable pandemonium during their exodus and more so after the monumental letdown. Our contemporary society is by no means immune to such irrationalism, as has been amply demonstrated by the Nazis of the Third Reich, the enforced mass suicides in Jonestown, and the recent fanaticism and terrorism of the Japanese Aum Shinrikyo movement.

To make matters worse, those who hold very strong beliefs cannot easily be shaken by contradictory evidence. (I do mean beliefs, not faith, which is a deep attitude of trust in the invisible Reality, the "implicate order.") On the contrary, psychologists have long known of a curious phenomenon among "true believers": that their cherished beliefs are not only not undermined by contradictory evidence but can in fact be strengthened by it. Repeatedly, leaders of the Jehovah's Witnesses sect prophesied a definite date for the eschatological event of the Lord's coming. When Judgment Day failed to arrive at the predetermined date, instead of feeling betrayed and collapsing, the sect's members felt an even greater commitment to their belief system. The leaders found a convenient explanation for their prophetic failure and deftly gave the ranks of believers a new date to prepare for. Psychologists explain this paradoxical behavior by means of the theory of cognitive dissonance, first formulated by Leon Festinger in 1957. The basic idea behind this theory is that we tend to rationalize away dissonance between conflicting ideas.[1]

The case of the Jehovah's Witnesses is a rather dramatic example of cognitive dissonance and of "believing is seeing" at work. But when we examine the minutiae of daily life, we might be surprised to discover how frequently our beliefs, or presumptions, come into play; how they determine the way in which we approach a person or situation and, in turn, how that determines the quality of a relationship or the outcome of a situation; and how hard it is for us to change our cherished beliefs.

A constructive way of looking at beliefs is to regard them as our little and big visions of things. The belief that we will receive our paycheck at the end of the month is what I would call a minor belief, unless we know the company is going bankrupt. So is the belief that we can always learn something new from reading Shakespeare or the Bible. Both beliefs entail a reasonable expectation based on past experience. They contain no major metaphysical assumptions.

By contrast, the belief that after death we will go to heaven to be reunited with our deceased relatives and friends is a major belief. So is the belief in a Creator-God or in the meaningfulness of existence. And so is the belief that *Homo sapiens* was created ten thousand years ago, which, according to a June 1993 Gallup poll, is held by a surprising 47 percent (!) of adult Americans. To entertain this kind of belief, we must make a considerable leap of faith. It is this type of belief that I want to discuss here.

To begin with, belief enters when knowledge is absent. The less we are sure of something, as Michel Eyquem Montaigne noted four hundred years ago, the more energy goes into our believing.[2] There is even an irrational urge in some people to believe when the object of their belief lacks not only evidence but plausibility. The third-century Carthaginian theologian Tertullian expressed this in his well-known statement *Credo quia impossibile*, "I believe because it is impossible."[3] He also said, *Credo quia absurdum est*, "I believe because it is absurd." And St. Augustine observed, *Credo ut intelligam*, "I believe in order to understand."

The only way we can understand this sort of irrationalism is by realizing that we believe something because there is some personal gain from our beliefs. A belief, even if it seems illogical, may make us feel good—as when we hang on to the Santa Claus myth even after we have recognized the face of a family member or friend under the white beard. Or a belief may support other beliefs we hold. If, for instance, we believe in the existence of angelic beings, we might find it comparatively easy also to believe that everyone has a guardian angel from childhood on. (This is only a convenient example; I am not arguing against the existence of angels here.) This all-too-human tendency prompted Caesar to write, "Men freely believe that which they desire!"[4] And Seneca made an identical observation, which rings true.[5]

The eternal skeptic Bertrand Russell spoke of beliefs as a man's "cloud of comforting convictions, which move with him like flies on a summer day."[6] Emerson expressed the same truth less acerbically and more poetically when he said, "A man bears beliefs, as a tree bears apples."[7] And, as we know, some apples are rotten while still attached to their branches. Moreover, some of the fallen apples will produce another tree of the same species of apple tree. That is to say, through our beliefs we tend to perpetuate ourselves. Therefore, if we are wise, we will carefully inspect our beliefs, discard those that would perpetuate merely our negative personality traits, and strongly cultivate those that have intrinsic merit and shape our destiny positively.

Some beliefs are patently wrong—that is, they do not correspond to anything in reality—and can be very destructive. George

Bernard Shaw saw very clearly that belief can be more damaging than disbelief.[8] Some people seriously believe that we do not live on the surface of the earth but in its hollow interior. And this despite satellite photographs of our beautiful blue planet, never mind the cinematographically recorded trips to other planets and the moon. This belief is quirky but relatively harmless, unless it were to trigger a militant crusade against those believing otherwise. A distinctly harmful belief not based in fact, however, is the gaunt belief in the superiority of the white race or of one segment of it. We have witnessed the horrifying destructiveness of this belief in the genocidal mania of the Third Reich, in South Africa's apartheid, and in the institution of slavery during the seventeenth, eighteenth, and early nineteenth centuries. The notion of white supremacy is increasingly rearing its ugly head again in American society and elsewhere in the world, and it is contributing to black people's own brand of racism.

What, however, are we to make of those who, like certain Christian fundamentalists, believe that it is desirable to withhold medication from a sick person even if that means certain death, since a person's fate is always in the hands of God? Or what are we to think of Dr. Jack Kevorkian's belief that it is right and proper to assist terminally ill individuals in committing suicide so as to end their suffering? Or how should we look upon the belief that abortion is right or that it is wrong? These are difficult questions that require us to wrestle with our own beliefs. They get down to the core of our basic view or vision of life, which to a large extent defines who we are.

It is no secret that our contemporary society is in such great moral upheaval because scientific materialism has, for the past hundred and fifty years, steadily eroded the belief system that once provided our forebears with a meaningful framework for understanding life. At the same time, the progress of communication between different cultures and traditions has given rise to a rampant pluralism that leaves many people in a moral and philosophical no-man's-land. Having grown taller than the fence of their own inherited religion, they can look into other fenced plots and be "comparative" in their approach. Thus, Christians delve into the Kabbalah; Jews read the Bhagavad Gita; Hindus read the Bible; and so on. Our contemporary paperback culture has placed all the world's sacred scriptures at our disposal. And people are more confused than ever!

TWENTY–TWENTY VISION FOR HAPPINESS

Right belief—or *right view* as I will call it henceforth—is therefore of signal importance. Siddhartha Gautama, the founder of Buddhism, realized this twenty-five hundred years ago. His noble eightfold path to enlightenment begins with right view *(samyag-drishti)*. What did he mean by this? In his very first sermon, known as the "Discourse of Setting in Motion the Wheel of the Teaching," the Buddha addressed a group of five ascetics thus:

> This, O mendicants, is the noble truth of suffering: birth is suffering; old age is suffering; illness is suffering; death is suffering; grief, lamentation, pain, affliction, and despair are suffering; to be united with what is unloved or to be separated from what is loved is suffering; not to obtain what is desired is suffering; in short, the five groups of grasping are suffering.[9]

The "five groups of grasping," also known as the "five aggregates," are the material body, sensation, perceptions, cognitions (thoughts and feelings), and consciousness. These factors compose, according to Buddhism, the human personality. They are infused with suffering because they are inherently impermanent. This implies that they are subject to decay and death and are incapable of creating true happiness. In other words, they are not worthy of our unqualified attention.

The way we see the world is also the way we view ourselves. Therefore, our view of the world has far-reaching consequences. It can lead us either to delusion, bondage, and unhappiness, or to mental clarity, freedom, and happiness. The Buddha was not concerned with mere opinions but the most powerful insights of which human beings are capable and that make or break our lives. In his analysis he went directly to the heart of the human condition. For, who does not want happiness? Yet, we typically look for it precisely in those things that the Buddha correctly described as being impermanent and hence incapable of yielding happiness.

He was not interested in the nature of the world as such, but only in our *experience* of the world, which is what affects us ultimately. The human personality, as he realized, is inherently unstable, without a permanent center of identity, and hence is a source of suffering. He did, of course, not deny that we also experience joy and pleasure in the course of our lives, but they are always fleeting. Often the harder we try to hang on to a pleasurable experience, the more we set ourselves up for frustration and disappointment.

The Hindu mystics arrived at the same conclusion. But they also pointed to an eternal Self beyond the personality, which, when realized, would bring unending happiness. The Buddha, however, refused to speculate about such an everlasting Self. He discouraged metaphysical thinking ("believing") among his disciples, asking them instead to focus on the task at hand: to penetrate the personality's machinations with the eye of wisdom and then to cultivate the mood of nonattachment, or nongrasping. He spoke of the state of full awakening, or Buddhahood, in paradoxical terms. As he put it, the being who has attained nirvana neither exists nor does not exist. He/she/it is beyond mental comprehension and description.

Technically, right view in Buddhism means understanding the four noble truths: that conditional existence is suffering, that suffering is rooted in craving and ignorance, that suffering can be transcended, and that the noble eightfold path of gradual self-transformation is the means of transcending suffering. Looked at differently, right view also means abandoning what the Buddhists call perverse views *(viparyasa)*, namely, looking for permanency in the impermanent, happiness in suffering, a stable Self in what is characterized as non-Self, and beauty in ugliness.

Another way of talking about right view, in the above sense, is in terms of wisdom. Wisdom is long-range understanding, deep insight into the nature of existence, or seeing the larger picture, which prompts a person to act in accord with such understanding. As many a poet has expressed, wisdom is born of suffering. It is distilled from human experience, but only by those who are able to reflect on their experience. In the final analysis, wisdom is rooted in self-understanding; hence the admonition of the Delphic oracle: "Know thyself!" But if wisdom springs from suffering, in its highest form it is also the means to ending suffering. And it is this message that unites many spiritual traditions—notably Buddhism, Hinduism, Jainism, Taoism, Gnosticism, and mystical Christianity.

"O mendicants, then and now," said the Buddha, "I teach only one thing: suffering and the termination of suffering."[10] He was a complete pragmatist in spiritual matters. This makes his teaching so appealing to us moderns. It helps us acquire twenty-twenty vision in our consideration of human existence, cutting through pet notions and delusions. Once we have come to appreciate the subtle but all-important distinction between pleasure and true happiness, we can readily see suffering at work in our lives. This, in turn, gives us the impetus to look for a way out, or what traditionally is known as the desire for liberation (mumukshutva). In the first instance, liberation is freedom from the wrong views that trap us in the many forms of suffering at which human beings seem to excel.

According to Eric Klinger, a professor of psychology at the University of Minnesota, we have about four thousand distinct thoughts in a sixteen-hour day.[11] Over a life-span of seventy years, this amounts to a total of roughly one hundred million thoughts! It would probably scare us to know just how many of these thoughts run along well-worn (karmic) grooves, perpetuating our condition of suffering. If we wish to enjoy genuine happiness and freedom, we must make our thoughts count more! To do so, we must first have a clear and realistic vision of life. "Without vision," we can read in Proverbs (29:18), "the people perish." The perilous crisis of our contemporary Western civilization, with its planetwide repercussions, is a sign that we lack vision—right vision.

The restoration of right vision is the single most important task confronting individuals and society today. It is the great challenge of a life dedicated to lucid waking. Addressing the social aspect of this problem, social scientist Duane Elgin writes:

> We cannot consciously create a future that we have not imagined. When our collective visualization is weak and fragmented,

then our ability to build a workable and meaningful future is commensurately diminished. To consciously evolve, we require a clear vision of a compassionate future that draws out our enthusiastic participation in life. The richness and reach of our social vision is a direct measure of our civilizational maturity.[12]

Moreover, the depth of our social vision—that is, the vision that informs our society at large—depends on the *spiritual* maturity of our social visionaries, their personal level of wakefulness and their degree of wisdom. As long as they continue to misunderstand the real nature of our present-day crisis, which is spiritual, and dabble merely in technological solutions, the future of the human race looks grim. So, where does this leave you and me? We cannot avoid being participants in the unfolding civilizational drama. Whether or not we are politically active to transform our society's social vision, our primary challenge and obligation as individuals is always to vigorously cultivate right vision in our personal life. By putting right vision into practice, we not only shape our own destiny positively but also, in ever widening circles, influence our fellow beings in benign ways. Willis Harman, one of the great practical visionaries of our time, observed:

Because of the interconnectedness of all minds with the universal mind, we can be sure that the tasks to which we are directed will be most effective in solving the world's fundamental illness, of which hunger and poverty and plague and pestilence and war are all a part. We need not fear that in pursuing our own real self-interest we will fail to contribute maximally to the real self-interest of others.[13]

As is clear from Harman's book, from which the above statement is excerpted, what he means by real self-interest is the pursuit of a life filled with peace, harmony, joy, and compassionate action for the benefit of others. What is *real* about this is that even as we promote the physical, mental, moral, and spiritual welfare of others we promote our own total well-being. Right vision, above all, honors the essential interconnectedness of all beings and things. It is ecological in the deepest sense of the word: mindful of the universe as our "home" (Greek: *oikos*), in which all beings are close relatives and in which there are no strangers or enemies.

8

INTUITION: THE OTHER WAY OF KNOWING

INTUITIVE PROMPTINGS

Occasionally, when the phone rings, I know who is calling before picking up the receiver. Judging from the testimony of my friends and acquaintances, this seems to be a fairly common experience. When my two sons were growing up, there were many times when I would suddenly feel compelled to check up on them, just in the nick of time to avert an injury or a minor disaster. I imagine there are few parents who have not had the same experience time and again.

Many years ago, a person very close to me was in the midst of arranging with a total stranger the breakout of a family member from behind the Iron Curtain. I was at the office at the time and had no idea that this conversation was taking place, but suddenly I felt a sense of foreboding in connection with her. I called her up to see whether she was all right. When she told me what she was about to do, I warned her and did not leave the phone until she had promised me she would consider the matter more carefully. In the end, she herself came to the conclusion that it would be best for all concerned if she dropped her risky plan, which had little chance of succeeding.

On October 17, 1989, I was supposed to drive to Oakland in the Bay Area from Lake County, California, where I live, and from there continue across the Bay Bridge to San Francisco. At the last moment I canceled my trip. When, on that precise day, the shock waves of the San Francisco earthquake rocked my home two hundred miles away, I knew why I had been feeling so apprehensive about the trip. Given my itinerary, I would probably have been crossing the Bay Bridge about the time the earthquake struck with such devastating force that a section of the bridge collapsed. In general, I seem to have a sixth sense about imminent earthquakes, even minor shakers. I often announce to my wife that it feels "earthquaky" again, only to experience or hear about a local quake within the next couple of days.

CREEPERS AND LEAPERS

Intuition, including forebodings of the kind just described, appears to be a universal human phenomenon. Its existence demonstrates, among other things, that we are multilevel beings. If we fail to see intuition at work in our own life, it is not because it does not exist but rather because we simply do not notice it. We all use intuition, though some of us do so more frequently and perhaps also more confidently than others.

Why do we not notice moments of intuition more readily? There is a cultural reason for this blind spot. Our Western civilization places a premium on rational thought, and consequently we tend to downgrade and ignore instances of nonrational mentation. Moreover, we are prone to deny our own and others' intuitive abilities. This amounts to the repression of a very significant aspect of the mind. Hence, in most of us intuition remains a largely undeveloped faculty.

However, not everyone who is blind to the mind's intuitive function is necessarily a hard-nosed rationalist. Some people, without feeling in the least guilty or awkward, actively invite nonrational modes of thought into their life. They know they are predominantly intuitive thinkers, and they are content and happy about this fact. By the way, it is quite incorrect to assume that women are more intuitive than men. Perhaps they feel fewer constraints about intuition and hence tend to make more use of it, but both genders have the same intuitive capability. It also appears to be incorrect to simply equate intuition with the right brain, as I will discuss shortly.

In his book *The Intuitive Edge*, psychologist Philip Goldberg notes that experiments have shown that men perform marginally better at spatial visualization, including geometry, and women are more sensitive to context, including comprehending nonverbal information and reading facial expressions.[1] He emphasizes, however, that these differences are statistical averages, not absolute values. Weston Agor, a professor of public administration at the University of Texas at El Paso, surveyed three thousand managers and found a national average score for intuitive ability of 6.9 for women and 6.3 for men,[2] although Agor's research has come under fire because it is not entirely clear what his questionnaire was testing. When science tries to dissect intuition to study its inner workings, it proves a rather elusive subject.

In terms of our thinking styles, we can distinguish between what I call creepers and leapers. The creepers are those whose mental processes crawl along in linear fashion, exploring this avenue and then that, without assurance of ever reaching a definite conclusion. The leapers, on the other hand, are like kangaroos; they can and will change direction in an instant to arrive at the desired destination in nonlinear, intuitive fashion.

For extremely rational types, intuition is an embarrassment that apparently threatens their entire worldview. In a way it does, for the very existence of intuition contradicts the fundamental belief of rationalists that authentic knowledge can spring *only* from correct reasoning. According to the rationalist interpretation of reality, there are only two valid ways of arriving at the truth: deduction or induction. Deduction is the argument from the general to the specific, deriving a particular truth from a general principle: "All human beings are mammals. Socrates is a human being. Therefore Socrates is a mammal." Induction, on the other hand, derives a general principle from particular truths: "Apples, raindrops, meteorites, and bombs fall toward the earth. Therefore all things tend to fall toward the earth (the law of gravity)."

Consensus opinion has it that the success of science has been largely due to inductive reasoning. However, some rationalist philosophers, such as David Hume and, more recently, Karl Popper, question or outright deny the validity of induction as a correct means of knowledge. Popper, a renowned philosopher of science, observed:

> I think that we shall have to get accustomed to the idea that we must not look upon science as a "body of knowledge," but rather as a system of hypotheses; that is to say, as a system of guesses or anticipations which in principle cannot be justified, but with which we work as long as they stand up to tests, and of which we are never justified in saying that we know that they are "true" or "more or less certain" or even "probable."[3]

If science is a "system of guesses," clearly intuition must be placed on a par with reasoning, and this opens up whole new vistas even for rationalists. Intuition should be an embarrassment to them—but rather an embarrassment of riches, because intuition opens up a vast store of knowledge that is not readily accessible to, or remains altogether closed to, analytical reason. Rational thought is plodding, slow, proceeding from A to B to C to D. The process involved in this form of thinking is very much like climbing stairs with low risers one by one when it is possible to take a bigger step, omit a few steps, and reach the top more quickly.

Intuition is such a leaping ahead. It is instantaneous and makes knowledge available suddenly, without noticeable intermediate steps called for by reason. For the rationalists this is scary, because they presume that knowledge must be acquired in a gradual fashion, following the laws of logic. They tend to distrust the intuitive process, and so, generally speaking, banish it from their work and life. But, to be sure, even rationalists have intuitive flashes, though they prefer to ignore, deny, simply rename ("lucky guesses"), or quickly forget them.

Similarly, there are those who insist that the only valid way of acquiring knowledge is through the senses. They are the staunch empiricists, for whom "seeing is believing," as it were. But much of our knowledge does not come through the conduit of the senses but is constructed on the basis of the countless concepts we carry around in our heads. Our nervous system is governed by those concepts. We have a concept of the ocean even if we have not actually been to the seaside and smelled the fresh ocean breeze or tasted the salty water.

Neither pure rationalism nor pure empiricism makes a viable philosophical explanation of how life really works. There is a significant piece missing in both of them. Sensory input and rational concepts are merely the tip of the iceberg. The large mass of the iceberg is immersed in the water of the subconscious, the unconscious, and the transpersonal bands of consciousness. And this is where much of our knowledge is derived and processed.

Since intuition is an integral part of human nature, when rationalists or empiricists deny intuition they also deny an important aspect of themselves. In fact, they deny that whole huge part of the mind that lies below the surface of conscious awareness. Basically they distrust themselves. To trust intuition is to trust ourselves. In the words of psychotherapist Frances Vaughan:

> Behind all emotions is the wisdom of intuition that can lead one to the full experience of the central core of being. The more you are willing to open yourself to the full awareness that is potentially yours, the more authentically you can live your life.
>
> A commitment to awakening intuition is a commitment to truth. It implies a willingness to listen to the still small voice which you can recognize as being true, even when you don't like what it says. It means a willingness to know yourself as you are, dropping pretenses and disguises no matter how successful your particular act may be in terms of getting approval from others.[4]

Intuition is a vitally important part of a life devoted to lucid waking. Without it, we cannot accomplish the task of psychological integration underlying spiritual life. We must come to appreciate just how remarkable the equipment is that we are given for the adventure of human life. We are born with all kinds of abilities, which are ours to cultivate and use. In his monumental work *The Future of the Body*, Michael Murphy has mapped a good many of these abilities, showing, in the words of Shakespeare, "how beauteous mankind is."[5]

THE BIG TURN-ABOUT

Once upon a time, intuition was the primary means of knowledge, and it still fulfills this function among certain tribal peoples who have not abandoned the old ways only to become top-heavy thinkers. Since the European Enlightenment and the ascent of rationalism and technology, there has been a growing reliance on the analytical intellect and a simultaneous belittling of the mind's other means of acquiring knowledge. Scientific ideology—known as scientism—made reason *(ratio)* into a golden calf, squashing all other modes of knowing. Scientists have pointed to their discoveries and the resulting miracles of technology as palpable evidence of the intrinsic value of rationalism. However, the shadow side of scientific progress has gradually become more visible, as in planet-wide pollution, the atomic bomb, nuclear waste, and the harmful side effects of electromagnetic fields.

As a consequence, the exaggerated rational approach of science is beginning to seem less enticing or convincing. Also, scientific studies on how scientists actually arrive at their most momentous insights have in fact revealed that the "irrational" power of the imagination plays a significant role in the process of discovery. Equally significantly, social scientists have pointed out the "irrational" elements that govern much of the scientific enterprise— from falsifying data to fit a theory to peer pressure brought to bear on dissenting members of the establishment.

Fortunately, intuition is making a slow but steady comeback. This is reflected in the increasing number of publications, lectures, and workshops on the subject and the closely related topic of creativity. In 1994, I helped launch *Intuition* magazine, which has since rapidly grown into a widely read periodical. Not only has it gained many readers, but also it has won the generous financial support of a retired industrialist fascinated with intuition. His interest in the magazine reflects the growing recognition of intuition as a valid tool for acquiring and synthesizing information in the business world—perhaps the last place one would associate with "soft-headedness." Psychologists probing into the inner workings of the managerial mind have acknowledged that the very best managers are those with a gift for intuition—the people with "hunches," "gut feelings," or a "sixth sense."

Business situations can be extraordinarily complex, and rational thought is seldom capable of clearly isolating all the variables required to see what is involved at a moment's notice. But even where this is possible, the complexities rarely allow for reliable predictions. We may have analyzed all the components of a situation but be quite unable to make sense of the larger picture. In order to put Humpty Dumpty together again, we need a more competent means of knowledge than mere reasoning. Thus, the business world offers an ideal testing ground for the intuitive thinker who simply *knows*. Where ratiocination fails, an intuitive leap can rescue the day. Good managers are bound to be good intuiters, though they may not always know this or label themselves as such.

In her book *Intuition Workbook,* Marcia Emery mentions the case of a manager who for many months had been struggling with the problem of reorganizing his staff.[6] Then one day, while working on a completely different problem, images popped into his head that clearly showed him how to solve the reorganization puzzle. Another executive interviewed the perfect candidate for a position but inexplicably postponed a decision because he kept having doubts about the applicant. The intuition proved justified when a third party provided the information that the applicant tended to be argumentative and disagreeable. Emery mentions many more examples, and presumably every business person could provide his or her own cache of stories.

Willis Harman, late president of the Institute of Noetic Sciences in Sausalito, California, told me in conversation that the increasingly widespread recognition of the usefulness of intuition amounts to a radical reassessment of the role of business. In a talk given at the 1988 IMI conference on intuition in business, Harman called the current interest in intuition among business executives "a coded message that implies a major transformation of global society."[7]

Intuition is also an integral aspect of the demanding mental work of mathematicians and theoretical physicists. No less a scientist than Albert Einstein admitted to leaping way beyond experimental evidence or known facts in formulating his theory of relativity. As he stated:

> For the creation of a theory, the mere collection of recorded phenomena never suffices—there must always be added a free invention of the human mind that attacks the heart of the matter.[8]

The eminent American physicist Heinz Pagels, in whose book *The Cosmic Code* the above quote from Einstein can be found, adds:

> A great deal of creative work in physics proceeds by this method, which places intuition at the very first step, a nonrational but verifiable aspect of scientific creativity.[9]

Quantum physics has in effect pushed the rational mind to its limits and, in the process, has rocked the very foundations of Newtonian physics. Instead of viewing science as an endeavor to eradicate mystery, more and more physicists are beginning to understand it as a particular encounter with the eternal mystery of existence itself. For instance, the British physicist Harold Schilling spoke frankly of the "mystery of both the glory and the unfathomability of existence."[10] For him, and many other physicists, the universe has not only spatial extension but also depth upon depth, or what he calls "interiority."

Precisely because of this collapse of inner and outer, Fred Alan Wolf—a scientist who left theoretical physics to dedicate himself to poetry and the pursuit of the sacred—was able to say, "My study of quantum physics made me realize that it is a psychological science as well as a physical one."[11] Of course, we will never get to the bottom of this mystery, though through experience (experiment), reasoning, and not least the intuitive imagination, we can discover ever-new levels of existence, adding to our breadth and depth of understanding and wonderment.

If "hard-nosed" business executives and "hard-headed" scientists invite intuition into their midst, so can everyone else. I believe the spell cast by extreme rationalism over our Western society has been broken. Most significantly, it has been broken in the very place from which it originated—the natural sciences, led by physics. Although the new mood (read: paradigm) that is brewing in scientific circles today is still rather tentative, there is no doubt that it is here to stay. Moreover, its presence will grow stronger and make itself felt throughout our culture. Among other things, we can expect it to bring about a sweeping reappraisal of intuition.

HOW DOES INTUITION WORK?

According to some authorities, rational thinking is an activity of the left cerebral hemisphere, whereas intuition is associated with the right side of the brain. However, this is an unfortunate oversimplification devised by those who popularized the split-brain model. More recent scientific evidence and thinking suggests that the brain is more like a hologram in which memory is not localized or resident in *either* one hemisphere *or* the other but found to be present throughout the brain. There is every indication that complex processes like intuition and reasoning involve both cerebral hemispheres.

This holographic theory of the brain was formulated by Karl Pribram, a professor of neuropsychology at Stanford University.[12] Although Pribram's model remains controversial, it offers a way out of the inadequate explanations of orthodox brain theories and therefore is being favored by many frontier researchers. Now, if the brain is a hologram where information is mirrored in every part rather than stored in a pinpointed area, we can readily see how the instantaneous knowledge of intuition can be possible, how we can have immediate access that does not require a chain reaction transmitting information from one neuron to another until we are conscious of the information.

The theory does not explain, however, how we can have intuitive knowledge of something we have never learned. For intuition includes the vast area of so-called psychic cognitive abilities, such as clairvoyance and precognition. While science may lag behind in its understanding of these processes, the esoteric traditions have long proposed their own answers. We may have to start to think of our whole being—indeed, of the cosmos itself—in terms of a hologram, and to admit that awareness is somehow woven into it all. There is even a scientific model to explain this in a rudimentary way: Nobel prize winner David Bohm's theory of holomovement. He maintained that awareness is woven throughout the holographic structure of the universe, observing that "deep down the consciousness of mankind is one."[13] Perhaps when we have come to fully appreciate the fact that cosmos and brain are of one mold, we will also realize that we do not have to spend billions of dollars to explore distant planets or travel to the nearest star, but that we can be psychocosmonauts, as earlier yogis were. As the ancients knew, microcosm and macrocosm are one and the same. It looks increasingly so.

Such concepts make little sense to the rational mind, however. They call for an intuitive leap. Reasoning works by fission. In its extreme linguistic form, we appropriately call it hair-splitting. Intuition, by contrast, is fusionary. It synthesizes and integrates information rapidly. As C. G. Jung put it, "In intuition a content presents itself whole and complete, without our being able to explain or discover how this content came into existence."[14] The American philosopher Dane Rudhyar noted that the best definition of intuition is "holistic perception." Intuition, he explained, is grounded in a process of identification by which a given whole—whether an inanimate object or a being—is identified with a particular quality. Rudhyar offered the following illustration:

> One knows intuitively that a man is honest, let us say. This means that in a peculiar way the man and honesty have been realized as identical. The quality, honesty, has superimposed itself on the concept of the man, and become one with it.[15]

Rudhyar believed that all intuitions can be explained in this way. This, basically, was also the point of view taken by the great nineteenth-century French philosopher Henri Bergson. In his book *The Two Sources of Morality and Religion,* Bergson considered how intelligence has entered into the life of an insect as instinct and into the life of the human being as reasoning. He wrote:

> It is true that intuition had had to debase itself to become instinct; it had become intent, as though hypnotized, on the interest of the species, and what had survived of its consciousness had assumed a somnambulistic form. But just as there subsisted around animal instinct a fringe of intelligence, so human intelligence preserved a halo of intuition.[16]

It is this "halo of intuition," Bergson suggested, that we must cultivate if we are to find a larger wholeness or sanity than could possibly be produced by mere intellectualism and rationalism. Intuition transcends intellect, as it transcends instinct. Bergson reminds us that in the evolutionary game, intuition required the intellect to move beyond the stage of pure instinct. Instinct resembles somnambulism inasmuch as it has consciousness dormant in it. Intuition, for Bergson, is instinct that has climbed to the level of self-awareness and is capable of genuine detachment from the world of objects and their demands.

Because of the central importance of intuition in Bergson's philosophical edifice, his approach has been characterized as a form of philosophical intuitionism. Not infrequently this label has been used to dismiss Bergson's outlook as antiscientific and merely metaphysical. While Bergson indeed did not shy away from metaphysics, he had a healthy respect for the sciences and believed that they should be placed on an equal footing with metaphysics. Be that as it may, this creative thinker has brought intuition to the attention of modern philosophers.

SCIENCE AND THE LIGHTNING FLASH OF INTUITION

Albert Einstein, whom many consider the greatest scientific genius of our century, arrived at his famous theory of relativity not by cumbersome linear thought but through a flash of insight. His intuition not only went beyond the available evidence but was not even verifiable through experiments at that time. Yet today, the theory of relativity is one of the cornerstones of modern physics. Later, Einstein reflected on his work thus:

> For the creation of a theory, the mere collection of recorded phenomena never suffices—there must always be added a free invention of the human mind that attacks the heart of the matter.

Clearly, the idea that intuition and science are incompatible is quite erroneous. Although many scientists consider themselves to be utterly rational beings and insist that their scientific interests are purged of such "irrational" pollutants of thought as intuition, in practice they are human beings first and scientists second. This means that they are not only subject to irrational modes (notably emotions, desires, biases, etc.) but also capable of small and large intuitive leaps.

Without such leaps, we would still be cutting the branches for our makeshift homes with stone axes. In fact, the invention of the stone ax itself was the result of a leap of the imagination. It was as daring and far-reaching a leap as Archimedes' discovery of the physical principle named after him. Archimedes, who has been called the greatest scientist of classical times, was given the following challenging assignment by his lord and patron, Hieron II, the ruler of Syracuse. Hieron had been given a crown of pure gold, but being of a suspicious nature, the tyrant asked Archimedes to find out whether the crown was indeed fashioned entirely of the rare precious metal or had been alloyed with some baser metal.

Archimedes knew the weight of gold per volume unit and could easily have supplied the correct answer if only he could measure the crown's volume. However, melting the treasure down or hammering it into an ingot was out of the question. But genius that he was, a solution occurred to him in a flash while he was taking a bath. He noticed that as he stepped into the bath his body made the water level rise. This is when he had his famous *eureka!* experience. It suddenly struck him that the volume of water displaced was equal to the volume of the immersed parts of his body. All he had to do now was to drop the crown into a known quantity of water and surprise Hieron with an answer to his question. After receiving Archimedes' test results, the tyrant had the fraudulent goldsmith executed.

The French mathematical genius Henri Poincaré invented, among other things, the theory of Fuchsian functions. His innovation is often quoted in the literature on intuition, because Poincaré provided a commendably lucid account of the moment of discovery. As he reminisced:

> One evening, contrary to my custom, I drank black coffee and could not sleep. Ideas rose in crowds; I felt them collide until pairs interlocked, so to speak, making a stable combination. By the next morning I had established the existence of a class of Fuchsian functions . . . I had only to write out the results, which took but a few hours.[17]

Poincaré went on to consider specific details of his mathematical theory, but he failed to find appropriate solutions to some problems. He welcomed the interlude of a geological excursion. The answers came to him out of the blue when he stepped on the bus that was to take him to the geological site. He did not have the time to verify his insight then, but he felt utterly certain of its correctness.

He reported a similar *aha!* experience in regard to a difficult arithmetic problem. He had been working on solving it for days and, in frustration, took a day off to walk on the beach. Again the solution popped effortlessly into his head when he least expected it. "The idea came to me," he wrote in his book *The Foundations of Science*, "with just the same characteristics of brevity, suddenness, and immediate certainty." On many other occasions, intuitive flashes of insight came to Poincaré's assistance. Comparable first-hand reports were made by other eminent mathematicians, such as André Marie Ampère and Karl Friedrich Gauss.

An oft-mentioned example of an intuitive flash of insight that revolutionized science is Friedrich August Kekulé's discovery that organic compounds are closed chains. Like Archimedes in his bath, Kekulé was in a rather relaxed mood when he had his own *eureka!* experience. In fact, he had drifted off into sleep and was dreaming of atoms forming long snakelike structures. One of these dream snakes curled around and bit its tail. He woke up instantly, with a complete understanding of the implications of this dream image for his chemical research.

THE FAR SIDE OF INTUITION: PSYCHIC PHENOMENA

The idea of solving scientific problems in one's sleep seems very attractive. "Let us learn to dream, gentlemen," Kekulé advised his fellow scientists. Dreamwork has in fact become an important part of many therapies and approaches to self-understanding, though it is not yet popular in scientific circles. Dreaming, which is an altered state of consciousness, is a significant gate to the hidden recesses of the mind—where we find both the unprocessed or half-processed garbage of our everyday experiences and those rare gems of insight that give our lives and efforts special meaning. Sometimes this distinction is expressed in terms of the unconscious and the superconscious, with the former being pictured as a twilight dumping-ground and the latter representing a lofty luminous level from which creative ideas are funneled down to brighten our ordinary awareness and understanding.

Montague Ullman, founder of the dream laboratory at the Maimonides Medical Center in Brooklyn, New York, has found incontestable evidence that dreams bridge our everyday reality and the hidden levels of the holographic universe.[18] He sees in them a fountain of life-enhancing and even life-sustaining wisdom. In numerous experiments, he has been able to demonstrate that even seemingly quite "unpsychic" individuals can have extrasensory experiences in the dream state.

The topic of intuition and dreams brings us to the realm of nonordinary states of consciousness. It was Bergson who first thought of intuition in the context of psychic phenomena and parapsychology. He mentioned the case of the woman who stepped into the elevator only to be abruptly pulled back by the repair man, whom she had not noticed before.[19] When she looked more closely she discovered that she had been about to take a step into an empty elevator shaft. Remarkably, there was no repair man at all. She had hallucinated him, just as she had imagined the elevator to be on her floor. Of course, some people might interpret this as an instance of angelic intervention.

Bergson speculated that the "instinctive or somnambulistic self, which underlies the reasoning personality" had jumped into action to save the woman's life. This vestigial instinct is imbued with the same kind of intelligence that also is present, in a different form, in reason. It is essentially intuitive, although, according to Bergson, it represents a lower form of intuition. Higher intuition, he rightly insisted, reveals the reality that is the familiar terrain of mystics. My own story, related at the beginning of this chapter, of canceling a trip that might otherwise have taken me to the epicenter of the 1989 earthquake in San Francisco, is another example of psychic activity, extrasensory perception (ESP), or what Bergson called the lower form of intuition.

Of course, not all parapsychological activity can be explained in terms of instinct or intuition. Conversely, however, ESP may be an occasional or possibly even a common component of intuition. This was first suggested by C. G. Jung, who considered intuition a separate function of the mind, along with thinking, feeling, and sensation.

To Jung, intuition was an irrational ability of the psyche, which arrives at insights purely on the basis of complex unconscious processes. Interestingly, he typified feeling as a rational psychic function, because it finds its fulfillment only when it is in consonance with rationality. Here feeling must not be confused with emotion, which definitely does not follow the laws of reason. Feeling allows us to appraise a situation without recourse to slow logical analysis. In this sense it is rather similar to intuition, and both functions are deeply rooted in the unconscious. Hence, Jung's distinction between feeling as a rational function and intuition as an irrational function has far from convinced all psychologists.

INTUITION IN THE HIGHEST OCTAVE:
SPIRITUAL ILLUMINATION

To Bergson, the highest form of intuition was rightly the one that wells up from the deepest foundations of human consciousness— from that region of the being that is the home of the mystics of all ages and cultures. Mystical intuition, he wrote, "is presumably a participation in the divine essence."[20]

Some psychologists believe that we use far less than our full brain power, and in this they include our potential for intuitive insight and the highest intuition of spiritual illumination. According to the testimony of the world's mystics and sages, spiritual illumination in fact transcends the brain and thus puts us in touch with reality as it is, without our customary cerebral filters. Therefore, some authorities have rejected labeling enlightenment as a form of intuition, which they define as a mental process. Bergson argued this point in the following way:

> If our body is the matter to which our consciousness applies itself it is coextensive with our consciousness, it comprises all we perceive, it reaches to the stars.[21]

In more modern language, we *are* the total hologram that presents itself in ever new ways to our perception. At any rate, enlightenment goes beyond all the illusions conjured up by the conventional brain, and hence it must inevitably transform our view of the world and our stance in the world. This is exactly what the spiritual traditions have claimed all along: that the genuinely enlightened person is present in the world but not of it, and that he or she walks lightly on this planet, having the welfare of all beings at heart. To quote psychologist and educator Philip Goldberg again:

> In a high state of consciousness, actions are said to be spontaneously right. The intuitive impulses that inform and guide the enlightened mind would be appropriate for both the individual and the environment, since the mind would be resonating with the deepest impulses of nature.[22]

Social scientist Willis Harman calls this higher creativity. His phrase brings out the close association between intuition and creativity. As Harman observes in his book *Higher Creativity*, coauthored with Howard Rheingold, human behavior columnist for *Esquire* magazine:

> According to the mystics, when one comes to truly know oneself, the pull of the material body and ego personality becomes greatly decreased and one finds that the deepest motivation is to participate fully, with conscious awareness, in the evolutionary process and the fulfillment of humankind. To put it another way, one becomes aware that what appeared to be driving motivations were mainly illusory ego needs and that the desires of the true Self are one's real needs—this sounds a lot like the phenomenon we have termed "higher creativity."[23]

As conscious beings we are not merely subject to the process of evolution but are challenged to lucidly—that is, cocreatively—participate in it. However, we are able to do so only when we call upon our inner knowing, our intuitive function, which will furnish us with the deeper and broader understanding necessary to act wisely in the world. Intuition and creativity both seem to bubble up from the same living spring within us. To enjoy their life-enhancing gifts, we must simply remove the obstructions that prevent them from freely enriching our lives. When we have learned to trust life, to trust ourselves, both intuition and creativity will flow. Our innate genius will manifest itself. Such genius, as Ralph Waldo Emerson knew, "sheds wisdom like perfume." In his essay "The Method of Nature," his own genius poured forth when he said:

> And what is Genius but finer love, a love impersonal, a love of the flower and perfection of things, and a desire to draw a new picture or copy of the same? It looks to the cause and life: it proceeds from within outward, whilst Talent goes from without inward. . . . Genius sheds wisdom like perfume, and advertises us that it flows out of a deeper source than the foregoing

silence, that it knows so deeply and speaks so musically, because it is itself a mutation of the thing it describes. It is sun and moon and wave and fire in music. [24]

9

CREATIVITY: SELF-ACTUALIZATION AND TRANSCENDENCE

The Courage to Create

"Creativity is a necessary sequel to being," writes the American psychiatrist Rollo May.[1] This appears to be a contemporary way of saying, in the words of the Bhagavad Gita (III.5), that to be alive means to be active and thus to participate in the creative process of life itself. Life, or nature, is endlessly creative. "Createdness," wrote the Russian philosopher Nicolas Berdyaev, "is creativity."[2] As human beings we are an integral part of the ebb and flow of this natural creativity of creation. The question is whether our participation is unconscious and ego-driven or conscious and self-transcending. As long as we are merely pushed and pulled by life, our creativity is simply nature's creativity. In this case, we are "doomed to creativity," as Henryk Skolimowski puts it.[3]

However, to the degree that we identify with consciousness, as a constant beyond the realm of nature, we transmute the *necessity* of natural creativity into *free cocreative participation*, thereby modifying our own destiny and the destiny of nature and evolution itself. In this case, we are not doomed but challenged to creativity. "Participation," writes Skolimowski, "is a matter of context." He explains:

> Context is a subtle phenomenon, invisible to the ordinary eye. Yet it binds things together, determines their nature, determines the nature of the relationships in which they are to each other, makes them belong to specific configurations (and not to any other kind of configuration), makes them perform their role according to the design of the whole.[4]

If the context is shallow, it signifies only shallow participation. By contrast, we can create a deeper context by participating deeply. Deep participation in society is often handicapped by severely limiting hidden rules, which demand our participation yet give us no creative freedom. For example, we are asked to show concern for those who are underprivileged, yet there is a stigma attached to actually interacting with a vagrant. Or we are expected to have compassion for the sick, yet we feel awkward about demonstrating empathy toward a mentally handicapped individual, again because of a hidden rule that taboos such contact. Only cocreative participation is full participation, as it permits us to creatively change the rules themselves. Skolimowski even envisions a still deeper form of participation through which the geniuses of our species are able to fashion creative works "bordering on miracles." He sees in cocreative participation "a path leading to God."[5]

Evolution apparently does not proceed by random mutations alone but also seems to call on spontaneous individual adaptation even at the level of bacteria. Thus, as the British botanist Rupert Sheldrake explained in his book *The Rebirth of Nature,* "when starving bacteria are in the presence of a sugar they are constitutionally unable to use, genetic mutations occur at frequencies far above chance levels to give the bacteria particular enzymes they need, just when they need them."[6] This kind of spontaneous adaptation is a creative reaction that is still unconscious but is purposive nonetheless. In the human being, endowed with self-conscious awareness, it can blossom into a fully conscious and cocreative response. Sheldrake, who is well known for his theory of morphic resonance, introduced the idea of three models of creativity. The first model has creativity emerge from the "mother principle," that is, nature's blind, unconsciousness processes governed by chance. The second model sees creativity as originating with the "father principle," that is, the higher transcendental intelligence (be it called "God" or *nous*). Thus, for Pythagoras, the laws of creativity are ultimately mathematical, since the eternal mathematical realities precede all manifestation. The third model, favored by Sheldrake, views creativity as resulting from the interplay between the father principle and the mother principle:

> It depends on chance, conflict, and necessity, the mother of invention. It arises in particular environments, at particular places and times; it is rooted in the ongoing processes of nature. But at the same time it occurs within the framework of higher systems of order.[7]

Human creativity, then, unfolds at the interface between consciousness and the hidden dimension of the mind (whether the unconscious or the transpersonal levels of consciousness). It draws on higher-order faculties while at the same time yielding to the promptings of the submerged part of the psyche: the unconscious or subconscious. Whatever universal features it may have, it always represents a unique personal gesture, calling for an unstinting investment of the creative individual's energies and thus a singular kind of courage.

Leaning on the great Protestant theologian Paul Tillich, Rollo May spoke of the "courage to create." Specifically, he meant the courage to create consciously or with the awareness of one's actions as creative. Many people are afraid of being creative because they lack confidence in themselves. They habitually shy away from innovation because deep down they fear failure or censure. Yet, we are constantly creative, whether we realize it or not. However, by and large, our creativity expresses itself in the automatic re-creation (read: duplication) of the familiar patterns and forms. Another way of stating it is to say that we are creatures of habit. Every time we act, we create or, rather, re-create ourselves.

Thus, it is never a question of being creative or not being creative, but of being consciously cocreative or unconsciously creative (replicative). To choose the former implies both courage and faith. According to May, the courage to create (or, rather, cocreate with nature or the unconscious) presupposes centeredness. But what is centeredness? It is the condition of feeling at one with oneself and, by extension, with the world at large. It is the sense of rightness about one's life, an affirmation of one's being. To be centered means to be concentric with what is real about oneself. Without centeredness, as May noted, there would be only a vacuum—which is precisely the unfortunate condition suffered by so many people. Psychological vacuum spells self-centeredness or egocentricity. True centeredness, however, is connected with the higher self, the Being-Consciousness or *atman* in which all beings inhere and are interconnected.

In keeping with Tillich's thought, May understood courage as "the foundation that underlies and gives reality to all other virtues and personal values."[8] Courage, then, is a matter of tapping into the core of our being—the Self—and allowing oneself to be dynamized and sustained by it. The Swiss cultural philosopher Jean Gebser referred to this attitude as "primal trust,"[9] or trust in the Origin, which is ever-present and inalienable.

May's book, though being for the most part an anecdotal account of creativity, proffers several valuable insights. The first useful point he makes is that the discovery of new forms or patterns, which is essential to creativity, is intrinsically difficult. It is difficult because we need to clear the ground, removing old forms and models to make room for the new. But, as May insists, it is difficult also because it implies what he calls a battle with the gods. The creative act is an analog to the act of creation itself, which has traditionally been reserved for God. As C. G. Jung, ever insightful, observed:

> Man is indispensable for the completion of creation; he himself
> is the second creator of the world, who alone has given to the

world its objective existence. . . . Human consciousness created objective existence and meaning, and man found his indispensable place in the great process of being.[10]

While it is true that as conscious beings we inevitably cocreate the world, this cocreative act fulfills itself only when we assume full responsibility for it. In that case, we will approach our individual existence and also our collective (sociocultural) life in the same manner with which an artist approaches a work of art: From a relatively amorphous mass, we will carefully draw forth a form and give it beauty. The Bulgarian spiritual teacher Omraam Mikhael Aivanhov, who was one of the great adepts of the twentieth century, made these inspiring comments:

> The artist *par excellence* is he who takes his own flesh as material for his sculpture, his own face and body as a canvas on which to paint, his own thoughts and feelings as clay to be modeled. He wants all the beauty and harmony of creation to flow and be expressed through his being. An artist such as this creates the art of the new culture which is dawning.[11]

Aivanhov continued:

> A human being who becomes a living masterpiece, who writes the book of himself, does far more for mankind than all the libraries, museums and works of art in the world, for they are dead and he is alive![12]

All too often, creative people ignore the fact that in the creative process the opportunity presents itself not only to create wonderful new external forms but also to re-create themselves. In the present discussion, I will bear both these meanings of creativity in mind.

The courage of creative individuals manifests itself in their ability to challenge the idols of "gods" in their own psyche and in their cultural environment. Creativity always tends to threaten the established order, for it carries the seed of destruction of the *ancien regime.* At least potentially, it calls in question the status quo, the current definition of reality. More than that, as May recognized, creativity is "a yearning for immortality."[13] But in the ordinary creative person, who is not aware of self-creation in every moment, this yearning expresses itself in the false hope that some kind of perpetuity is assured through his or her creative product. We speak of great "immortal" artists—the Shakespeares and Beethovens of our species—and yet they all have succumbed to mortality. Nor is there any guarantee that their works will be remembered and enjoyed forever, or even beyond the next century or millennium. At any rate, postmortem fame is a poor substitute for personal immortality. Less creative individuals fall prey to the same illusion when they hope to perpetuate themselves through their offspring. Neither creativity nor procreativity ensures personal continuity.

THE SPIRITUAL DIMENSION OF CREATIVITY

Immortality transcends both creativity and procreativity, as it transcends the notion of individuality. Only the Spirit, or the ultimate Reality, is immortal. Therefore, to "become" immortal, we must simply "be" present as Spirit, prior to our human conditioning, prior to Nature and the pathways of evolution. No amount of creativity can take us there, though through our creative works—especially when we experience them in the context of lucid waking—we may gain glimpses of the immortal dimension. Creativity need not be an obstacle to immortality. It traps us only to the extent that we identify with our creations, forgetting our true nature as the immortal Spirit.

Berdyaev, who thought more deeply about creativity than anyone else, felt that creativity was of the Spirit itself. "Where the Spirit is," he wrote, "there is freedom and there, too, is creativeness."[14] He continued:

In creativeness the divine in man is revealed by man's own free initiative, revealed from below rather than from above. In creativeness man himself reveals the image and likeness of God in him, manifests the divine power within him.[15]

Creativeness, for Berdyaev, continues the work of creation. However, as this Christian philosopher saw it, true creativeness is possible only after redemption, since the Fall weakened our powers of creativity. He believed that we are "standing on the threshold of a world-epoch of religious creativeness, on a cosmic divide."[16] However, in his 1926 preface to the German edition of his work, he confessed that he had become more pessimistic, announcing a period of barbarization before the new light could dawn. By "religious creativeness," Berdyaev meant the kind of creativity that proceeds on the basis of ecstatic self-transcendence. He viewed this new epoch as the "third revelation," following the revelations of the Old and New Testaments. If such a culture of true creativity can be realized, it will dwarf all previous creativity of the human species.

It is true that in the creative process, individuals reach out beyond their finite form. It is also true that in many ways by re-creating reality, they symbolically re-create themselves. For the creative process is the cocreation of the outer reality and the inner reality. But in what sense do creative individuals re-create themselves? We only need to read the biographies of famous artists to see what form their re-creation tends to take. All too often their lives are tortured and twisted by their own afflictive emotions—notably anger, envy, jealousy, avarice, revenge, hatred, and fear. All too often their lives are marked by a singular absence of harmony, dignity, and beauty. They are driven by the creative process, and, because they sense themselves deprived of freedom by their own drivenness, at times are even in deep conflict with their creativity, which merely increases their agony. In this way, their creativity merely re-creates their neurotic (karmic) patterns of engaging life. This is the mechanism by which the phenomenal reality *(samsara)* is kept in motion. "A creative person," stated Carl Gustav Jung, "has little power over his own life. He is not free. He is captive and driven by his daimon."[17] Tellingly, he added, "This lack of freedom has always been a great sorrow to me."

Many highly creative musicians, artists, writers, and scientists are embroiled in a lifelong struggle with their creativity. We just need to remember geniuses like Michelangelo, Beethoven,

Dostoevski, and Flaubert. By and large, we can say that this is so because they do not relate correctly to their creativity, which is the exercise of their imagination. To be sure, all creativity is a form of exertion, or self-application. Even the divine act of creation is universally associated with the idea of work, or labor. Thus, Genesis, the opening book of the Old Testament, furnishes us with the Hebrew version of the myth of creation, which includes the Creator's desire to rest on the seventh day, the sabbath. In the many cosmogonies of India the act of creation is described as a form of penance *(tapas),* causing the Creator-God Brahma (not to be confused with *brahman*) to sweat so profusely that in the process he emanates the universe. There is a difference, however, between this type of self-exertion and the struggle experienced by so many creative individuals. They may go from periods of creative frenzy to periods of stagnation, both of which are really forms of suffering, since there is an absence of harmony and balance. As Pablo Picasso confessed:

> I am exhausted if I don't work. It fills up the void of nothingness. Sometimes it seems as if all the forces in the world are united to prevent me from getting to my work. Then I am like a furious beast.[18]

Another genius painter, Joan Miró, made these telling remarks about his creative process:

> You mustn't interrupt the flow of work. Even a short interruption can cause weeks getting back into it. I awake and "think" paintings from four to six in the morning. I sleep again briefly—and to work. I work best when I am angry, or annoyed.[19]

It would surprise creative individuals to hear that their creative struggle is, for the most part, a product of their inadequate imagination. For they fail to recognize their drivenness as a disguised form of what Ken Wilber called the Atman Project, or, if they recognize this correctly, they fail to act on it appropriately.[20] Another way of expressing this is to say that creativity is a peculiar manifestation of the impulse to transcend everything that is not the Spirit. When creativity is taken as an opportunity to re-create ourselves in the highest light, it can not only transform us but also imbue our creations with that same light, and thus lead to genuine de*light* in others. Put differently, when we take the business of self-transcendence in and through creativity seriously, our creations will reflect a corresponding spiritual luminosity that does more than give aesthetic pleasure to others; it also communicates with them at the deepest level of their own being, triggering as it were their own spiritual response system.

True creativity, or creativity engaged in and through lucid waking, is the exercise of our inherent freedom. It is not in the least karmic. As Berdyaev so clearly understood, "Creativity is inseparable from freedom."[21] Therefore he did not hesitate to speak of it as in every way equivalent and, for modern humanity, even superior to the old way of asceticism. As he put it:

> The experience of creative ecstasy as a religious way is not revealed in the consciousness of the Church Fathers or in the consciousness of the old mystics. The creative experience, the creative ecstasy, is either denied completely by religious consciousness as "worldly" and of the passions, or else is merely admitted and permitted. At the best, religious consciousness justified creativeness. . . . Creative experience is something primary and hence justifying. Creative experience is spiritual, in the religious sense of the word. Creativeness is no less spiritual, no less religious, than asceticism.[22]

Berdyaev's insistence on the spiritual nature of creativity notwithstanding, the creative process, as psychoanalytic studies have shown, is frequently associated with feelings of guilt and anxiety rather than natural acceptance and ecstasy. The creative act throws the individual into a state of limbo: He or she has deliberately abandoned the old forms and now faces the unknown prior to the emergence of new forms. This sense of uncertainty creates the necessary tension for the creative process to ignite. However, for some creative individuals this essential uncertainty is rather anxiety-provoking—a reaction that is presumably rooted in their personal history, such as past experiences or feelings of abandonment. More than that, the question that consciously or unconsciously plagues the creative individual is: What right do I have to play Creator? The greater a person's genius, the more likely he or she will suffer from such feelings of guilt.

Still, if the creative process were attended only by pain and torment, only masochists would immerse themselves in it. Many creative people, by contrast, have testified to moments of great joy in the midst of their creative frenzy. Undoubtedly drawing on his own personal experience, May wrote:

> There is a curiously sharp sense of joy—or perhaps better expressed, a sense of mild ecstasy—that comes when you find the particular form required by your creation.[23]

But experiences like this are little more than intimations of bliss—of the intense joy that results from complete self-transcendence, of bursting through the boundaries of the ego-personality and breathing the freedom of the Spirit. There is nothing "mild" about actual ecstasy. It is a radical shift of consciousness, fusing subject and object and revealing Reality as it is prior to all mental constructs.

Bliss is the fruit of truly renouncing all ego-driven desires and motives. In his *Art and Artist*, Otto Rank argued that the creative individual can never be at peace with his or her creativity unless that creativity—indeed, the individual's entire life—is offered up to the Divine as a gift.[24] This conclusion, which is perhaps astonishing for a psychoanalyst, is in perfect consonance with the spiritual traditions of the world. To end with a quote from Meister Eckehart, whose thought epitomizes the spiritual perspective beautifully:

> In all his works, a person should turn his will toward God and have God alone in sight. And thus he should proceed and harbor no fear . . . then one arrives where one should, and all is well.[25]

10

HIGHER CONSCIOUSNESS

WHO DO YOU SAY I AM?

How do you define yourself? Do you think of yourself as a biological organism, a particularly clever mammal known as *Homo sapiens*? Or do you regard yourself as an immaterial and immortal Spirit inhabiting, for a relatively brief span of time, a material body? The first view is that of scientific materialism, which treats consciousness or mind as a by-product of matter, a result of the play of material atoms. The second view, which is less "scientific" but enjoys great popularity in religious and New Age circles, is that of spiritualism.

Those who look to physics and chemistry for explanations of life's complexity will treat spiritualism with contempt, dismissing its premises, procedures, and conclusions. No surgeon, materialists typically argue, has ever discovered an immaterial entity—call it soul or spirit—within the body. Therefore, they conclude, "soul" and "spirit" are simply meaningless labels. They do not correspond to anything in reality. Moreover, for them, the consciousness to which we attach such great importance is a purely material process dependent on the nervous system. When the brain and nervous system no longer function, the person is dead. Period. End of argument. Nothing survives the demise of the body. The most we can hope for is a kind of substitute immortality through our children or our works. According to the materialist opinion, consciousness is as impermanent as the mist caused by our breath on a cold winter's day.

Those who are more inclined to be inspired by the arts rather than the hard sciences are likely to dismiss the materialist explanation as cold, reductionistic, and absurd. They will instead argue that the death of the body is not the same as the destruction of our essential being. Something intangible survives the corruption of the flesh. There is some sense of identity, or consciousness, remaining after we drop our mortal coil. We are like a butterfly emerging from its cocoon and flying into a new freedom. Of course, the materialist laughs this off as wishful thinking or hopeful romanticism. Similarly, the spiritualist looks down at the monochrome world of materialism.

The fact, though, is that neither the materialist view nor the spiritualist view represents the whole truth. (To be sure, no point of view does! But some views are plainly wrong, while others are more or less plausible.) In any case, *as extreme positions*, both perspectives are mere caricatures that capture only a portion of the whole truth. The spiritualist point of view, however, has the distinct advantage of fully acknowledging that life is not a flat pancake but has depths of meaning that lie beyond the visible realm.

Yet, the most important point about all this is that whatever view we adopt, we must realize that it will influence our life as a whole. In other words, it matters greatly how we define ourselves, for our self-definition is fundamental to our attitudes, motivations, hopes, desires, and goals. If I were to identify with my roles as a writer, scholar, husband, father of two children, board director, and so on, then that is what I would be. As a consequence, I would bite my nails from worry over book contracts and book sales, my wife's happiness and well-being, my parental responsibilities, my children's future, and the future of the businesses with which I am involved. I would in all probability also be upset about having to pay taxes, the monthly bills, and the state of the world in general.

Is not all this normal enough? So it is. *But*—if we believe that there is nothing more to life than these ordinary roles and the daily

round of chores and problems, then we are unlikely ever to experience anything else, and we will remain trapped in our diminutive
picture of ourselves. For our self-definition acts as a filter for our
experiences. Another way of putting it is that we are programming
ourselves to realize only a portion of our potential and of life's
possibilities.

If, however, I believe that I am not just a writer and scholar, not
just a husband and father, not just a board director, and not just
worried about taxes, bills, and the state of the world, then I am
open to live a much fuller, richer, and more rewarding life. More
than that, I am likely to experience the joys of real human growth,
creativity, and perhaps even ecstatic self-transcendence beyond all
conceivable roles.

Our definition of ourselves is crucial to our happiness. The
materialist view of human life is distinctly impoverished and drab.
It compares to a picture painted in shades of gray when we have at
our disposal a whole range of splendid colors. On the other hand,
the spiritualist view, as ordinarily understood, tends to be romantic
and can lead to self-delusion and greater egotism. If I think I am
only this particular body-mind, I unnecessarily limit myself to the
visible band of the huge spectrum of existence. If I think I am only
a disembodied, transcendental Spirit, I exclude the most obvious
part of my existence and set myself up for much disappointment
and pain. As I have shown in an earlier chapter, embodiment is an
undeniable and highly significant aspect of human existence. It
must not be denied. But what is the body without the enlivening
Spirit if not an empty shell?

"Who do *you* say I am?" asked Jesus of Nazareth when his disciples reported to him that people rumored he was the reincarnation of John the Baptist, Elias, or Jeremias. His question, as recorded in Matthew 16:15, was not a casual inquiry, as is clear from their
answer: "You are the annointed one, son of the living God," replied
Simon Peter, unequivocally affirming the spiritual reality of Jesus'
life. Before answering the question "Who am I?" we would be wise
to consider Simon Peter's response carefully and do so in conjunc-
tion with Jesus' disclosure to his disciples that the heavenly kingdom lies within.

SCIENCE AND THE REDISCOVERY OF
NONORDINARY REALITY

Irrespective of the centuries-long quarrel between materialists and spiritualists, what is certain is that we are more than we seem to be. That at least is the unanimous testimony of all the great philosophers, religious thinkers, mystics, and sages of the world, past and present. It is also the preferred view of the new breed of scientists who have succeeded in breaking away from the antiquated nineteenth-century model of the universe as a gigantic clock, or super-machine—people like physicists David Bohm, Jack Sarfatti, and Fred Alan Wolf, as well as biologists Rupert Sheldrake and James Lovelock, and brain researchers Karl Pribram, John Eccles, and Wilder Penfield. Indeed, there is a remarkable convergence between the most advanced ideas of modern science, especially quantum physics, and the highest teachings of the great spiritual traditions of the world.

The new physics has furnished us with an exhilarating image of the universe and thus of ourselves. The cosmos is now conceptualized as an infinite ocean of energy that is organized into extraordinarily complex patterns within patterns, of which the human body-mind is just one configuration of energy. Unfortunately, this new image has not yet filtered down to the general public, partly because it has not yet made its proper impression on most physicists themselves. The reason is not far to seek. Scientists are first and foremost human beings and therefore as likely as anyone else to turn a blind eye to the full implications of what they do when those implications demand personal change. The fact is that when we translate the new cosmology into daily life, we are challenged to behave like saints or *bodhisattvas*. For, if everything is interconnected and if the view that our ordinary reality is made up of discrete objects is largely a construction of our minds, then we must stop behaving as if we are islands unto ourselves and assume our essential oneness with everything and everyone. Suddenly, traditional ideals such as compassion, generosity, selfless service, forgiveness, and patience loom large.

For some four hundred years, science has developed under the spell of the ideology of materialism ("matter is the ultimate touchstone of reality"). By the end of the nineteenth century, that spell had become so overpowering that many scientists—known as positivists—even went so far as to deny the existence of consciousness! Psychology, which supposedly deals with phenomena of the mind, was turned into a study of human behavior, without mention of the psyche, or consciousness. Not until the 1960s was this bizarre trend reversed, and under the impact of the youth counterculture with its psychedelic experimentation, psychologists began to look into so-called altered states of consciousness. This opened up new areas of inquiry and creative thought. It also led to a new tolerance among scientists toward those things that are not immediately obvious or measurable but are nonetheless important to a fuller and worthier human life. Concepts like "new paradigm" and "Aquarian conspiracy" captured the changed mood, or zeitgeist.

The hodgepodge category of altered states of consciousness comprises a whole range of fascinating states, such as sleep, dreaming, daydreaming, hypnagogic consciousness (between wakefulness and sleep), hypnopompic consciousness (between sleep and wakefulness), drug-induced hallucinations, hysteria, meditation, trance, psychic phenomena, transcendental experiences, loss of self, and so on.[1] *Altered* really means anything that is not the "normal" waking consciousness marked by mental alertness, rationality, and ego-fixity.

Today, well over a generation after the countercultural explosion of flower power and hippiedom, we can talk relatively freely about other levels of mind or states of being. One of the phrases often heard is "higher consciousness." But what is it? How is it related to our ordinary mind and psyche? How does it differ from altered states of consciousness? What does it have to do with the ultimate Reality that some call "God," others "overself," yet others "transcendental Spirit," and so forth? Why is it important to us?

Whereas the phrase "altered state of consciousness" merely suggests a state that is different from the ordinary waking consciousness, "higher consciousness" implies something more. Not

only is it different from the normal consciousness or mind, it is
"higher" in relation to it. But "higher" in what sense? Our mind is
so arranged that we can think of things only in terms of their posi-
tioning in space-time. Thus, we think of the objective world as
being "out there," or of God as "up there," or of the Self as "in
here." Frequently we take these metaphors too seriously, which
is when the trouble begins. For what happens then is that we fix
something in space or in time that really has no location. Thus,
the objective world is not merely "out there." Outside what? Is the
body itself not part of the so-called objective world? Similarly,
the idea that God is "up there" hails from the time when we still
thought of the heavenly vault as the upper limit of the cosmos, with
paradise stretching into infinity beyond the starry heavens. Nor is
the Self only "within." Within what? As the new physics makes
plain, our body is not a container but a rather complex pattern of
energy in the midst of an immeasurable sea of energy.

By the same token, higher consciousness is not spatially higher, even though when speaking of it most people automatically
point somewhere above the head. Rather, *higher* suggests priority:
higher consciousness is higher because in the nature of things it is
senior to our everyday, ordinary consciousness. It is higher also
because we value it as such—at least in principle, if not in practice.
Higher consciousness is nonordinary or extraordinary. We presume
it to be something more primary, powerful, and magnificent than
our work-a-day consciousness. Often when we speak about higher
consciousness we use the term rather vaguely. At times, we mean
the mysterious creative drive that prompts us to compose a poem
or a song, or to create a painting, a sculpture, or a beautiful flower
arrangement. At other times, we mean our intuitive capacity or the
sense of guidance we experience in making life decisions. Both of
these interpretations of higher consciousness are too limited, but
they do suggest that higher consciousness is a part of our nature
that goes beyond our egoic consciousness. That is, it is "larger"
than our ordinary self-identity and lies outside the immediate control of the ego. In his book *The Highest State of Consciousness*,
John White explained higher, or rather highest, consciousness
thus:

It is beyond time and space. . . . One's socially conditioned sense of "me" is shattered and swept away by a new definition of the self, the I. In that redefinition of self, I equals all mankind, all life and the universe. The usual ego boundaries break down, and the ego passes beyond the limits of the body. The self becomes integrated with what Emerson called the Oversoul and what Arthur Clarke in *Childhood's End* called the Overmind. Self becomes selfless . . . and the ego game ends.[2]

Strictly speaking, higher consciousness is not a *state* of consciousness at all. It *is* consciousness happily bereft of the usual chasm between subject and object, between cognizer and cognized. This paradox is equivalent to the eye seeing itself. Higher consciousness is what in earlier chapters I have called Spirit.

THE EGO REFLEX

Sometimes it is useful to delineate a concept by describing what it is not. In the present case, higher consciousness is most definitely *not* the ego-embroiled consciousness. This statement warrants explication. The egoic personality—that which we typically regard ourselves to be ("I am a writer, scholar, husband, father, etc.")—is also sometimes called the lower self. It is concerned with (and concerned about) our survival as biological and social beings. The ego is a peculiar invention of nature by which we move about in our various environments as conscious agents. This is a useful enough arrangement. When we accidentally touch a hot stove with our fingers, we withdraw our hand to avoid burning ourselves. When we see a wall in front of us, we walk around it to avoid crashing into it. When we are hungry, we eat. The ego is a kind of reflex. John White spoke of it as "bound consciousness":

It is the notion of separate selfhood, personal autonomy, independence from the nurturing matrix of society and environment which support individualized life. It is limited identity. It is self-conceived as being apart from God or Ultimate Reality or Cosmic Wholeness. Thus, the ego—the illusion of separate self—is hell.[3]

Yet, as White concedes, the ego has its usefulness. In his own words, it is an anchor "to which latent abilities become tied in place for action."[4] He cites Dane Rudhyar, who in his book *The Planetarization of Consciousness* aptly characterized the ego as a scaffolding that is "necessary for the adequate, timely, and efficient transportation of the building materials to where they belong." As Rudhyar explained, we build a temple with the help of a scaffolding, but once the temple is completed, the scaffolding should be dismantled.

The trouble begins when we treat the scaffolding as the temple or, to use another metaphor, when we treat the ego as king, as if it were our exclusive identity. The result is ego-obsession or egomania—a widespread affliction. When the ego gets the better of us, we become self-conscious, righteous, intolerant, stubborn, rigid, opinionated, extreme, fanatical, proud, unreasonable, pompous, self-seeking, self-indulgent, aggressive, envious, greedy, wasteful, or lazy. These qualities subside the moment we relax our egoic hold on life, that is, when we cease to identify ourselves with the various roles we assume in order to get along in life—that of employer or employee, husband or wife, father or mother, know-it-all or sucker, Mr. Nice Guy or Ms. Nightingale.

The ego is a great actor with an astonishing repertoire. The "I" can masquerade as just about anyone or anything—from street bum to president, from seductress to mother superior, from rogue to philanthropist, from hillbilly to cosmopolitan. The ego, as Alan Watts once pointed out, is a social fiction.[5] The fiction starts when we identify with a particular body-mind—a habit that we grow into even as we outgrow our infancy. Then, as we pile up experiences, this habit gets reinforced and becomes stronger. In the end, we live and die as "true believers" in the limited body-mind as our ultimate reality.

When I speak of the ego as being a king or an actor, this of course is merely a convenient linguistic artifice. It does not mean that the ego is an entity all its own. That is only a popular illusion, by which we are apt to make excuses for our shortcomings and character flaws. In effect, the ego is a *process*. It is our activity of differentiating ourselves from "other" beings and things. It is the way in which we choose, in every moment, to relate to the world as separate identities. No one has emphasized the processual nature of the ego more strongly than the American adept Da Free John, who, almost to prove the point, has adopted half a dozen names during his career as a spiritual teacher. In *The Paradox of Instruction,* one of his earliest and finest books, he wrote:

> Ego, soul, inner self, or separate, defined consciousness is not an entity, an *actor.* It is simply another version of the same universal *activity* in which every form and function in manifestation, or manifest experience, high or low, participates. It is the single activity of contraction, which shows itself as the complex of objective definition, differentiation, independent form, separation, opposition, subjectivity, and contradiction or dilemma.[6]

Prominent as the ego is, it does not exhaust human nature or consciousness. For instance, in sleep, which makes up a good portion of our lifetime, the "I" is mostly submerged. Either it disappears without a trace (as in deep sleep or coma) or it is present in a modified and weakened form (as in dreaming). Even during the day, as George Ivanovich Gurdjieff and other spiritual teachers have reminded us, we live largely in a semiconscious condition, as sleepwalkers.[7] Only for brief moments are we actually awake and fully present as conscious personalities. The rest of the time we are "on automatic," daydreaming, or engaged in internal monologues, during which the ego is less prominent though not altogether absent.

Gurdjieff distinguished between two forms of extraordinary consciousness. The first form he called self-consciousness, a state in which a person is highly wakeful but without the delimiting ego. He or she does not feel separate from the immediate environment, though there is a mood of coolness to it. This state of self-remembering occurs in momentary flashes. The second form, which is "higher," Gurdjieff called objective consciousness, where everything is experienced with uncommon lucidity. It is accompanied by deep knowledge (wisdom) and ecstasy. This consciousness may burst forth spontaneously as a result of inner work, and in the great adepts it becomes permanently established. This event may be equivalent to what the Hindus and Buddhists know as *sahaja-samadhi*, "spontaneous ecstasy," or ultimate enlightenment.

Throughout our life we experience many different states of consciousness. In some states the force of the ego is fully present—as in righteous anger—while in others the ego's force is blunted, as when we sleep or pass out. But the ego-habit is ingrained in us and readily asserts itself with a vengeance as soon as adequate wakefulness or awareness returns.

APPROACHING HIGHER CONSCIOUSNESS

In higher consciousness, as I would like to define it, there is no trace of the ego at all. It is transcended, or "gone beyond." This absence of the ego is what radically distinguishes higher consciousness from altered states of consciousness like sleep or hypnosis. We all experience sleep and we all dream. Most of us have experienced alcoholic inebriation or the effects of nicotine, which are also altered states of consciousness. Many people have experienced other drug-induced states of mind—from the lows of barbiturates to the highs of marijuana, cocaine, and LSD. As children we unknowingly altered our consciousness by twirling excitedly—an exercise that the dervishes of the Middle East have developed into a mystical art. Later we more deliberately held our breath for as long as possible to achieve a similar effect. We may also experience an altered state of consciousness when making love with full abandon or when listening with rapt attention to a piano concerto, an Indian raga, or a jazz improvisation.

Creative individuals typically enter into an altered state of consciousness in the course of their creative work. It is reported of Aldous Huxley that he used to go into what he called a state of "deep reflection." While he was in it he might, for instance, answer the telephone or respond to someone and seem quite normal, but he would remember nothing of it later.

Meditators regularly and quite deliberately exit from the ordinary waking consciousness. For a period of time they reduce their sensitivity to external stimuli, such as sounds or light, by focusing on their inner environment. Phases of the meditative state are not unlike the state we experience just before falling asleep.

But what about higher consciousness? When do we experience it? What is our evidence for it? Remarkably, we don't experience it! Experience presupposes a subject and an object. But whenever higher consciousness is fully present, "we" are not there. Higher consciousness is not an object of experience. It is our essential identity: It is what we are when the ego illusion is dispelled, when our many role identities drop away.

Unlike our egoic personality, higher consciousness is not concerned with individual survival. It is not even a response of the body-mind, a characteristic of the nervous system or brain. It has no location in space-time: It transcends the knowable world of forms and the mind grasping them. In a way it is even misleading to speak of higher consciousness as consciousness. We do so only because it is not an object outside of the perceiving mind, nor is it merely a thought or concept. We call it consciousness because it is not insentient like a rock or vaguely intelligent like a mammal (including human beings), but it is super-awake. It is super-wakefulness.

It is what there is. In philosophical language, it is not a being but Being itself, Reality as a whole. As such it is the matrix of space-time, the omnipresent soil in which all things and beings grow and die.

How do we know all this when we cannot experience higher consciousness through the mind? Here is the simple answer: As with so many things, we can infer its existence and nature from other experiences. This is a perfectly valid procedure. What is more, our inference is strengthened by the testimony of those who have either temporarily or permanently awakened as higher consciousness—the great mystics and adepts of the different religious traditions. Their accounts and descriptions are the most important evidence we have for higher consciousness. Easily the most remarkable thing about them is that across centuries and cultural boundaries, they are astonishingly similar. Six characteristics are typically mentioned:

1. It is impossible to describe the transcendental realization, or enlightenment, in satisfactory rational terms,

because it is full of paradoxes. Of course, mystics and realizers have seldom kept silent but have typically endeavored to communicate their realization in many different ways in order to illumine others about their great discovery.

2. The sense of individuality is abolished, an event often spoken of as "ego-death." One's identity is the Identity of all.

3. It is not a fall into unconsciousness but an ascent to perfect wakefulness.

4. It is an utterly blissful and benign condition of being.

5. It feels overwhelmingly real, and by comparison with it, our ordinary state of consciousness appears puny and illusory.

6. It is completely attractive and desirable.

Once we accept the idea that there is this higher consciousness or transcendental identity, other things begin to make more sense. For instance, we can understand how it is that in our social "play" we can so readily assume different role identities: because consciousness is prior to our role playing and supplies it with continuity. We can also better understand deep sleep. It is well known that the most refreshing sleep we can get occurs when our consciousness sinks below even the dream level. Psychologists speak of this as the delta state because of the slow brain waves accompanying it. Every night, we enjoy about four hours of deep sleep. The rest is taken up by dreaming, in which our subconscious "works" with all the submerged material of the day, notably our fears and desires. Meditators can cut down on their dreaming time by up to three hours, but they still need the rejuvenating effect of deep sleep.

The reason for this was given centuries ago by the yogis and yoginis of India. Long before psychologists became interested in altered states of consciousness, the practitioners of Yoga explored all the different niches of the human mind and psyche in incredible detail. In the course of their experimentation, they naturally also encountered higher consciousness and even developed sophisticated approaches to realizing it.

What they discovered was that in deep sleep, when the ego consciousness is the most relaxed, we get in touch with higher consciousness. We are never completely out of touch with it, of course, because it is our essential identity. But ordinarily our false self-image (as egoic personalities) does not allow higher consciousness to be a more direct influence. The problem about deep sleep is that our awareness, together with our ego-consciousness, is greatly reduced. As a result, we rarely awaken from deep sleep with a sense of having been in touch with great joy, peace, or light. But sometimes we do, and those occasions are particularly memorable and enriching. Perhaps if we understood them rightly, we would value them even more and use them as guides to a more wholesome life.

Higher consciousness is sometimes said to guide us. Thus, the Hindus refer to it as the inner ruler *(antaryamin).* But what does this mean? Is higher consciousness a kind of personality? The answer must be that it is far beyond anything we could conceive as either personal or impersonal. It certainly cannot be less than the personal, being at the summit of the entire cosmic evolutionary process. It is the superpersonal, superconscious, superintelligent, superluminous Reality.

For practical, emotional reasons we may want to personalize higher consciousness and speak of grace, or divine guidance, or an infallible inner sense of direction in terms of our personal growth. Yet, it is just as valid to look upon it as an impersonal force *(shakti* in Hinduism) whose sheer presence, rather like the sun, obliges us to move and grow in a certain way—toward it. Plants grow toward light. We humans grow toward higher consciousness. Light is omnipresent, yet it has apparent foci like the sun or the other stars. So also higher consciousness is nonlocal, but it appears to have focal points—in enlightened beings, in sacred places or objects, or within our inmost self.

In fact, the analogy with light is a good one, because those who have caught a glimpse of higher consciousness in unitive or mystical experiences, or those who have permanently realized it, describe their transformative state as luminous, illuminating, or enlightening.

We can intuit or even temporarily become that higher consciousness in ecstatic states of awareness. But, in fact, we are encountering it even now in our ordinary experience, because it is not different from the events of the present moment. We are never not it! We only *presume* ourselves to be something else—a presumption that is hypnotically powerful and shapes our destiny.

Enlightenment occurs when we awaken to the truth that everything is higher consciousness, or Spirit. This realization, however, is not a mere intellectual exercise. Rather, it is a bodily and mental transformation that shatters all our intellectual presumptions about it. It sweeps us up and grasps and transfigures our entire body-mind. What gets blown to pieces is the idea that we are different from that Reality—that we are an I, an ego, a finite personality. In our realization of higher consciousness, we do not merely conceive it, or speculate about it, or even intuit it. We *are* it. Or, to put it differently, it is all there is.

For the ego-personality, our ordinary self, this is a rather frightening prospect. Indeed, for that realization to occur, we must pass through and beyond the fear of our "own" death, the disappearance of the ego-identity to which we are so attached. On the other side, however, infinite bliss, delight, beatitude, and unqualified love await us. However, these are not distinct qualities but merely different ways of describing what is essentially indescribable.

Finally, how can we realize higher consciousness? The simple answer is: There is no way from here to there. There is nothing the ego can *do* to *achieve* higher consciousness. No amount of meditation, fasting, or consciousness-raising practices can, strictly speaking, get us there. All such practices are simply means of purification, of setting the stage for the real task of remembering of who we really are. We must constantly recollect that we presently *are* higher consciousness and thus go beyond the ego-presumption in every moment. It is the way of self-transcendence, which must not be confused with self-denial or self-repression. It is the disposition of unsentimental love, of being merely but fully present.

As can readily be seen, anyone desiring to realize higher consciousness faces a formidable and mind-bending paradox. Logic tells us that we cannot haul ourselves up by our bootstraps, and yet we must do exactly that if we are to find lasting happiness. That it can be "done" has been demonstrated over and over again by the great mystics and adepts of the Eastern and Western esoteric traditions. The important thing is that we take the first step by letting go of the clench of the ego whenever we notice it (and to notice it more and more often), by loving more, by being more in relationship to everything, by remaining in our feelings, by strongly remembering the larger picture, namely, that we are more than we seem to be.

11

THE ART OF SELF-UNDERSTANDING AND SELF-TRANSFORMATION

THE MIRROR OF THE MIND

Human consciousness has built into it the capacity to mirror itself. We are aware not only of objects but also of the fact that we are aware. This peculiar feature of our mind is known as self-consciousness or, better, self-awareness. We pride ourselves on this reflective nature of our mind, and we even lay an exclusive claim to it. The fact, however, is that orangutans and chimpanzees apparently share this psychological trait with us. As for sea mammals like whales and dolphins, it also seems increasingly likely that they possess self-awareness.[1]

While in our own case, self-awareness is beyond dispute, the nature of the self represents something of an enigma. This is indeed a pivotal problem in psychology. Upon closer inspection, there does *not* appear to be a stable, unchanging self, which immediately calls into question concepts like self-consciousness or self-awareness. As the Scottish philosopher David Hume noted long ago:

For my part, when I enter most intimately into what I call myself, I always stumble on some particular perception or other, of heat or cold, light or shade, love or hatred, pain or pleasure. I never can catch myself at any time without a perception, and never can observe anything but the perception.[2]

Hume's reading of the situation was anticipated two millennia earlier by Buddhist psychologists, whose astonishingly detailed analyses have been preserved in the *Abhidharma:* texts of the Buddhist canon. Today psychology, psychoanalysis, and cognitive science are trying to comprehend the mystery of the elusive self.

Now, if there is no actually enduring self, how can we be aware of it? We obviously cannot. What we are aware of is our construction of a successive self-sense arising from and within our field of experiences and those experiences themselves. The ephemeral nature of the self is an alarming discovery only for those who, for one reason or another, place great store in the self. The spiritual traditions are unanimous in recognizing the self as chimerical and in prescribing methods for its transcendence. In this respect, they seemingly clash with contemporary schools of psychotherapy, which emphasize the need for creating a strong or healthy self-sense. But this contradiction is more apparent than real. For the spiritual traditions also clearly recognize that a neurotic, weak-willed individual (lacking a healthy ego) is incapable of engaging the process of self-transcendence. In other words, we must first have a well-articulated self before we can overcome it. We must have completed our psychological development to the point where we are relatively integrated, whole, mature persons before the great work of self-transformation can truly begin.

The fact that introspection reveals no permanent self does not negate the mirroring or recursive ability of consciousness. Certainly this self-reflective capacity of the mind is fundamental not only to psychotherapy but also to philosophy and spirituality. To grow spiritually, we must gain insight into the play of forces within ourselves. Such self-understanding depends on self-observation. This must not be confused with anxious self-watching, which, to use psychological jargon, is a function of the super-ego (the inner authority monitoring us). While self-watching is essentially neurotic and self-involved, self-observation is an objective, healthy process.

The distinction between self-watching and self-observation is an important one. Charles Tart, one of the pioneers of transpersonal psychology, made a similar differentiation when speaking of the "observer" versus the "Observer." The former refers to the sporadic observation of one's behavior or inner states, which is mixed with evaluation and thus not entirely disentangled from the observed processes. The latter, by contrast, refers to disciplined *witnessing*, as it is conducted in certain meditation practices. This form of self-observation (or what Tart called self-Observation) is to a high degree, if not completely, independent from the observed psychological states. He wrote:

> It is not always easy to make this clear distinction between the observer and the Observer. Many times, for example, when I am attempting to function as an Observer, I Observe myself doing certain things, but this Observation immediately activates some aspect of the structure of my ordinary personality, which then acts as an observer connected with various value judgments that are immediately activated. I pass from the function of Observing from outside the system to observing from inside the system, from what feels like relatively objective Observation to judgmental observation by my conscience or superego.[3]

Both types of self-observation have their usefulness. The former allows us to initiate self-correcting behavior; the latter enhances our capacity for detachment and renunciation. Both are necessary on the spiritual path.

By cultivating the habit of observing ourselves (our self) in action, we little by little gain insight into our particular mental patterning. In the absence of such insight, we are condemned to merely replicate our karmic (psychological) conditioning. Self-understanding, however, serves as a portal to the higher processes of spirituality, namely intentional self-transcendence and self-transformation.

Before I go on to discuss these higher processes, however, two crucial questions remain to be answered. First, how does the demand for self-observation tally with the claim that in enlightenment we live completely spontaneously? Does not self-reflectiveness interfere with being spontaneously present? In his widely read book *Flow*, Mihaly Csikzsentmihalyi relates various anecdotes of people who, engrossed in their favorite activity (climbing, long-distance ocean travel, motorcycling), experienced moments of spontaneity—"flow"—marked by the absence of the self. "In flow," he writes, "there is no room for self-scrutiny."[4] But the kind of self-scrutiny he is talking about is the egg-on-the-face variety, attendant with a vague feeling of alienation; it is not self-awareness pure and simple. Even in a state of spontaneity, self-consciousness is not absent; we simply lose our rough edges so that we seem to be one with the circumstance and environment. As Csikzsentmihalyi explains:

> The absence of the self from consciousness does not mean that a person in flow has given up the control of his psychic energy, or that she is unaware of what happens in her body or in her mind. In fact the opposite is usually true. . . . A violinist must be extremely aware of every movement of her fingers, as well as of the sound entering her ears, and of the total form of the piece she is playing, both analytically, note by note, and holistically, in terms of its overall design. A good runner is usually aware of every relevant muscle in his body, of the rhythm of his breathing, as well as of the performance of his competitors within the overall strategy of the race.[5]

Thus, what is lost in the flow state is not consciousness, not even the self, but our consciousness of the self, the often painful feeling of identification with certain aspects of our total being.

The second question is this: If there is no stable self anywhere to be found within the workings of the mind, and we can know and be aware of this fact, then *who* or *what* is doing this witnessing? For the Buddhist psychologists—as for many, if not most, modern investigators of the human mind—this question itself is misleading. Not so for the Upanishadic sages and many adepts from other

spiritual traditions. Within Western philosophy, it was Immanuel
Kant who tried to make sense of the unicity of consciousness by
postulating a transcendental ego. This corresponds to the *atman,* or
transcendental Self, of the Hindu sages and to the *dharma-kaya* of
the Buddhist masters. Both Buddhists and Hindus base themselves
on experience rather than on mere theory. The Buddhists point to
the ever-changing nature of what they call the five aggregates
(skandha) composing the human person, namely forms (i.e., the
sensory faculties and their objects), sensations, perceptions, dispo-
sitional factors, and awareness. The Hindus point to the continuity
of awareness in the enlightened adepts, who, having realized the
fourth state *(turiya),* remain the "same" in the three states of waking, dreaming, and sleeping.

The Buddha himself declined to speculate about the enlightened
or liberated condition, preferring instead to focus on the mechanics
of the path to liberation. For the Hindu sages, the *atman* doctrine
was and is fundamental to their spiritual methodology, which
revolves around disidentifying oneself from everything that is not the
transcendental Self. I see the practical benefit of both these
approaches, even though they are metaphysically irreconcilable.
Interestingly, spiritual experience itself has proved persuasive enough
to lead, within Mahayana Buddhism, to the creation of philosophical
schools favoring a position akin to the *atman* doctrine of Vedanta.

KNOW THYSELF: PERSONAL GROWTH
THROUGH SELF-UNDERSTANDING

"Know thyself," *gnothi se auton.* These words, inscribed on the
temple of Apollo at Delphi, echo through the ages. Self-knowledge,
made possible by the mind's facility for mirroring its own activities,
is still the most priceless possession a person can have. It is indispensable on the spiritual path. But what is self-knowledge or self-
understanding? First and foremost, it is insight into those behavior
patterns by which we maintain the illusion of our separateness from
all other beings. In other words, it is insight into the mechanism of
the ego contraction—the peculiar psychological habit that gives rise
to the ideas of "I," "me," and "mine."

The moment we are born, we relate to life in an intensely self-centered fashion. But this neonatal self-centeredness is not yet egoic in the strict sense. The ego emerges only gradually as we get older. The newborn has as yet no sense of himself or herself as a separate being. In fact, the neonatal experience is one of undifferentiated insertion into the world. Infants behave as if their desires are those of the world at large. When they are hungry, the entire world is hungry. When they are in discomfort, the whole world is in discomfort. "This archaic-autistic stage," as Ken Wilber put it very well, "is not 'one with the world in bliss and joy,' as so many Romantics think, but a swallowing of the world into the self: the child is all mouth, and everything else is merely food."[6] This neonatal voraciousness tests even the best parent, and emotionally immature parents, who have not outgrown their own narcissism, can barely handle the demands made on them.

The differentiated self, or ego, crystallizes gradually in the course of childhood and is firmly in place by the time the child has acquired the ability to distinguish not only between himself or herself and the surrounding world but also between himself or herself and the various roles he or she enacts. This coincides with the emergent capacity to think logically or rationally, that is, to allow the mind to go beyond the immediately given data and correctly recognize the abstract connections between things.

The crystallization of the ego inevitably brings its own set of problems. Adolescents are typically strongly opinionated, defending their ideas with great passion and impatience. Unless they learn to apply their newly gained reasoning capacity to their own world of experience, they will grow into dogmatic adults. Also, unless they learn to properly delimit their newly won self-sense, they are destined to become narcissistic. The truth is that few people complete their psychological growth, and therefore they remain stuck in adolescent and even childish forms of behavior. Thus we get adults who are perennially rebellious, implacably sulky, or obnoxiously self-referring.

Those who continue their personal development beyond adolescence are known as self-actualizers. This concept was introduced by Abraham Maslow, one of the founders of humanistic psychology. He characterized the self-actualizing individual as follows:

Self-actualizing people are, without one single exception, involved in a cause outside their own skin, in something outside of themselves. They are devoted, working at something, something which is very precious to them—some calling or vocation in the old sense, the priestly sense. . . . All in one way or another devote their lives to the search for what I have called the "being" values ("B" for short), the ultimate values which are intrinsic, which cannot be reduced to anything more ultimate. There are about fourteen of these B-Values, including the truth and beauty and goodness of the ancients and perfection, simplicity, comprehensiveness and several more.[7]

Self-actualization is not possible without self-understanding. It is a commitment to growth, and this always calls for a cool-headed appraisal of where we as individuals are at in any given moment. "One cannot choose wisely for a life," wrote Maslow, "unless he dares to listen to himself, *his own self*, at each moment in life."[8] This listening is a form of understanding, which demands that we transcend the ego and its fears and do so with uncompromising honesty and integrity. When we listen to ourselves, we tune in to the wisdom of our body, which is in a fascinating reciprocal relationship to the mind. Bioenergetic therapist Stanley Keleman captured this link between body and mind in the phrase "Your body speaks its mind," which is the title of one of his books.[9] The body always speaks "its" mind, though we need to learn its language. For instance, when we make a decision, we should check in with the body to see how our body is reacting. We may *think* our decision is the "right" one, but our bodily sense may tell us a different story. A decision may turn out to be intellectually correct but somatically wrong. The body is a reliable ally on the path of self-understanding.

LOOKING INTO THE MIRROR WITH OPEN EYES: THE FINE ART OF SELF-REMEMBERING

If self-observation is a rudimentary form of disciplined awareness leading to self-understanding, then self-remembering is the next higher level of cultivating lucid waking. This concept plays a vitally

significant role in the teachings of Gurdjieff, who clearly understood that the ordinary consciousness is multiply fragmented. As
we have seen, the self is really a constantly shifting sense of I-ness,
attaching itself to this and then that thought or emotion. Our psyche tends to be rather scattered. Through self-remembering, or sustained self-awareness, we can create a more stable psychological
unity within ourselves. Why is this desirable when the self, as noted
earlier, is the root cause of our suffering? It is desirable for the same
reason that it is desirable to cultivate a strong, healthy ego before
going about transcending it.

Self-remembering disrupts the automaticities of the ordinary
consciousness, which rumbles along its well-worn grooves, contin-
ually replicating its familiar states. It creates instead a focal point in
consciousness that shapes the disparate psychological elements into
a more cohesive pattern. This process of self-remembering can be
compared to the fakiristic rope-trick: Sharing a collective hallucination, the onlookers see a boy climb up the rope and disappear in
the distance. The fakir climbs after him with a blade between his
teeth. Shortly afterward, the boy's severed head and limbs fall to
the ground one by one. Then the fakir reassembles the limbs, and,
to the utmost astonishment and disbelief of the onlookers, they
once again behold a smiling boy. "Parts of our minds are dismem-
bered, lost to us," explained Charles Tart, "and we have to re-member ourselves."[10]

At the core of the spiritual process is the kind of deconstruction of ourselves that is analogous to the fakiristic dismember-
ment. Another way of expressing the same thing is self-purification, or catharsis. But at the same time, the spiritual process is
reconstructive, for the Old Adam is being replaced by the New
Adam, the spiritually regenerated person. Self-remembering is an
important aspect of the reconstructive task. In his book *Waking
Up*, Tart described a specific exercise by which we can re-member
ourselves. This consists in paying attention to various parts of the
body, bringing them one by one into the orbit of our consciousness. We sense our toes, feet, hands, arms, trunk, etc., but without passing judgment on any of our sensations or trying to change
their quality. Then, gradually, we sense more and more of our

body altogether. Then the senses other than the kinesthetic sense
are similarly activated and integrated.

Tart compared attention with a muscle that needs to be trained.
At first, it is quite difficult to sustain attention, but with practice it
becomes easier to apply oneself to this exercise of what he calls
"sensing, looking, and listening," without tiring so quickly.

> Eating, walking, talking, swimming, making love, arguing, uri-
> nating, praying, feeling good, feeling bad—all are material for
> sensing, looking, and listening.[11]

Self-remembering, which corresponds to the Buddhist practice of mindfulness, is like a searchlight cast upon the often murky
contents of our own consciousness. It reveals what is actually
going on with us, which, for the most part, is quite uninviting but
also very sobering. Yet it also creates the necessary conditions for
remembering who we really are, beyond the ever-changing flux of
thoughts and emotions. It clears the ground for inner peace and
joy. It creates detachment without dissociation. Thus, it is an
important step toward integration and wholeness in the context of
lucid waking.

In one of his early talks, given in 1924, Gurdjieff emphasized
how difficult it is to observe ourselves objectively:

> When you try, the result will not be, in the true sense, self-
> observation. But trying will strengthen your attention, you will
> learn to concentrate better. All this will be useful later. Only
> then can one begin to remember oneself.
>
> If you work conscientiously, you will remember yourselves
> not more but less, because self-remembering requires many
> things. It is not so easy, it costs a great deal.[12]

Gurdjieff taught that the exercise of self-observation was sufficient for several years and that one should not attempt anything
else during that period. He also believed that practiced conscien-
tiously, it would lead automatically to the next step on the spiritual
path.

TRANSCENDING AND TRANSFORMING THE SELF

Self-transcendence is as common an experience as self-observation, though both normally occur sporadically and without our conscious intention. Every time we fall asleep, we transcend the self that characterizes our waking state. Every time we awaken, we transcend the self that was present during our sleep, especially in our dreams. Every time we reach out to ease someone's pain, or allow our love to flow to our partner or to our children, we transcend the self that typically seeks to insulate itself from everyone else. When we stop smoking, go on a diet, or take up regular physical exercise, we transcend the habitual self. When we adjust to a new sociocultural circumstance (through relocation of one's home or in wartime), we transcend the self. When we fall ill, we likewise transcend the customary self. We are thus quite familiar with the phenomenon of self-transcendence, though we seldom think of it in these terms.

At a higher octave, self-transcendence is the transcendence of the ego in mystical states of consciousness in which the split between the subject and the object is lifted. This type of self-transcendence is fundamental to enlightenment, or what in the Hindu tradition is known as self-realization *(atma-jnana)*. Other forms of self-transcendence are, as it were, trial runs, training us for the moment of full ego-transcendence in mystic fusion.

In 1969, one year before his death, Maslow formulated what he called Theory Z. According to this psychological theory, there is a type of self-actualizing person who is also a transcender. In other words, he or she actualizes not merely the possibilities of the normal human personality but also *transpersonal* (or spiritual) potential. Ordinary accomplished self-actualizers can still be relatively caught up in their own programming. Their pursuit of excellence, beauty, justice, and so on is still colored by the perceptions of the conventional consciousness and may be tinged by a degree of self-centeredness. By contrast, self-transcending individuals align themselves with their transpersonal nature, the Spirit, or Divine. They are motivated by the desire to realize their true identity, which is the identity of all beings and things—the transcendental Self *(atman)* of the Hindu tradition.

The spiritual path, which leads to the redisovery of our true nature, is a path of progressive self-transformation. But the work of self-transformation does not end with enlightenment. On the contrary, only then can it be pursued with an intensity that is impossible while the ego is still intact and fearfully monitors or even blocks change. After enlightenment, when the ego is dethroned, we can fully dedicate ourselves to the transformation of the world, which coincides with our own transformation. This is the Mahayana ideal of the *bodhisattva*, who works untiringly for the enlightenment and happiness of all others. The *bodhisattva* practices virtues like compassion, generosity, and patience to perfection, not shying away from risking life and limb in the service of others.

Where does it all end? While self-transcendence is a permanent accomplishment in the state of enlightenment, self-transformation is in principle endless, because there is an infinite number of beings and worlds in need of help on many levels. But the enlightened being is not daunted by this prospect, for he or she also knows that there is infinite time to accomplish the liberation of all.

12

THE SHADOW OF ENLIGHTENMENT

WHAT IS ENLIGHTENMENT?

To juxtapose "shadow" and "enlightenment" seems a glaring contradiction. Yet, we know from our everyday experience of the physical world that wherever there is light there also is shadow and that, depending on the intensity of the light, the shadow is proportionally darker and sharper. The spiritual event or condition of enlightenment, or illumination, has its own umbra. How we explain this shadow depends on our definition of enlightenment. Some people mean by it little more than a flash of illumination, while for others it is a mystical vision or a state of higher knowledge. For instance, a renowned Buddhist scholar, who is otherwise known for his precise terminology, speaks of it misleadingly as a "peak experience."[1] But enlightenment is no experience at all! Just as it is not a state of mind. Strictly, it is a state of being. Then, of course, there are those who reduce enlightenment to mere intellectual cleverness, which presumably goes back to the European philosophical movement of the seventeenth and eighteenth centuries that bears this name. This particular explanation completely ignores the spiritual usage. Here is my own definition:

Enlightenment is the permanent condition of consciously realized freedom based on the transcendence of the ego habit and
coinciding with the manifestation of certain virtuous qualities,
notably compassion, wisdom, generosity, kindness, and
patience.

This is a minimalist definition, which highlights the single most
important feature of enlightenment: the permanent shift that occurs
in a person's sense of identity. To use Hindu language, the shift is
from self-identity to Self-Identity—from *ahamkara* ("I-maker") to
atman ("Self"), or from *asmita* ("I-am-ness") to the transcendental
aham-bhava ("I-State"), or from conditional *citta* ("conscious-
ness/mind") to transcendental *cit* ("Awareness/Consciousness"). In
Buddhist terminology, enlightenment is "awakening" *(bodhi)* or
"full awakening" *(sambodhi),* namely, the awakening from the
dream of consensus reality as a result of the recovery of one's true
nature, or Buddhahood. In Tibetan, enlightenment is called *byang-
chub-sems*, meaning literally "pure, autonomous awareness." This
indicates that enlightenment is not a state of unconsciousness, as
some critics have suggested. It is the conscious realization of Being-
Consciousness, or pure Being-Awareness, as the fundamental truth
of our nature.

I prefer to speak of temporary realizations of the enlightened
condition as enlightenment *experiences* rather than enlightenment
proper. In Japanese Zen Buddhism, fleeting intuitions of our true
nature are known as *satori,* meaning literally "awakening." In certain schools of Hinduism, such as the school represented by the
Tripura-Rahasya, they are called *kshana-samadhi* ("fleeting ecstasy"). According to this Sanskrit work, fleeting ecstasies occur all
the time but remain undetected because we are not expecting them.
These are moments when we are free from thought and other mental activity, brief pauses in the inner chatter. If we become consciously aware of them, we can begin to enjoy and dilate them
more. For that, we must be in the present, ever mindful.

Here I want to focus on enlightenment as a permanent realization. For it is this realization, which is also called liberation, that is
the avowed goal of authentic spirituality. Momentary conscious

immersions into the enlightened condition are important sustenance for travelers on the path, but they do not give us lasting happiness and peace. For the same reason, we also should not allow other forms of ecstasy *(samadhi)* to sidetrack us, however fascinating, uplifting, and even revealing they may be. No experience is ultimately liberating. Only the kind of radical shift in our identity that comes with full enlightenment has the power to remove the karmic causes of our suffering.

It is important to understand that enlightenment is not merely a matter of awareness—certainly not of awareness in the conventional sense. Since it is a state of being—an unbounded state—it also has an energy aspect. This has been clearly recognized in Tantric Buddhism. In one of his talks, the Nyingma master Tarthang Tulku said:

> Enlightenment is not really something mysterious or other-worldly, but rather the result of an unrestricted and subtle awareness within the activity of our body, speech and mind. It is a subtle energy that is not easily detected because of our own internal blockages. The current is stopped, dammed up within us. Though we speak of these energies on a physical level, they are not necessarily dependent on the laws governing physical substances. This Enlightenment quality is not a "thing": it has no fixed position, no substance we can point to . . . its nature is more like "open space." It is never an awareness of some "thing," which could just be another projection of our self-image—it is neither a subject- nor object-oriented "looking."[2]

In other words, enlightenment is not a new state that is called into existence by our efforts. It is not even a state that is external to ourselves and can be attained. The enlightened condition is always true of us, but there are veils in our mind that prevent us from recognizing this truth. These veils are energetic blockages that have karmic causes. As we purify ourselves through spiritual discipline, these inner obstructions are gradually removed, and then, one day, we suddenly face the inner sanctum of the universal Mind, which is our own nature and the inherent nature of everything else.

Enlightenment and the
Persistence of the Personality

Enlightenment is a radical event that shatters our entire self-image. While we are caught in the unenlightened state, we can only barely intuit what this entails, and we must rely on the testimony of those who have broken free from the cycle of conditioned existence *(samsara)*. All traditional sources, however, are agreed that this rupture does not do away with nature and its forces as they manifest themselves in the physical body. Just as a loaded cart, once set in motion, continues to roll downhill, the karmic causes responsible for the appearance of the human body likewise continue to follow their momentum. Enlightenment only cuts the bonds of future karma and thus negates the possibility of future suffering as an ego-bound individual. Karma already set in motion will run its course until it is exhausted—an event that coincides with the death of the physical body.

This raises an important question: Since the human personality is not merely the product of social conditioning but—as we are learning more and more from genetic research—is also shaped by a person's genetic endowment, what does this mean in the case of an enlightened being? The answer that suggests itself is that so long as the enlightened being has a body, certain features of his or her personality can be explained as a result of the karmic momentum. In other words, while enlightenment lifts the spell of the ego, it does not erase the personality or character. The "shadow" of bodily and mental existence remains. This is obvious when we look at the history of spirituality with its abundance of colorful masters, each of whom had his or her unique way of being in the world. As I observed in my book *Holy Madness*:

> That the personality of enlightened beings—just as of advanced mystics—remains structurally largely intact is instantly obvious when one examines the available biographies and autobiographies of adepts past and present. Each one manifests his or her specific psychological qualities, as determined genetically and by his or her life history. Some are more inclined toward

passivity; others are spectacularly dynamic. Some are typically gentle, others congenitally fierce. Some have no interest in knowledge and learning; others are great intellectuals.[3]

We might add: some have a devotional bent, others favor a more sober approach; some are solitary by nature, others are more sociable; some prefer the middle path in everything, others are naturally eccentric. However—and this is an all-important qualification—the personality of an enlightened being can be expected to sparkle with qualities that in the ordinary person would be deemed great moral virtues. For, with the transcendence of the ego there simply is no room for the lower emotions, such as anxiety, cupidity, greed, slothfulness, gluttony, pride, arrogance, competitiveness, jealousy, envy, resentment, bitterness, meanness, and aggressiveness. These can arise only in association with the ego-contraction. Transcendence of the ego removes the humus in which these powerfully negative emotions ordinarily thrive. Instead it creates an open space where virtues like peace, happiness, contentment, humility, patience, loving-kindness, compassion, love, and wisdom can grow and flourish in abundance.

In *Holy Madness*, I scrutinized the life of well-known adepts from various eras and various spiritual traditions in an attempt to understand their post-enlightenment behavior. I focused on adepts who, in their attempt to guide others to the same spiritual realization, availed themselves of a rather unorthodox teaching style known as crazy wisdom. I explained:

On the most general level, that which tricksters, clowns, mad lamas, Zen masters, holy fools, rascal gurus, and crazy-wise adepts have in common is an *active* rejection of consensual reality. They behave in ways that outwardly manifest the reversal of values and attitudes intrinsic to all genuine spirituality.[4]

Thus, there are the "fools for Christ's sake," like St. Simeon or Mark the Mad, who practiced self-effacement to perfection and endured any amount of mockery and physical abuse to demonstrate the virtue of a sacred way of life. Then there are great Sufi madmen *(majzub),* like Shibli or Abu Sa'id, who, risking their life, went against the grain of Muslim monotheism when they ecstatically preached their perfect identity with God. Next there are Tibetan crazy-wise adepts, like Marpa, who manifested a fierce temper to plunge their worthy disciples into the kind of despair that can lead to a genuine spiritual breakthrough, or like Drukpa Kunley, who liberally used sex to boost the spiritual life of beautiful maidens. We also have Hindu *avadhutas* like Zipruanna or Nityananda, who offended public sensibilities by walking around naked and sitting on garbage heaps to demonstrate the utter insignificance of conventional notions of propriety.

By no means are all crazy-wise adepts enlightened. However, if they are authentic, "their eccentric or antinomian behavior is at least informed by their intuitive appreciation of the enlightened condition."[5] The question that immediately poses itself is whether crazy-wise behavior is pathological rather than methodological. I have tried to answer it fairly and squarely in *Holy Madness.* My conclusion was that as long as an individual is not fully enlightened, psychopathology is always possible. Thus, many of the *masts* ("madcaps") of India would seem to inhabit the borderline between saintliness and insanity. In the case of an enlightened being, however, eccentric behavior should clearly be understood to be metamotivated, that is, powered by wisdom and compassion rather than neurotic compulsion. I refrain from repeating the arguments presented in *Holy Madness,* which I still consider to be essentially valid.

Here I would simply like to reiterate that post-enlightenment behavior, though metamotivated, is nevertheless filtered through a human personality. This personality, though transformed through long spiritual discipline and the elevated being-state of e_lightenment, is essentially continuous with the personality prior to enlightenment. Thus, while enlightenment changes our self-image (or self-identity) and the psychological structures underpinning it, it does not abolish or even transmute all structures.

CASTING LIGHT ON THE SHADOW

In *Holy Madness* I went so far as to argue that enlightenment does not automatically integrate the shadow, in the Jungian sense, and that such integration is in fact a lifelong task even for the enlightened being. I wrote:

> The claim has been made by some contemporary adepts that in the breakthrough of enlightenment, the shadow is entirely flooded with the light of supraconsciousness. The implication is that the enlightened being is without shadow. This is difficult to accept as a statement about the conditional personality. The shadow is the product of the near-infinite permutations of unconscious processes that are essential to human life as we know it. While the personality experiences life, unconscious content is formed simply because no one can be continuously aware of everything. The uprooting of the ego-identity in enlightenment does not terminate the processes of attention; it merely ends the anchorage of attention to the apparent center of the unenlightened body-mind, which we style the "ego" or "ego-identity." Moreover . . . the enlightened being continues to think and emote—both processes that leave an unconscious residue, even when there is no inner attachment to them. The important difference is that in the realizer the unconscious residue is not experienced as a hindrance to ego-transcendence simply because ego-transcendence has already been accomplished.[6]

After further consideration, I feel it necessary to modify and refine my earlier view somewhat. There is no question that after enlightenment, the enlightened being's personality is rendered transparent to himself or herself. What this means is that the personality becomes a fine-tuned instrument for the exercise of compassion and wisdom in the world. Enlightened beings acknowledge that they have a particular personality or character but accept that this not only is necessary for being present in the world but also serves the larger good. Therefore, they do not tend to tinker with their personality in the sense of seeking to somehow improve it. They live wholly spontaneously, allowing their actions to be determined by the wisdom arising within them, which is the wisdom of Reality itself.

In the above quote, I used the term *shadow* in a broader sense. In Jungian psychology, it has a more circumscribed meaning. I would like to take a closer look at the Jungian notion of the shadow to determine more precisely its relevance to the present consideration. The shadow is that part of our psyche that is ignored or denied. Specifically it is those inbuilt traits or talents that, for lack of exercise, retreat into the unconscious. For instance, a person at home with the intellect may neglect the feeling function of his or her psyche. Consequently, the feeling function retreats—goes underground, as it were. The aggregate of all these repressed innate abilities forms a dark counterpart of the conscious personality. The shadow is like a negative image, an antimatter duplicate of our daytime psyche, which seems to have a life of its own that is yet connected with the daytime psyche. We can see its workings in the in-between world of our dreams, and when we do not understand or ignore the signs, the shadow will jump the dream barrier and enter into our waking life and haunt us like an inseparable ghost.

The more we deny an aspect of ourselves the more it becomes energized in the unconscious. When the charge reaches an intolerable level, the unconscious, predictably, lets off steam. For example, a person who has suppressed his anger ever since childhood and never been able to express his feelings finally explodes and in an outburst of rage commits a heinous crime of senseless violence.

Another way in which the shadow manifests itself is through projection: the unknowing attribution to others of exactly those qualities that we deny in ourselves. Many social interactions are charged with the energies of our individual shadows, and international politics is also something of a shadow play where the other is typically seen as an evil antagonist who must be conquered and subdued.[7]

The shadow, then, represents a peculiar division in our human nature. By definition, the enlightened being is undivided and whole. He or she is the same One that is the true nature of everyone and everything. As all the great spiritual scriptures affirm, there is no room for otherness in the enlightened being. Enlightenment is literally en-*light*-enment, the condition of being lit up, or illumined. Where does this leave the Jungian shadow? Is the enlightened being completely free from darkness?

Most traditional accounts insist that this is so. However, more sophisticated presentations insist that the enlightened being transcends light as much as he or she transcends darkness, entering a dimension of existence that is beyond good and evil (which, in psychoanalytical terms, is beyond personality and shadow). For instance, the *Lankavatara-Sutra,* an early Mahayana Buddhist work, has this relevant passage:

> False imagination teaches that such things as light and shade, long and short, black and white are different and are to be discriminated; but they are not independent of each other; they are only different aspects of the same thing, they are terms of relation, not of reality. Conditions of existence are not of a mutually exclusive character; in essence things are not two but one. Even Nirvana and Samsara's world of life and death are aspects of the same thing, for there is no Nirvana except where is Samsara, and no Samsara except where is Nirvana. All duality is falsely imagined.[8]

What does it mean, then, to be beyond light and darkness, beyond good and evil? Essentially, it means to transcend these mental categories that are the typical constructs of the dualistic mind. The enlightened being is as little good or evil as nature itself. Unless we indulge in poetic metaphor, we do not speak of a tornado that devastates a village, that maims and even kills people, as evil. Nor do we literally regard a sunny day as morally good. Similarly, we ought not to attribute conventional moral categories to the enlightened condition. As the Hindu and Buddhists scriptures affirm, it is difficult to fathom the behavior of the adept who has transcended the ego. What we can be sure of, however, is that no enlightened being has any other ultimate purpose than to illumine others. From the unenlightened perspective, this of course appears as being morally good. From the enlightened perspective, it simply is the case.

Whatever paradox we may perceive in the enlightened being, we must always remember that this is purely of the dualistic mind.

The One is perfectly comprehensible to itself, though its comprehension is not a matter of mental understanding but of sheer thought-free obviousness. Hindu metaphysicians speak of the self-luminous *(sva-prakasha)* nature of the One. This kind of descriptive statement takes us to the very edge of meaningful rational discourse about Reality. It is necessarily inadequate and leaves the keen intellect unsatisfied. As the *Taittiriya-Upanishad* (II.4.1) declares, Reality is that "from which words bounce back together with the mind."

Now, to question the testimony of the enlightened adepts of the world is to question not only their veracity and integrity but also the raison d'être of their respective wisdom traditions. There is no reason to do so, but very good reason to accept their self-reports as true and valid. At the same time, the experience of undivided wholeness in enlightenment does not necessarily mean that the enlightened being has actualized his or her full *human* potential. We must clearly distinguish between the feat of transcending the ego and the capacity for expressing and developing innate abilities and talents as a human personality. While the enlightened being does not suffer the dividedness of a shadow split from the conscious personality, he or she is still capable of self-actualization. To the extent that the enlightened being does not express or develop his or her own innate abilities and talents as a human being, we, from an evolutionary (and admittedly unenlightened) perspective, may be justified in seeing this as a shortcoming. Thus, in a modified sense, enlightened beings may have a shadow (unexercised psychological potential), but this shadow does not manifest itself as an antagonistic force in their psyche and perturbs only unenlightened critics rather than the enlightened beings themselves.

If our highest potential is to realize the enlightened condition, then why should the enlightened being be at all concerned with developing his or her ordinary human abilities? Another way of putting this question is: If enlightenment is the highest form of self-fulfillment, why should the enlightened being feel motivated to return to lower levels of self-fulfillment or self-development? Most enlightened beings in fact do not seem to experience a need for this. They apparently regard their present personality as sufficient for expressing themselves. Yet, personal growth after enlightenment is desirable for the simple reason that a more rounded and competent personality is a more useful instrument for accomplishing the liberation of all beings, which is the great ideal of the *bodhisattva*. The post-enlightenment task of further personal growth is perfectly compatible with the enlightened state, which is neither diminished nor enhanced by it but which, it would seem, can be communicated more completely by a personality endowed with advanced skills and abilities. Maybe this is exactly what the Buddhist ideal of *samyak-sambodhi*, or perfect enlightenment, implies.

This assessment of potential for further personal growth in enlightened beings receives significant support from at least one major spiritual tradition. I am referring to the centuries-long controversy between Mahayana and Hinayana Buddhists. The former have vehemently criticized the ideal of the *arhat* ("worthy one") held high by the Hinayana monks. From the Mahayana point of view, the *arhat*, though enlightened, is not entirely unselfish, as he or she does not have the spiritual welfare and ultimate enlightenment of all beings at heart. The Hinayana authorities have always dismissed this attack as unjustified. Strictly speaking, the accusation makes no sense because enlightenment implies self-transcendence. I do not mean to take sides here, however, but merely wish to highlight the significant fact that apparently within the Buddhist tradition it is considered possible to be enlightened and yet to be subject to further inner growth.

If my analysis of enlightenment and post-enlightenment personal growth is correct, we have the exciting prospect of a future breed of enlightened beings who have not only transcended the human condition but also push its innate functional capabilities to their limit. Who would not welcome enlightened artists, enlightened scientists, enlightened philosophers, enlightened inventors, enlightened craftspersons, enlightened writers, enlightened physicians, enlightened composers, enlightened lawyers, enlightened sports champions, and enlightened educators?

13

FREEDOM, DESTINY, AND THE QUANTUM REALITY

FREEDOM IS OUR NATURAL CONDITION

Many years ago, after meditating in the temple of a Sufi teacher for half a day, I found myself suddenly thrown into a state of incomparable joy. Whatever I did, joy was infused into it; whatever thought occurred to me, it was bathed in utter delight; whatever I saw with my eyes, heard with my ears, or touched with my skin, it felt completely joyous. I went for a walk under one of those rare sunny skies of Britain, and the wind playfully bent the flowers toward me. The wind and the flowers were joyous too. Everything was gathered together in the same universal happiness. And I felt completely free within myself. After returning from my walk, I sat quietly on the sofa wrapped in unspeakable bliss, and the thought lazily drifted into my mind that my happiness would not in the least diminish if the ceiling were to drop on my head and the house collapse around me. Joy and freedom would persist under any circumstance.

My mystical euphoria was not a particularly advanced experience on the path, though it did palpably remind me of the fundamental fact that we are inherently free and blissful. This indeed is the message of all the great spiritual traditions. This is the very marrow of the state of mystical union. Our apparent bondage, our daily experience of subjection to the forces of destiny, is merely a temporal inconvenience, yet an inconvenience that causes us tremendous suffering while it lasts.

Our state of imprisonment is a self-made arrangement for which each individual alone is responsible. Nobody is depriving us of our innate freedom; rather, we are our own jailers. There is no external agency, no *deus ex machina*, casting us into the prison of self-divided existence. Our own mind, our own imagination, is the source of all the constrictions by which we hem ourselves in, living in painful separation from all other beings and things. We are the sole architects of our bondage and misery.

Our enslavement to conditional existence, or what the Hindus and Buddhists call *samsara* ("flux"), is a product of inadequate imagination. Put differently, it results from wrong use of our free will. That we are free to choose the direction and quality of our life in every moment is guaranteed by our innate freedom, which is the freedom of the Spirit. We are free to make wrong choices. That freedom is not a mere philosophical postulate formulated in the ivory tower of intellectual abstraction. On the contrary, it is the actual experience of those who, in their consuming passion for liberty, have rattled the prison door and discovered that it was never locked. Even if we were not inherently free, we would have to assume our essential freedom lest we should succumb to the bleakness of fatalism, give up on ourselves, and passively wait for death to end our wretchedness.

How strong our intuition of inner freedom tends to be is borne out by the many people who, despite appalling adverse circumstances (such as internment in a concentration camp, life in a ghetto, imprisonment, or prolonged hospitalization) have not lost their sense of dignity, their hope, or their courage. They know that even within their limiting conditions, they can exercise their free will. At the very least, we can always demonstrate our inherent freedom by cultivating inner peace in the face of a very difficult but unchangeable situation. Paul Tillich gave this attitude philosophical expression when he spoke of our "finite freedom":

Man is essentially "finite freedom"; freedom not in the sense of indeterminacy but in the sense of being able to determine himself through decisions in the centre of his being. Man, as finite freedom, is free within the contingencies of his finitude. But within these limits he is asked to make of himself what he is supposed to become, to fulfill his destiny.[1]

But if all we had was finite freedom, we would not be truly free at all. However, as is the unqualified testimony of the great spiritual teachers, in our essential being we are *unconditionally* free. That fundamental freedom makes itself felt in our finite circumstance as a call to exercise our free will.

Free choice is in fact one of the obsessions of our modern world, which is powered by our idolatry of individualism. Yet, seldom do we exercise our free will wisely—that is, exercise it in order to break through to the level of our fundamental freedom. More often than not, our choices push us deeper into consensus trance, which is a state of bondage and suffering. By and large, we remain unaware that the highest and noblest expression of our free will is to choose freedom itself by transcending the finite body-mind and its karmic destiny and by recovering the Spirit, our infinite nature as Being-Consciousness. This very possibility, validated again and again by adepts and mystics throughout the millennia, implies that our freedom is not finite but unqualified, or unlimited.

We must not confuse freedom with social, economic, or political liberty. We have sought freedom from toil, oppression, and persecution. We also have fought for economic, political, and even religious freedom. Today, model democratic constitutions guarantee all kinds of freedoms. The Preamble to the Constitution of the United States of America speaks of securing "the blessings of liberty to ourselves and our posterity." And the Declaration of Independence mentions life, liberty, and the pursuit of happiness as inalienable human rights.

These freedoms are held dear by all beneficiaries of the democratic system. But we ought not to exclusively pursue these freedoms—which can conveniently be summarized in the concept of liberty—and remain ignorant of our fundamental freedom. This ignorance deprives us of the opportunity to grow beyond karmic necessity and to realize genuine peace and abiding happiness in the midst of whatever situation we may find ourselves in. This does not mean that we should not feel free to oppose oppression, inequality, and injustice or to support all the other values that we have learned to treasure in our democratic society. But the freedoms defended through social activism are secondary to our essential freedom. As long as we have not recovered our innate freedom, we cannot even be sure that our notions of liberty and our programs for safeguarding or restoring liberty are built on the necessary wisdom. The history of social and political revolutions, which are typically touted as means of improving our lot, is characterized by a prevalence of misjudgment, folly, and destructive excess.

Nor must we confuse freedom with license. We are indeed free to pursue whatever we want, but we must be careful to anticipate the consequences of allowing free reign to our desires. As long as we merely chase after the fulfillment of all our whims, we remain entrapped by the force of habit. And habit is the antithesis of freedom. To realize our inherent freedom, we must freely choose to deploy our imagination in such a way that we reduce the influence of habit, or karma, in our lives through the cultivation of lucid waking. However, all too often we choose that which further delimits us and increases our suffering. As Jean Jacques Rousseau knew, "Man is born free, yet he is everywhere in chains."[2] This has prompted some thinkers to dismiss free will altogether. Yet, the imprudent exercise of free will is itself an integral part of our freedom.

Billions of individuals may be quite unaware that through the application of their free will they continuously determine their destiny. As Frederick Franck observes:

> My inner freedom then consists in accepting the fruits of past karma, all the while remaining aware of and putting full trust in *my human capacity to give a new twist to thought and action at this and every other moment.*[3]

That "new twist" was spelled out long ago in the Bhagavad Gita (II.47). After affirming that while we exist we cannot help but be active, the God-man Krishna divulges the great secret of ego-transcending activity to his disciple, Arjuna, as follows:

> In action alone is your rightful interest *(adhikara)*, never in its fruit. Let not your motive be the fruit of action, nor let your attachment be to inaction.

In another verse (II.50), Krishna defines Yoga, the unitive path, as skill in action. Action that is colored by selfishness (the ego principle) yields unwholesome states of consciousness. However, when we act in the world with dispassion *(vairagya)*, or nonattachment, we will not be bound by our deeds. Even seemingly good works are karmically binding when they are not completely free of selfish motives, whether these are conscious or not.

Beyond the generation of good or bad karma there is, then, a third alternative. This is the creation of karma that in the words of the *Yoga-Sutra* (IV.7) is neither black nor white. This third type of karma is the province of the ego-transcending person striving for liberation. Such a person moves in the world without attachment and therefore creates no negative subconscious deposits that subsequently sprout forth as ego-driven activities. By maintaining the mind in emptiness, as the Mahayana Buddhists would say, the self-transcending practitioner gradually eliminates all those karmic factors that give rise to our experience of the conditional world *(samsara)*.

If our own mind imprisons us, it also is the source of our liberation—that is, the springboard for recovering our inherent freedom and blissfulness. As the *Amrita-Bindu-Upanishad* (1-2) declares:

> The mind is said to be twofold; pure and impure. The impure [mind is driven by] desire and volition; the pure [mind] is devoid of desire.

> The mind alone is the cause of bondage and liberation (moksha) to humans. Attached to objects, [it leads] to bondage; devoid of objects, it is deemed [to lead] to emancipation (mukti).

THE QUANTUM PERSPECTIVE
OF FREEDOM

According to Freudian psychology, we are enslaved by the instinc-
tual forces of our unconscious. According to Marxists, we are driven by the blind forces of economy and history. Both views are the
ill-begotten children of the mechanistic Newtonian paradigm that
has us living in a wholly deterministic clockwork universe. This
paradigm, which has reigned in Western thought and culture for
the past three hundred years, was undermined with the advent of
quantum physics. However, its hold on our culture is still strong,
and the findings of quantum physics have not yet percolated down
to the level of daily life. Even Einstein's theory of relativity, formulated a few years before quantum mechanics shortly after the turn
of the century, has so far been only an insignificant factor in the
thinking of the lay public. We like to reiterate that "everything is
relative," but beyond this we are largely ignorant about and
untouched by Einstein's discoveries. In his posthumously published
Notebooks, Paul Brunton spelled out the philosophical and spiritual implications of relativity theory thus:

> Such is this relativity of all things to their knower that because
> the world we experience is *our* mental world, we never see the
> world as it really is in itself or as a being who was observing it
> from outside would observe it. The consequence is that we
> never see the world without unconsciously seeing the world
> mixed up with the self. The "I" plus something other than the
> "I" constitute our field of consciousness. We never know the
> world-in-itself but only the world-in-a-state-of-interaction-with-
> the-self. We never know the self-in-itself but only the self-in-a-
> condition-of-interaction-with-the-world.[4]

Brunton also noted:

> The relativity theory brings space and time together as having
> no existence independent of each other. Mentalism explains

why this is so. They are both inherent in one and the same thing—imagination; they are two ways in which the creative aspect of mind functions simultaneously.[5]

"Mentalism" is Brunton's shorthand term for metaphysical idealism, which asserts that everything is pure mind, or pristine consciousness. This position, which is the position of the perennial philosophy, does not deny the existence of the world, merely its reality. Where common sense believes in solid objects, mentalism sees the play of consciousness. Without using this term and not necessarily being in complete agreement with Brunton, Ken Wilber ably restated the philosophy of mentalism in his preface to the new edition of *Spectrum of Consciousness* as follows:

It has been almost twenty years since I wrote *Spectrum*, and the intervening two decades have convinced me more than ever of the correctness of its essential message: being and consciousness exist as a spectrum, reaching from matter to body to mind to soul to Spirit. And although Spirit is, in a certain sense, the highest dimension or level of the spectrum of existence, it is also the ground or condition of the entire spectrum. It is as if Spirit were both the highest rung on the ladder of existence *and* the wood out of which the entire ladder is made—Spirit is both totally and completely immanent (as the wood) and totally and completely transcendent (as the highest rung). Spirit is both Ground and Goal.[6]

And:

The realization of our Supreme Identity with Spirit dawns only after much growth, much development, much evolution, and much inner work . . . only then do we understand that the Supreme Identity was there, from the beginning, perfectly given in its fullness.[7]

In his superb *Sex, Ecology, and Spirituality,* the first volume of a projected trilogy, Wilber offers the following additional observation:

When the yogis and sages and contemplatives make a statement like, "The entire world is a manifestation of one Self," that is *not* a merely rational statement that we are to think about and see if it makes logical sense. It is rather a description, often poetic, of a direct apprehension or a direct experience, and we are to test this direct experience, not by mulling it over philosophically, but by taking up the experimental method of contemplative awareness, developing the requisite cognitive tools, and then directly looking for ourselves.[8]

Many, if not most, of the metaphysical statements of the mystics and sages are intended to be both descriptive and prescriptive. For, in their effort to convey transcendental truths, they always try to evoke the kind of response that will lead respondents to their own personal realization of those truths. Significantly, when we deeply ponder the truths of relativity theory and quantum theory, we are ultimately led to the boundaries of rational thought and to the contemplation of a profoundly mysterious universe, which seems linked to our own consciousness.

Many writers have commented on the curious convergence between "Western" avant-garde physical theory and "Eastern" metaphysics. An early commentator, physicist Fritjof Capra, made these remarks:

In contrast to the mystic, the physicist begins his inquiry into the essential nature of things by studying the material world. Penetrating into ever-deeper realms of matter, he has become aware of the essential unity of all things and events. More than that, he has also learnt that he himself and his consciousness are an integral part of this unity. Thus the mystic and the physicist arrive at the same conclusion; one starting from the inner realm, the other from the outer world. The harmony between their views confirms the ancient Indian wisdom that *Brahman*, the ultimate reality without, is identical to *Atman*, the reality within.[9]

In trying to account for the parallel insights of modern physics and traditional spirituality, Capra points out that both employ an empirical methodology and both deal with aspects of reality that are not accessible to the ordinary senses. The realities of the sub-atomic realm investigated by physicists could not in fact be more remote from everyday experience. They cannot even be pictured, never mind described other than in highly abstract mathematical formulae.

Einstein's general theory of relativity undermined the naive expectation that our ordinary sensory experience of the world can serve as a valid yardstick for all situations. He demonstrated that our experience based on three-dimensional space is applicable only to certain circumstances. More specifically, he showed that the rules of Euclidean geometry, previously thought to be ironclad, are by no means universal. The rules of mechanics likewise do not hold true in a four-dimensional space-time continuum. Both ordinary geometry and mechanics are useful only in a limited context (called an inertial system), but they are rather like a shorthand version, or even a caricature, of the real thing. Another far-reaching conclusion of the general theory of relativity is that gravitation does not exist as an actual, independent force in the universe. It is a mental construct. The moon does not circle around the earth because of some invisible attractive force, but its pathway is determined by the local curvature of space-time itself.

A still more radical break with the Newtonian worldview was effected by quantum theory. It was pioneered by Max Planck (who in 1899 discovered that heat radiation comes in energy packets, or what Einstein called quanta), Niels Bohr (who in 1913 applied the notion of quantum to atomic theory and in the process formulated the classic version of quantum theory, and in 1927 formulated the principle of complementarity), Werner Heisenberg (who in 1925 invented matrix mechanics and two years later formulated his principle of indeterminacy, which is fundamental to quantum reality), Erwin Schrödinger (who in 1926 devised the theory of wave mechanics), Paul Dirac (who in 1926 showed that wave mechanics and matrix mechanics were complementary aspects of quantum mechanics), and Max Born (who, also in 1926, introduced the idea of quantum waves as waves of probability).

These scientists and their successors have created a vision of the universe that entails many mind-baffling paradoxes and that continues to be refined and even challenged by new research and thinking. Quantum theory effectively overturned the idea that the universe is made up of discrete solid objects that behave according to strictly deterministic laws of Nature. The "interior" of atoms and the "space" between atoms are a vast emptiness, and yet our sensory experience confronts us with objects that appear to be stubbornly solid. To be sure, at the subatomic level, reality is rather weird. Subatomic actualities appear to be interconnected, and this interconnectedness manifests itself to the observer only as probabilities. In contrast to the Newtonian worldview, which insists on the complete separateness of the observer from the observed, quantum theory includes the observer in the observed: The quantum interconnectedness extends to the observer, who is an integral part of the overall web of relations that we call the world. For instance, it depends on the observer (the experimental setup) whether the subatomic relations appear as particles or as waves. The classical ideal of objective description is thereby rendered obsolete. Moreover, it is impossible to simultaneously know the position and the momentum of a particle, as is formally expressed in Heisenberg's uncertainty principle.

A further paradox is contained in the fact that while quantum theory and relativity theory each yield useful experimental results, they are theoretically incompatible. To put it simply, relativity theory is deterministic (calling for continuity and strict causality), whereas quantum theory is founded on the ideas of noncontinuity, noncausality, and nonlocality. So far, all attempts to find an overarching unified field theory have been frustrated. This should be a forceful reminder to us that reality is larger than the intellectual categories we can superimpose on it. One of the great physicists and thinkers of our time, Carl Friedrich von Weizsäcker, made this poignant remark:

> The genuinely real is what cannot be thought conceptually. Because of this, one cannot even apply the predicate "being" (itself a concept) to the "genuinely real." Physics is possible only against the background of negative theology.[10]

In other words, we cannot say anything about Reality without
obscuring it. Whether we refer to it as Being, Void, or
Consciousness, all these terms have more or less definite associa-
tions for us, none of which comprehensively captures Reality.
However, in the interest of communication, Weizsäcker himself, a
great Plato scholar, did not hesitate to apply Platonic terminology
to the quantum reality, referring to it as the One. He continued:

> The mystics have in fact found the philosophy of the One to be
> an interpretation of their experience. And it seems obvious
> that, conversely, those who reject the possibility of this experi-
> ence or consider it irrelevant would find the philosophy of the
> One to be incomprehensible or confusing, and would find a
> way of escaping from this state into some oversimplifying inter-
> pretation. On the other hand, mystical experience itself is as
> remote from being philosophy as sense perception is from
> science.[11]

Thus, mysticism and philosophy relate to the One each in its
own way. But whereas philosophical theory can at best bring us
intellectual conviction, mysticism alone gives us the gift of peace
and happiness. For, in realizing the One through direct experience,
we step beyond the fragmented self and world that are the cradle of
our suffering. When we have recovered our identity as the One, we
are free. In mystical experience, this recovery is only temporary.
Therefore, if we want to not merely suspend but completely eradicate our suffering, we must aspire to permanent enlightenment as
the final fruit of a life lived on the basis of lucid waking.

The choice is always ours. The human mind, in the language of
contemporary physics, is itself an aspect of the quantum reality and
thus has the ability to make free choices. Yet, like the electrons
spinning inside the atom (a somewhat outmoded description), our
mind or mental energy tends to behave largely according to habit.
Habit requires little energy and is the preferred functional mode of
nature. To knock an electron out of its regular orbit, we must introduce energy into the atom. Similarly, the exercise of conscious self-
determination, or lucid waking, demands concentrated high energy.

So while we are inherently free, we seldom exercise our freedom but choose habitual pathways instead. That choice is our destiny, or karma.

By animating the witnessing state, our observer function, we are able to focus our attention more. This in turn empowers us to break the pattern of habit. But first we must see an alternative to our present condition, using the facility of our imagination. As long as we sleepwalk through life preoccupied with survival, we merely squander the great opportunity of exercising our free will and discovering our intrinsic freedom. We may not even realize that none of the freedoms for which we struggle and even sacrifice our lives truly set us free. Finally, at death, unenlightened individuals realize—or maybe not even then—that they have lived out their life in self-chosen bondage. Only the sages, the adepts, who enter the death process consciously, with utmost mindfulness, are masters of their own destiny both here and now and in the great beyond.

14

THE QUEST FOR WHOLENESS

FIXING THE WORLD

The fundamental quantum-theoretical assumption that reality is an undivided wholeness, spoken of in the preceding chapter, is very much a reflection of our present-day preoccupation with integration, or wholeness. This concern can be understood as a response to our contemporary experience of fragmentation—the atomization of knowledge, the shattering of the ideals and idols of our preindustrial heritage, the political fractioning of the world's nations, the steady granulation of the earth's resources, and not least the schizoid self-dividedness of our perplexed postmodern psyche: Humpty-Dumpty has fallen off the wall. But can we put him together again? And will he look as before? More fundamentally: *should* we put him together again?

Several more or less ingenious approaches to our crisis situation have been proposed in our century. These I intend to classify under the following five categories: techno-fixing, eco-fixing, socio-fixing, psycho-fixing, and ideo-fixing. First and foremost is the approach of the *techno-fixers*, those stalwart optimists who, upholding the nineteenth-century philosophy of progress, propose to us that whatever is wrong with our civilization, technology will sooner or later find a remedy for it. Computer technology, nano-technology, and virtual reality are among the latest panaceas peddled in the marketplace. Perhaps the greatest spokesman for technolog-ical rationality was R. Buckminster Fuller, whose "comprehensive anticipatory design science" aimed at educating people "to realize that what we are going to have to do to make the world work is to get all of humanity on to the consumer-implementing payroll in progressively greater magnitude in direct proportion to the swiftly evoluting, increased capability of world-integrated productivity."[1] Fuller was a brilliant generalist, who made significant contributions not only to architecture but also to engineering, cartography, and not least technological methodology. While he rightly and valiantly fought against overspecialization, he remained truly a child of nine-teenth-century rationalism. His exclusive reliance on reason in determining humanity's destiny is almost quaint when we bear in mind the complexity of human nature and the multidimensionality of our consciousness, as disclosed for instance by Jean Gebser's psychohistorical reconstructions.[2] In general, the techno-fixers' faith is shared by fewer and fewer nonspecialist thinkers, with the possible exception of some science-fiction writers who continue to foster this hope.

The "state of the world" reports produced by such organiza-tions as the Club of Rome and the World Watch Institute give us little cause for optimism: The deterioration of our environment is outpacing technological intervention. Likewise, in the social arena, problems continue to pile up for already incompetent or inade-quately responsive governments—the rapid spread of AIDS and the resurgence of diseases thought to have been conquered being the latest threat to the shaky equilibrium.

This brings me to the second camp, the *socio-fixers*, or social reformers, who insist that the situation must be handled through organizational renewal. A good example is the communist revolu-tions of Russia and China. While they have undeniably brought about sweeping changes, they have failed to give birth to the utopias that were their underlying inspiration. More than that, they have caused a vast number of socioeconomic and political problems of their own. Even the widespread ideological "reeducation" of individuals, especially in China, has not succeeded in making the communist ideals come true. It has succeeded even less in creating authentic psychological and political wholeness. The collapse of the Soviet Union can be seen as an upshot of the failure of communist ideology. Of course, the Western capitalist ideology has its own tragic shortcomings, bolstered as it is by the egocentric ideal of competition and serving as it does the military-industrial complex.

A third group of reformers, which I call the *eco-fixers*, put their faith in cleaning up the environment and restoring a healthy ecological balance on our home planet. They address a great variety of problems, simply because our sprawling human civilization has, in the short span of three or four generations, managed to pollute every last corner of the globe. The eco-fixers seem to be fighting a losing battle, however, because the mind-set and institutional forces that are responsible for the ecological disaster continue to thrive and wreak havoc with the environment. Above all, the eco-fixers do not sufficiently appreciate the pervasiveness of the human ego as a potentially destructive force.

This, among other things, furnished the stimulus for the creation of deep ecology, which recognizes that in our quest for human maturity, we must neither separate ourselves from other life forms nor seek to dominate them, but rather live cooperatively with all other beings, human and nonhuman. Such cooperative or cocreative living is possible only when we actively aspire to transcend the ego. Commendably, deep ecology strives to provide a profound philosophical and even spiritual framework for the science of ecology. However, what is known as the deep ecology movement is, as Ken Wilber has pointed out, still handicapped by its rejection of natural hierarchy.[3] The danger of indiscriminate holistic thinking, as evidenced in ecological and also New Age circles, is that it is basically reductionistic and can easily sink into totalitarian ideology. The critique of anthropocentrism by deep ecologists is marred by the antihierarchical mode of thinking, and their analysis of the humanity–nature relationship has remained problematical on the theoretical and practical levels.[4]

A fourth group of reform-oriented people—the *psycho-fixers*—place great hope in the renewal of the individual human being—

whether through psychotherapy (à la Freud, Jung, Maslow, or Assagioli), body therapy (à la Löwen, Reich, Rolf, or Alexander), or designed behavior modification (à la B. F. Skinner, inventor, among other things, of the teaching machine and the mechanical Air Crib, a mechanized baby tender). Usually what is at the bottom of the therapeutic orientation is the objective of enhancing, raising, or expanding a person's self-awareness. But as Edwin Schur noted in his book *The Awareness Trap*, awareness training or "personal growth" may indeed improve a person's well-being, but it does not necessarily create good interpersonal relations or solve national and international problems.[5] It appears that in some cases heightened awareness is inversely proportional to such old-fashioned values as humility, empathy, and social concern.

Theologian William A. Johnson, in his book *The Search for Transcendence*, made the further point that in regard to Jung's approach (though his criticism applies to most other psychotherapeutic approaches as well), the creation of a psychologically healthy member of society is not tantamount to wholeness.[6] Johnson called this the holistic fallacy, by which he means the assumption that the whole is no more than the sum of its parts. Johnson put it boldly and bluntly thus: "Psychic wholeness does not necessarily contribute to rational collective behavior. There have been many psychologically healthy individuals who have started wars and who have initiated racial strife."[7] He went on: "Wholeness can come about solely through an act of grace by the ultimate source and ground of man's being."[8]

While Johnson's argument is somewhat opaque in its details, and while it is doubtful that a psychologically healthy person would deliberately initiate war or racial strife, it does point to the fact that what is usually understood by psychic wholeness is still only a partial wholeness. Comprehensive wholeness, or authentic integration, requires the inclusion of transcendence into our psychic life, or, rather, the voluntary transcendence of our (whole) psychic life in favor of the larger Reality (Whole), which some call God and others term the Self.[9] This is of course an imponderable alternative for most activists, who tend to espouse a secularist philosophy that attempts to rescue either civilization, the environment, or the individual. But for those in whom a more embracing view of life is making itself felt, self-transcendence is the cornerstone of any authentic effort toward a wholeness that revitalizes person and planet.

The behaviorist approach, as exemplified by the Skinnerians, bypasses awareness and insight and attempts to bring about inner change through operant conditioning. The benefits and also the inherent limitations and dangers of such a Skinnerian technology of behavior have been discussed at length in the psychological and philosophical literature, and I will not detail them here. Suffice it to say that a large part of our personality is "on automatic," but this does not mean that we cannot go beyond our automaticities. Above all, we are not merely a passive product of our culture but are capable of actively transcending culture and the personality shaped by it. In the late sixties, educator George Leonard, who was by no means blind to the constructive power of Skinnerian behaviorism, summed up the situation well when he said, "The human potential is infinitely greater than we have been led to believe."[10]

A fifth and final group is composed of the *ideo-fixers*. Their principal argument is that what is lacking is an overarching philosophy, a new synthesis that would integrate the massive amount of information that is now available to us only in fragmented form. A respectable representative of this camp is the philosophy professor Oliver L. Reiser, author of *The Integration of Human Knowledge* and several other works.[11] While there is undoubtedly a need for the integration of knowledge, the attempts made so far have been "unifications" (the term used by Reiser himself), which, in light of Jean Gebser's work on the archaeology of human consciousness, suggests not a breakthrough to an integral reality-perception but a magical bonding of disparate elements.[12] This is not the place to justify this conclusion in detail, but in any case, works like Reiser's raise the question whether the kind of grand philosophical synthesis that was possible and perhaps even desirable in, say, the time of an Aristotle or a St. Augustine is possible and desirable today. My own inclination is to think that our knowledge base has widened so incredibly that no single theory can account for all the known facts. What is called for is penetrating insight, or wisdom, that takes us to the very heart of everything and allows us to live sanely, creatively, and harmoniously in the midst of the chaos created by the knowledge explosion.

THE HEALING POWER OF MYTHOS

My main misgiving about the five orientations just described is that to the degree that they seek to "fix" the situation they are unlikely to succeed. Fixing is always tinkering with broken pieces. But there is no glue to stick together the broken parts (and hearts) of our civilization. We cannot wipe out the brutal historical facts of war, political hypocrisy, worldwide economic mismanagement, ecological breakdown, or racial strife. These are a sad but undeniable aspect of our contemporary reality. They will always be there in our historical consciousness to remind us of our errors in growth, our evolutionary failures. They are our shadow, as Jung called the dark side of our human nature. I am not saying that we should not work, and work hard, at eliminating war, poverty, pollution, racism, and all the other evils of our time. But we should do so from the position of wisdom, the intelligence born in the stillness of an ego-transcending life, rather than merely from accumulated knowledge and abstract theorizing.

Rather than trying to fix things, which is always a piecemeal undertaking at best, I believe we should invest our energies in creating new beginnings. We must set down new roots that will help us outgrow the withered limbs of our civilization. And the roots we must set down are spiritual roots. As long as we pay overmuch attention to the diseased aspects, we cannot cultivate new strengths. In the face of the chaos surrounding us, it is all too easy to succumb to despair. But depression is no cure. While the problems are very real, there are also those individuals, the doomsday philosophers of our day, who magnify them beyond proportion, perhaps because they derive energy from pondering the possibility of ultimate obliteration. This is mere hypochondria, and hypochondriacs seldom get better, because they have so much invested in being sick.

Obviously, we cannot ignore the serious imbalances in the sociocultural, ecological, and psychic dimensions of contemporary

life. But we can adopt a new attitude toward them. We can give the
image of wholeness and well-being priority over the image of death
and destruction. We can look upon the complications of our present-day situation as teething troubles that have arisen as a part of
humankind's evolutionary struggle for a new self-definition.

Our contemporary concern with wholeness is all too frequently merely a function of our existential neurosis, our fear of the
future, and our inability to cope with the present. Increasingly,
wholeness is becoming a slogan that sells ideologies, goods, and
gadgets. But the ideal of wholeness has evolutionary merit only to
the extent that it is a *mythos:* a genuine myth, not merely a fiction
that has no guiding power. As a mere slogan, which is a dangerous
form of cynicism, it simply reinforces the fragmentation that it pur-
ports to overcome. As a mythos, however, the ideal of wholeness is
a true psychic force that can empower real growth.

We need mythos rather than mythology, which all too often
remains for us on the level of mere allegory. Entrenched as most of
us are in what Jean Gebser called the mental-rational consciousness, we seldom experience the life-giving power of myth. If we do
not demythologize (raticnalize) the mythic content, we reinterpret
the deep symbolism of myths to conform to our intellectual perspective. Thus, our understanding of ancient civilizations and their
spiritual traditions has remained rudimentary. In recent years, symbolist research has endeavored to remedy this shortcoming, but it
has succeeded only to a modest extent.[13] How far removed we still
are from understanding archaic symbolism and myths can be appreciated when we try to translate the Rig-Veda, the oldest literary
document of which we have knowledge. The Rig-Vedic hymns,
composed in an archaic form of Sanskrit, pose formidable problems
to even the most symbol-sensitive translator.[14]

We cannot escape the fragmentation of our world. We are the
world we have created. But we can learn to transcend it by integrating the fragments into a larger, spiritual vision. To begin with,
we must become more alert to those instances when *mythos,* which
makes us hale, is reduced to a hollow slogan or ideology. That task
is a personal obligation. Yet, since the external world and the inner
psychic universe are not separate, it is also a social and political

obligation. The contemplation of authentic wholeness cuts across all compartments, departments, and other angularities. It proceeds from the single person, but it is a species-wide challenge.

This may sound less than concrete, because what I am talking about begins in the dimension of human intuition and feeling, from there filtering down into our thoughts and actions. And this is not something we can expect to take shape overnight, either in our personal life or in the world at large. But surely it must take shape.

15

THE NEW AGE: REGRESSION OR POSSIBILITY?

THE NATURE OF CRISIS

Ever since Oswald Spengler's apocalyptic prophecy of the decline of our Western civilization in the early 1920s, seemingly confirmed by the two world wars, it has become fashionable to reiterate that ours is an age of great crisis. In light of the unabated devastation of the environment, the continuing population explosion (by the year 2025 A.D. our planet, we are told, will have eight billion mouths to feed), and the shocking fact that more wars have been fought in this century alone than in all previous eras put together, Spengler's prophecy seems reasonable enough. Who today would seriously deny that our human species is in deep trouble?

And yet, the abyss that so many observers of our era see yawning before us, is just that: an abyss, a chasm, which is nothing without the solid matter bounding it. Valleys are formed by the mountains surrounding them. The space inside a jar is defined by the shape of the containing material. Both go together. The abyss is only one side of the historical truth. The other side is that we are still on the march and do not need to take the fatal last step that would hurl us into oblivion. We can pause. We can bypass the imminent historical chasm, or, to employ a different metaphor, we can create a bridge that will see us safely across the ravine. Thus, the abyss that we perceive, and which some extrapolate or prophesy as being our inevitable destiny, is more a threshold—steep, to be sure, but by no means insurmountable.

Let us recall that every crisis is, by definition, indeterminate. It contains elements that foreshadow both negative and positive outcomes. Crisis moments have a highly unstable structure that is peculiarly susceptible to input from the outside, as Ilya Prigogine brought to our attention through his work in chemistry.[1] Human crises, therefore, represent not merely a threat but an opportunity for the intervention of human intelligence. But this has to be clearly understood. We cannot sit back in a "democratic," infantile stupor, allowing things to flow their supposedly predestined way and trusting blindly that everything will work out for the best. Rather, we need to harness whatever creative, constructive forces are available to us. We must want to pass through the crisis and emerge hale. Psychiatrist Roger Walsh writes:

> As the old saying goes, "Life will either grind you down or polish you up," and which it does is now our choice. On one hand, we may respond with an exacerbation of the fear, defensiveness, and aggression that created our dilemma, and thereby regress in even more dangerous ways. On the other, we may use the situation to spur ourselves to rethink our values and choices, to explore and resolve the psychological dynamics with which we endangered ourselves, and thereby accelerate our individual and cultural maturation. Never in the course of human history have the stakes been higher.[2]

But rethinking our values and options does not appear to be a priority with the world's political leaders, who, with exceedingly few exceptions, make little more than token gestures toward solving the massive problems facing every country on earth today. As Robert L. Heilbroner pointed out, many members of our civilization even seem to have succumbed to an unconscious death wish:

> This is the danger that can be glimpsed in our deep consciousness when we take stock of things as they now are: the wish that the drama run its full tragic course, bringing man, like a Greek hero, to the fearful end that he has, however unwittingly, arranged for himself. For it is not only with dismay that Promethean man regards the future. It is also with a kind of anger. If after so much effort, so little has been accomplished; if before such vast challenges, so little is apt to be done—then let the drama proceed to its finale, let mankind suffer the end it deserves.[3]

As we are learning from the healing arts, human intention is a wonderfully magical tool. We are able to heal ourselves, but we must want to be healed. We must envision ourselves as hale and whole. If our intention is self-punishment, a twisted sense of atoning for our collective guilt—whether real or imagined—by condemning our species to extinction, then this too can become our horrible reality. Thinking, intention, visualization, or imagination *will* make it so.

On the other side, however, we can also not afford to abandon ourselves to the adolescent ardor of elitist, blueprint social engineering. True, we must reform and even recreate many, if not most, of our social institutions. But this can be accomplished effectively on a large scale only when there is a general readiness for personal transformation. Personal and institutional change must go hand in hand, and they must be informed by higher values and not merely be forced on people from the outside by some political fiat. The environmentalists have duly appreciated this fact: Social action begins at home—by putting a brick in one's own water closet to reduce water consumption, switching off unneeded lights in one's home, composting vegetable waste matter, or solarizing one's own house.

The great sociocultural revolutions of the past—and communism is a good example—failed essentially because the sweeping changes enforced by them were not willingly and intelligently embraced by the larger social body, which was insufficiently prepared to engage the difficult work of *personal* transformation. Apart from this, the communist revolutions were bound for bankruptcy because they had no grounding in higher values but operated on the basis of a reductionistic anthropology. In the case of communism (as with capitalism), the guiding anthropological image is that of *homo economicus*. Only the material, visible side of humanness is taken into account. Matter is hailed as the ultimate principle. Consequently, religion, which typically enshrines the highest spiritual and moral principles of our species, is dismissed as an opiate for the masses.

If revolutions are not the answer, do we then need to allow the status quo to play itself out, without ever challenging it? I believe there is a middle path between lethargy and revolutionary zeal. And that *via media* is the discipline of lucid waking powered by an alert, self-critical intelligence that can inspire appropriate action. This is the route of a life dedicated to self-transcendence and self-transformation for the benefit of all sentient beings.

The million-dollar question is how this third alternative can be made to appeal to a sufficient number of people to mobilize the energy necessary to create new order out of the existing sociocultural chaos. As Prigogine has shown, in highly unstable systems (such as our present-day global civilization) even a comparatively small input can cause major change (leading toward either total chaos or a new order). But no one knows how this translates into human terms. Speculation about the "hundredth monkey principle" has been rampant, but this idea is part of modern mythology rather than established scientific fact. Even plant biologist Rupert Sheldrake's concept of a "morphogenetic field" is at this stage only a theory awaiting full validation.[4]

Spengler's reading of our situation was ingenious, premature, and lopsided. In being hypersensitive to the negative aspects of our crisis, he failed to see its positive potential. His *Decline of the West* was so amazingly successful in the German-speaking world because it expressed the frustration, despair, and paranoia about the future felt by his contemporaries. While Spengler still has his bedfellows, today's zeitgeist is more one of hope against all the odds. The mood of uneasiness about the state of the world is far more widespread than it was in Spengler's days. But the populace at large still generally refuses to ponder deeply their concerns and fears about the state of the world and prefers to repress them. On some level, the hope is that the problems will magically go away.

Among those whose intelligence does not allow them to blink out the stark realities of our era there are many who feel that the inadequate solutions attempted by the political leadership will not stop the massive hemorrhaging of our civilization. Yet, they simultaneously entertain the belief or hope that we will not bleed to death but, after a drastic purging, will recover our strength. By and large they place their faith in technology.

LAYING NEW FOUNDATIONS

Some members of our Euro-American civilization interpret the present-day crisis as the birth pangs of a new and brighter era for humanity. They believe that we will summon our creative abilities in time to avert the worst disaster and then usher in a reign of harmony, peace, and plenty. Many entertain the view that this *metanoia* will occur as the inevitable result of cosmic (astrological) triggers. Others associate it with outside intervention by aliens, whom they believe to be in contact with us already. The advent of the optimistic New Age ideology in the 1970s is definitely proving to be an increasingly significant cultural phenomenon.[5] That is not to say, however, that the "Aquarian front" is correct in its interpretation of our contemporary crisis, where the maverick historian Spengler was wrong. To predict the death of a patient in the throes of a serious crisis can turn into a self-fulfilling prophecy. Having heard or overheard the medic's prognosis, the patient loses hope and obliges by dying. I have talked about the power of imagination in a previous chapter. Likewise, however, a prediction of full recovery, which is the gospel of the New Age, can be equally farfetched and foolish: Unimpressed by the doctor's misplaced optimism, the patient gives up and dies anyway.

Much in New Ageism smacks of misplaced enthusiasm, wishful thinking, fashion, gimmicks, and half-truths. A whole new ideology has sprung up that is reminiscent of, and in its function homologous to, the mythologies of premodern periods. However, it clearly entails a regressive tendency, a flight from reality into fantasy and fiction, and hence a sacrifice of much-needed lucidity. It will not do to build imaginary bridges across a real gulf. This would only amount to nihilism as well. I do not wish to dismiss all New Age preoccupations. Far from it. There is much that is healthy and necessary, but only the "true believers" will fail to see the regressive component in New Ageism. Neurotic traits are in evidence both on the side of the exploitative leaders of this movement and on the side of their gullible victims, who, in their hunger for meaning, immolate their own intelligence and integrity.

One need not resuscitate logical positivism to countermand the kind of irrationalism witnessed in the popular and quasi-scientific literature of New Ageism. What is called for instead is simply (though not easily) a healthy measure of clarity, in which both reason and faith (rather than mere belief) have their rightful function.

And when we look clearly at today's civilizational crisis, we can detect a great deal that is potentially destructive and much that is potentially constructive. In quantity, the destructive elements seem by far to outnumber the constructive aspects. But how can we assess their respective qualitative weighting? It is impossible to say, particularly in view of the intellectual and spiritual resourcefulness and the immense adaptability that characterize our species.

Therefore, instead of portraying either gloomy or glorious scenarios for the future, it seems to be more appropriate and useful to consider how the positive criteria can be strengthened and the negative criteria overcome, and then act accordingly and in consonance with the highest human potential: the capacity for self-transcendence and self-transformation.

Of course, we will inevitably have an overall image integrating all the elements that we identify as positive or negative. However, we ought not solidify that image into an icon—that is, an ideology that then merely dims the acuity of our reality perception. Indeed, such an icon would be detrimental to our very intention to turn the present-day crisis to our advantage. For ideology encourages habit rather than human maturity, creativity, and responsible action, which are cornerstones of the bridge that we must now construct and that, I believe, is in the process of being built. A great challenge and a profound obligation for individuals and institutions alike!

I have already talked about our tremendous capacity for creativity and cocreativity. The question is: What do we mean by "human maturity" and "responsible action?" And how can they be realized? Whatever our answer or answers may be in detail, they must include self-transcendence and self-transformation as central values. This idea is not new, of course. But that makes it no less important and timely. For, despite the preoccupation with personal transformation in the new therapies and humanistic psychologies, self-transcendence does not appear to play a prominent orientational role in most of them. In this respect, they are trailing behind the sagacious insights of Abraham Maslow, father of the so-called third force in psychology, who fully acknowledged, certainly in his later work (see his "Theory Z"), that self-transcendence is an important aspect of the higher forms of self-actualization.[6]

Our society, as a whole, still has to discover that, in the words of theologian-philosopher Bernard Lonergan, "Man achieves authenticity in self-transcendence."[7] Only through conscious self-transcendence do we awaken from the consensus trance and begin to transform ourselves and our world in the light of Higher Consciousness. The realization of a New Age must occur in every moment, or it means very little. Besides, not everything that is new is necessarily desirable. It depends on us, on our integrity and lucidity, whether the new age will resemble the Golden Age of mythology or merely be the fulfillment of the nightmare of the Dark Age prophesied in the Hindu and Buddhist scriptures of long ago. Each one of us codetermines the future of our species.

In the second edition of his eminently readable book *Memories and Visions of Paradise,* Richard Heinberg makes the point that in our choice we face a considerable handicap, which is that as a species and individually we are traumatized beings:

> It seems to me that we human beings, and particularly we civilized humans, are wounded and sick. We reproduce catastrophe because we ourselves are traumatized . . . beginning at

birth. Because we are wounded, we have put up psychic defens-
es against reality and have become so cut off from direct participation in the multidimensional wildness in which we are
embedded that all we can do is to navigate our way cautiously
through a humanly designed day-to-day substitute world of
symbols—a world of dollars, minutes, numbers, images, and
words that are constantly being manipulated to wring the most
possible profit from every conceivable circumstance. The body
and spirit both rebel.[8]

However, Heinberg does not succumb to pessimism. He
believes that we can heal ourselves and recover our inner freedom
and learn to remember again "how to feel, love, and wonder."
Because, as he emphasizes, at our core we are "pure, brilliant, and
innocent beings"; we simply have to remember "paradise" rather
than struggle to invent it. This is indeed the path of lucid waking.

Through the yoga of participation to which we are called, we
will decide the destiny of literally billions of our fellow humans and
possibly trillions of other life forms on our home world.[9] It
behooves us, therefore, to take the sacred obligation of lucid waking, or mindfulness, seriously and meet it with great wisdom and
joy.

16

TOWARD INTEGRAL CONSCIOUSNESS

THE EVOLUTION OF CONSCIOUSNESS AND PERSONAL DEVELOPMENT

From the discussion in the preceding chapters it should be clear that we cannot meaningfully engage the process of personal growth without keeping the larger picture in mind. Part of this larger picture is the fact that human consciousness and culture share an interdependent history of gradual unfolding. The way we see the world sculpts our social relationships, economy, politics, art, architecture, and every other facet of cultural life. These in turn reinforce our perceptions of the world. This interconnectedness between individual and culture is studied by psychohistorians. Now, we must distinguish between two separate but compatible approaches to psychohistory. In the first approach, the comparative discipline of psychohistory deals with motivation in history. It uses introspective psychology, especially psychoanalytic theory, to understand historical patterns and developments, and it emphasizes the importance of shared modes of child rearing in forming personality types.[1] Personality types, in turn, help us comprehend the motivational forces impelling individuals and whole groups. In the second approach, psychohistory is the comparative study of history as a manifestation of modes of consciousness. This approach is best illustrated in Jean Gebser's *The Ever-Present Origin*, Ken Wilber's *Up From Eden*, Duane Elgin's *Awakening Earth*, and my own *Structures of Consciousness* and *Wholeness or Transcendence?*[2]

When we look back in time, we can detect a series of cultural styles that are reflective of cognitive styles, and vice versa. We can readily appreciate that the world experienced by our ancestral hunter-gatherers was markedly different from our own. Indeed, we can barely comprehend their consciousness and world experience. But we do not even need to travel so far back in our historical imagination to encounter a consciousness and culture strikingly distinct from our own. The so-called primitives of our own era represent a cognitive/cultural style that in its sharp differentiation from our own gives us ample material for self-reflection. A great deal has been written about this fertile subject in the anthropological literature.

However, seldom has the discussion taken into account the fact that consciousness, like culture, has evolved in discernible stages. One of the few scholars to pay attention to this matter was the Swiss cultural philosopher Jean Gebser, who has shown that human consciousness is undergoing continuous mutations. He was able to demonstrate the emergence (and persistence) of four major mutations, or cognitive structures, in human history. Most importantly, he also demonstrated that we are witnessing today the birth of a new structure of consciousness, which he called the integral consciousness. His developmental model, incidentally, was formulated long before it became popular to speak of a "new paradigm." The core idea underlying his model came to him in an intuitive flash as long ago as 1932, and the first part of his magnum opus, *The Ever-Present Origin*, was published in German seventeen years later.

In our efforts today to tap into the spiritual potential of the human species, we ought to be aware of the overall quality of our cognitive set and cultural setting. Understanding our culture and its particular style of consciousness is an indispensable part of any genuine self-understanding. What, then, is the flavor of our life world and its constituting consciousness? Following Gebser's model, we can characterize the world we live in today as being increasingly shaped and dominated by the mental-rational consciousness, which had its birth in the Renaissance. When we look back beyond that fecund era, we encounter a cognitive and cultural style that is qualitatively different from our familiar world. And the further back in time we go, the more obvious that difference becomes, until our comprehension falters. The cave world of the Neanderthals and Cro-Magnons leaves us puzzled, perhaps even disoriented.

The new consciousness of the Renaissance came to fruition in men like Petrarch, Boccaccio, Dante, Ockham, da Vinci, Copernicus, Pico, Columbus, Erasmus, Dürer, Vesalius, Michelangelo, Galileo, and Bacon. They essentially created a new cultural style corresponding to a novel way of experiencing the world. In fact, they laid the foundations for our own contemporary world. One of the most significant and most symbolic achievements of the Renaissance was the discovery of perspective, first theoretically formulated by Leonardo da Vinci, one of the greatest geniuses of humankind. This discovery perfectly encapsulates the spirit of the Renaissance. It corresponds to the emergence of a new, more sharply defined self-sense (or ego), serving as the vertex point of perspectival perception. Hence, Gebser spoke of this as the "perspectival consciousness" or the "mental-rational consciousness." He wrote:

Space is the insistent concern of this era. . . . Copernicus, for example, shatters the limits of the geocentric sky and discovers heliocentric space; Columbus goes beyond the encompassing Oceanos and discovers earth's space; Vesalius, the first major anatomist, bursts the confines of Galen's ancient doctri.ies of the human body and discovers the body's space; Harvey destroys the precepts of Hippocrates' humoral medicine and reveals the circulatory system. And there is Kepler, who by demonstrating the elliptical orbit of the planets, overthrows antiquity's unperspectival world-image of circular and flat surfaces (a view still held by Copernicus) that dated back to Ptolemy's conception of the circular movement of the planets.

It is this same shape—the ellipse—which Michelangelo

introduces into architecture via his dome of St. Peter's, which is elliptical and not round or suggestive of the cavern or vault. Here, too, we find a heightened sense of spatiality at the expense of antiquity's feeling of oceanic space. Galileo penetrates even deeper into space by perfecting the telescope, discovered only shortly before in Holland, and employing it for astronomical studies—preparations for man's ultimate conquest of air and suboceanic space that came later and realized the designs already conceived and drawn up in advance by Leonardo.[3]

Perspective requires the eye as its source point. The emphasis on sight and on space in Renaissance thinking is well known, but Gebser for the first time made sense of it in terms of the evolution of consciousness. The discovery of perspective could not have occurred prior to the rise of the mental-rational consciousness, which is linear, spatial, quantifying, and ocular in the extreme ("seeing is believing").

The narrowly rational consciousness, which reigns supreme today, represents the deficient mode of the mental consciousness, though we could think of it as a structure or cognitive modality in its own right. Confusingly, the rational consciousness has little to do with reason or logic as they are applied in philosophy, mathematics, or ethics. Rather, it is a warped kind of rationality, which is egocentric and therefore quite myopic in its divisiveness and destructiveness. Gebser rightly held it responsible for our contemporary social malaise.

Other structures preceded the mental-rational consciousness ushered in by the Renaissance. Thus, Gebser distinguished between the archaic, the magical, the mythical, and the mental consciousness.

The *archaic consciousness*, as the name suggests, is the most ancient of all the psychohistorical configurations. It takes us back to the very beginnings of humanity, some three million years ago. This is the time of *Australopithecus africanus* and *Homo habilis*. Gebser himself was reluctant to fix this early structure chronologically, because it is not associated with any time awareness. The archaic consciousness corresponds to the consciousness of deep

sleep, which lacks even dreams. Since all structures, once actualized, remain part of our species' psychological heritage, the archaic structure is thematized when we experience a temporary eclipse
of the self-sense in orgasm or certain mystical states, or when we
experience what Gebser called nuclear dreams (of which we can
remember the details very clearly but not their sequence because
they presented themselves synchronously).

The *magical consciousness*, which is an amorphous group consciousness, made its appearance with *Homo erectus* some one and
a half million years ago. This modality of consciousness feels itself
a part of nature, though it does not yet have a differentiated sense
of space and time. Thinking is visceral, and communication is largely ritualistic. The emphasized sense is hearing (just as seeing is the
emphasized sense of the mental-rational consciousness), which
explains the origin of music during that evolutionary epoch. We can
get a sense of the simplicity of the magical consciousness and its
"prelogical" cosmology when we look at the psychological world of
a toddler.

The *mythical consciousness*, which probably coincided with
the full lateralization of the brain and the invention of syntactical
language, flowered at the time of the late Cro-Magnons. This consciousness contributed an enhanced capacity for imagination and
social empathy. It invented religion crystallized around tribal myths
and focused on the worship of the Great Mother. The style of thinking associated with this consciousness is logical but polarized
rather than dualistic, as is the case with mental consciousness.
Anyone who has read the Vedas, the Pyramid texts, or other truly
ancient scriptures readily recognizes the difference, even though
these cultural artifacts belong to the transitional phase between the
mythical and the mental consciousness rather than to the mythical
consciousness par excellence. The time sense of the mythical consciousness is organic (rhythm-sensitive) rather than abstract, and
its spatial sense is still "flat," as can be seen from the absence of
perspective in early art from any culture.

The *mental consciousness*, marked by the ability to think dis-
cursively in linear logical fashion, is intensely dualistic and spatial-
izing. It experiences even time in spatial terms, as an "arrow." Its

favored tools are dialogue and dialectics, which were developed to a fine art in ancient Greece and, simultaneously, in India. The mental consciousness is responsible for the invention of mathematics, astronomy, geometry, grammar, jurisprudence, and the other sciences based on "measured" thinking.

All four structures or modalities, according to Gebser, are spontaneous mutations, which have the ever-present Origin as their eternal backdrop. Each subsequent structure is built upon the accomplishments or qualities of the preceding structure or structures. Thus, the mental consciousness includes the capacities acquired through the unfolding of the archaic, the magical, and the mythical consciousness. For instance, we are capable of not merely logical thought (mental structure), but also instinctive knowing (archaic structure), knowledge by emotional resonance with the object (magical structure), and mythological or "poetic" thinking (mythical structure). However, because of the exaggerated emphasis on rationality in our modern version of the mental consciousness, we tend to devalue and repress the other structures, and this inevitably gives rise to a sweeping psychological imbalance.

Most, if not all, of the social problems we face today are the direct result of the *rational consciousness*, which is inherently defective. For it is ego-fixated and experiences the world as basically hostile or antagonistic (a thing to be conquered). At the same time, the ego-fixity of the rational consciousness breeds psychological insularity or isolation. Its abstractedness from the living dimension of the world makes possible problematic developments such as mindless consumerism, overproduction, rampant technology, and cynical politics. All these can be understood as negative manifestations of the denied or repressed structures of consciousness.

Unlike his contemporary Oswald Spengler, however, Gebser did not capitulate to pessimism.[4] His analysis of twentieth-century culture, sciences, and the arts gave him cause for cautious hope. In his own words:

> When something breaks, new powers follow closely. It is then a matter of becoming aware of them, of allowing them to take effect, and of trusting them.

Our time is a time of fragmentation, and new powers seek to shape themselves through us: We of today are doubly on trial. In order to pass the trial, we must become conscious of the new powers, must accomplish a new intensity of consciousness, which enables us to realize the new reality.[5]

Furthermore:

And there can be no question that our task will be resolved, since it originates in necessity. The only open question is whether it will be resolved soon; if not, the solution would demand unthinkable sacrifices of those who are surrendering themselves. The number of those who will experience the solution depends on the temporal intensity of the emergent consciousness structure. If the task is not accomplished in time, it will lead to an almost complete self-surrender of mankind.[6]

That is, a new modality of consciousness is trying to push through, and we can either assist this process by cultivating lucid waking or obstruct it by choosing to remain asleep in the consensus trance spoken of by psychologist Charles Tart.[7] Depending on our response, we will either suffer more or suffer less.

THE EMERGENT INTEGRAL CONSCIOUSNESS

Gebser believed that today we are witnessing and suffering the birth pangs of a new modality of consciousness, which he named the "integral consciousness." He reached this momentous conclusion long before it became fashionable to speak of a New Age and after carefully examining the latest developments—"new concepts"—in physics, mathematics, biology, economics, sociology, psychology, philosophy, literature, music, jurisprudence, painting, sculpture, and architecture. The new consciousness represents a mutation, a leap out of the existing structures, with all the discontinuity that this implies. Yet, Gebser understood that this process is spontaneous rather than automatic. As he repeatedly emphasized, we must work hard on ourselves for the new consciousness to become fully crystallized and effective.

Gebser also stressed that the emergence of the integral consciousness has nothing to do with an expansion of consciousness. If anything, it is an *intensification* of consciousness, opening up a new way of perceiving ourselves and the world. It does not stretch itself over a larger area of space but lifts us above the linear mode of the mental-rational consciousness, which is hooked on spatial perspectivity. Nor does it come about through mere reactivation of the existing structures of consciousness. It is therefore not at all regressive. It does not consist in prerational instinctive spontaneity, which characterizes the archaic consciousness. Nor does it consist in some prerational magical union with nature or a human group, or in mythical imaginal inwardness. It also decidedly transcends the dualistic program of the mental structure of consciousness with its massive need for rational control. What the integral consciousness does accomplish is nothing less than the *integration* of all existing structures, which are given the opportunity to express themselves appropriately, that is, in harmonious interplay. Each structure is given its proper weight in any situation. None is denied expression; none is inflated.

As we have begun to more fully understand, the reigning mental-rational consciousness has caused us to suppress entire aspects of the human psyche. As Carl Gustav Jung noted:

Modern man does not understand how much his "rationalism" (which has destroyed his capacity to respond to numinous symbols and ideas) has put him at the mercy of the psychic "underworld." He has freed himself from "superstition" (or so he believes), but in the process he has lost his spiritual values to a positively dangerous degree. His moral and spiritual tradition has disintegrated, and he is now paying the price for his break-up in worldwide disorientation and dissociation.[8]

Movements like ecology, feminism, Eastern religions, neopaganism, and not least New Age are, to varying degrees, manifestations of the integral consciousness seeking to redress the psychological and cultural balance that has been upset by the mental-rational consciousness. Because these movements are largely uninformed about their place in the history of consciousness, however, they include regressive aspects that hinder rather than facilitate the emergence of the integral consciousness. Ken Wilber has addressed some of these in his brilliant work *Sex, Ecology, and Spirituality*.[9] He puts this in terms of what he calls the "pre/trans fallacy," that is, the confusion between prerational and transrational modes of consciousness. In the "pre" fallacy, transrational modes are reduced to prerational modes of consciousness. In the "trans" fallacy, prerational modes are wrongly elevated to transrational, transpersonal modes.

The great achievement of the integral consciousness is its transcendence of the spatialized concept of time and its discovery of time as an intensity. What this means is that through the integral consciousness, we overcome our relationship to time as something that is merely measurable clock time. We realize that in and of itself genuine time has nothing to do with space but that, depending on our mode of consciousness, it manifests itself as clock time, star time, cosmic time, rhythm, biological duration, and even psychological time. As Gebser has shown, our era is preoccupied with time: measuring it, living by it, having or not having it, or "wasting" it. We relate to time as if it were a thing, a quantity to be hoarded or squandered. We fail to see it as a creative force.

Each structure of consciousness has its own relationship to time. To the archaic consciousness, there is no time sense at all. The magical consciousness too is marked by timelessness. The mythical consciousness experiences time as quality in the form of the rhythms of nature. Only with the emergence of the mental consciousness did our time sense become the "arrow of time."

The integral consciousness is inherently time-free—it is not bound by any of the preceding forms of temporal experience. The integral perception reveals time to be, as Gebser says, an ever-present abundance. It also makes transparent the limitations intrinsic to the time sense in the other structures of consciousness. Because of the plenitude of genuine time, we need not fret over ever running out of it. *Zeitangst* (time anxiety) is one of the hallmarks of our era, and this ought to tell us something about the urgency of the task before us: namely to delve into our own consciousness, or psyche, in order to resolve the problem we have with time. "The time anxiety of our transitional era," noted Gebser, "is evidence of the fact that we have been overwhelmed by the time problem and are not able to confront it, and that we have not realized it or become conscious of it."[10] But this is exactly what we must do.

To express what he means by genuine time, Gebser availed himself of the Greek word *achronon,* which stands for the immeasurable intensity that transcends all manifestations of time. It is identical with the spiritual dimension of reality, the Spirit. Science of course knows nothing of this time-free dimension or, as Gebser preferred to call it, "amension." If relativity theory has shown that time is not independent of space, quantum theory has made time fuzzy and meaningless.[11] David Bohm, perhaps the most powerful and original dissenting voice in modern physics, argued against the quantum fuzziness of time. He maintained that quantum phenomena were rooted in what he called the implicate order, a level of reality in which the visible realm is "enfolded" and which also is the matrix of all forms of time.[12]

To free ourselves from our time anxiety as well as our greed for more time (*Zeitsucht*), we must free ourselves from the artifact that we call the ego. This does not mean we must abandon the ego, for this would be equivalent to regression, but we must truly overcome and master it through disciplined self-transcendence. The integral consciousness unfolds in and through freedom from the ego, which is the source point of the mental-perspectival consciousness. The integral consciousness is pervious to the ego-transcending spiritual reality, the Whole.

Yet, it is important to understand that the integral consciousness is not identical with mystical union requiring introversion to the exclusion of the external world. It is a new way of seeing, by which the world is rendered transparent like glass so that we can see the ever-present Origin shining through it. This integral perception is steadily unlocking the gates of the mental-rational prison in which we have found ourselves for at least two centuries. New disciplines like quantum mechanics, ecology, depth psychology, and parapsychology all have powerfully challenged many of the core ideas of our civilization that until now were held to be inviolable, including the idea of the supremacy of the rational mind and the notion of linear time. As we understand the present crisis more and more as a crisis of consciousness, we can expect this reconceptualization in the sciences to become still more comprehensive and radical. Inevitably, we will see the repercussions of this process in other areas of human knowledge and experience as well.

But the conceptual insights of the few will ultimately have to become the living reality of the many. The integral consciousness, as I said, requires the conscious participation of all of us. But how should we participate? Gebser wrote:

> Since the new consciousness is here, no ways can possibly lead to it. One also need not entertain any hopes about it. There is no place for means by which one could become conscious of it and its inherent reality. It necessitates no action, merely a corresponding and appropriate *attitude*. To adopt this attitude is still difficult today, because it requires complete trust in the invisible powers that preserve us and unconditional devotion to this particular inner attitude that neither the egoless nor the ego-bound but only the ego-free person is capable of realizing.[13]

More specifically, the integral attitude is a disposition that favors quiet and silence over haste and noise; spontaneity over goal-directed thinking; compassion and loving kindness over lust for power and manipulation; inner harmony and balance over mechanical organizing; unsentimental tolerance over prejudice; authenticity over blind conformism; delight in inner growth over fear of change; acceptance of life and death over mere avoidance. These attitudes typify what Abraham Maslow called the self-actualizing and self-transcending person.[14] They also describe the individual who, in traditional terms, is "on the path," that is, who practices the discipline of lucid waking. Thus, the integral consciousness, if (through our active participation) we allow it to emerge in full, will form the modal consciousness of our civilization in the third millennium.

On the basis of this ego-free, diaphanous consciousness cultivated through lucid waking, we will be able to tap into the vast
resources of inner space either through traditional spiritual systems
(minus their superseded dogmatic accretions) or through approaches not yet formulated. Moreover, the integral consciousness alone
will provide a sturdy launchpad for the exploration of outer space.
For, without it, we are bound to merely spread the virus of our present fragmented psyche to the stars. Before we think of "conquer-
ing" galaxies, we must first conquer ourselves. The challenge of the
philosophical life is upon us as never before. How we live our lives
today matters not only to us and to our children and their children
but to all living beings on our earth and to whatever other life-bear-
ing planets may exist in the deeps of space. We are surely not alone
in this vast universe. The only question is whether we will step
across the threshold of the ionosphere armed to the teeth, in fear of
imagined hostile aliens, or whether we can harness the necessary
intelligence to do so with reverence for all forms of life and a desire
to benefit rather than to use, abuse, or destroy them.

The integral consciousness is not an end point in our evolution,
but it is most definitely a promising beginning. Therefore, we
should nurture it with tender care in ourselves and our fellow
beings. "Each person," writes social visionary Duane Elgin, "is a
vitally important and unique agent in the process of planetary evolution."[15] We, as a species and as individuals, have reached a stage
in evolution where the only thinkable option is that of conscious
coevolution pursued in the context of lucid waking—the art of
mindful living—which calls for our utmost courage, energy, and
unrelenting dedication to our own transformation.

17

REMEMBERING THE FUTURE

To remember the future sounds like a paradox, if not an impossibility. But this appears so only to the linear mind, which insists on a strict causal trajectory originating in the past, moving through the present, and inexorably heading toward the future. Modern physics, however, has undermined the classic notion of the "arrow of time." According to relativity theory, the present moment is different for each observer. Hence, one person's present moment could be another's past or future. Assume an infinite number of observers and you have an infinite number of intersecting present and future moments. We are not only "pushed" by the past but also "pulled" by the future. To understand this paradox, picture a young man on a train going from town A to visit his girlfriend in town C via town B. At the departure point, the girlfriend calls him saying that unless he arrives by 1:00 P.M., she will not be at home, as she has to go to town B to pick up her new car. The train's departure is then unexpectedly delayed by one hour. The young man realizes that he will very probably not be able to reach town C by 1:00 P.M., so he gets off the train in town B with the intention of locating his girlfriend at the local car dealer. In his decision he was influenced by the probable future of arriving at his girlfriend's home in town C too late to be welcomed by her there.

Another example is furnished by what I call the millennium effect. A growing number of people share the belief that the turn of the millennium represents a significant threshold in human evolution. Some entertain apocalyptic fears, others utopian hopes. Even if December 21, 2012 A.D.—Terence McKenna's "Timewave Zero"—is otherwise a perfectly ordinary day, an arbitrary point along the timeline, the increasingly widespread belief in its higher significance can be expected to at least partially result in a self-fulfilling prophecy.[1] In other words, a belief by tens or perhaps even hundreds of millions of people that some future date is a highly significant marker in human evolution will have concrete repercussions, since they will very likely make decisions in their lives that reflect this belief and thus help it come true in whatever fashion and to whatever degree.

The French paleontologist Pierre Teilhard de Chardin believed that we are all marching away from the Alpha Point of subatomic particles and toward Omega Point, a kind of future attractor acting like a downstream waterfall that inexorably pulls the river of evolution toward itself. This onward march of evolution is one of increasing complexification, as he called it, leading to the emergence of the noosphere: the world of thought characterizing humanity. At this Omega Point, according to Teilhard de Chardin, the light of the Spirit will fully flood the earth and transfigure everyone and everything. This supreme consciousness, which is the end-time reality of Omega Point, is neither impersonal nor personal but suprapersonal. It is a Someone, not merely a Something. But that Someone is beyond all conception.

> Like a vast tide, Being will have engulfed the shifting sands of being. Within a now tranquil ocean, each drop of which, nevertheless, will be conscious of remaining itself, the astonishing adventure of the world will have ended. The dream of every mystic, the eternal pantheist ideal, will have found its full and legitimate satisfaction.[2]

McKenna puts it this way:

> History will end, and the transcendental object that has been drawing being into ever deeper reflections of itself since the

first moments of the existence of the universe will finally be completely concrescent in the three-dimensional space-time continuum. Then the moving image of time will have discovered itself to be Eternity.[3]

This eschatological event amounts to the literal enlightenment of all beings, which would be the ultimate fulfillment of the solemn vow taken by all Buddhist *bodhisattvas*. For both McKenna and Teilhard de Chardin—each coming from a different direction—evolution is a progressive intensification of consciousness, terminating in perfect illumination. To be sure, Omega Point and Timewave Zero are metaphysical and not scientific concepts, but this is not necessarily a disadvantage, as long as we find their explanations plausible. However, I must confess that while I think that cosmic evolution is likely to have a terminal point, I am entirely unconvinced that the end of history lies around the corner. This type of idea seems to me to spring from narrow anthropocentrism, as if the entire vast cosmos were dependent on earthlings for its salvation. The other problem I have with this notion is that it is difficult to imagine anything beyond that point. Therefore, if the day passes uneventfully, the believers will be deprived of a future. In the past, particularly at the threshold of 1000 A.D., this led to much despair and great personal and social chaos.[4] My own prediction is that the year 2012 will come and pass, and history will continue much as before. I am inclined to side with the British historian Arnold Toynbee, who remarked:

But if there have been a few transfigured men and women, there has never been such a thing as a civilized society. Civilization, as we know it, is a movement and not a condition, a voyage and not a harbour. No known civilization has ever reached the goal of civilization yet.[5]

In other words, let us endeavor to create a truly human civilization first before pinning our hope on a collective spiritual transfiguration. As I emphasized repeatedly in the earlier chapters, nothing is going to happen automatically. The only thing that can be expected to happen of its own accord is a continuing social and environmental deterioration on earth.

To assume, then, that 2012 A.D. will magically transform us is a false and dangerous hope. We must *work* on change. In fact, we must invest a lot of energy in conscious change. For a train to be able to move onto a different track, someone must switch the line and make the transition possible. Since I have used the word *work*, I need to qualify what I mean. Work, as I understand it in the present context, is not merely *doing* but also *being*, for silence and fully conscious repose can in some situations accomplish as much as toil and exertion.

The problem is that the energy for the kind of personal and collective change called for today must come from somewhere. It inevitably comes out of our present condition. So, it is reasonable to assume that more likely than not we will change only by comparatively small increments. The force of habit, or psychological lethargy, is too well established in most people for planned sweeping change to occur. Merely hoping for a better world is not enough. Wishful thinking does not have the energy necessary to change us and our reality. Fantasizing about the future is as ineffectual as romanticizing the past or losing oneself in the present. What is needed is to envision our future, but our envisioning must have a realistic base, that is, a context in the here and now. Only then will we be able to convert our vision into sane attitudes and sound actions.

Of course, it is always possible that through the appearance of an unexpected catalyst—such as ecological or economic collapse, war, a planetwide epidemic, or, more remotely, an alien invasion— a large number of people will be shocked out of the consensus trance and galvanized into constructive action. It is always possible, too, that through the actions of a large enough minority who believe in the special significance of 2012 A.D. (or some other date in the near future), our postmodern civilization may shift gear. How great such a shift would be, no one can foretell. In any case, whether or not we share the end-time hopes of people like Terence McKenna, José Arguelles, and other New Age optimists, the only way we can avoid unprecedented collapse is to take actions that help bring about a better future for our species and the planet as a whole.[6]

Through our imagination we can "hook up" with any number of possible futures for ourselves individually and for our species as a whole. This is in fact exactly what futurists, who consider possible future scenarios for humanity, are doing. In a sense, we must all become futurists. We must remember the future! But what does this mean? As Fred Alan Wolf explains:

> The river of time has two counterstreaming currents. Information coming from the future as well as from the past influences the present. Thus we pick up two bottles every time we reach down into that river, not one. And we find inside two messages.
>
> However, these bottles are strange. They don't really exist until we reach down into the river. If we could "see" what the river actually contained we would see countless ghostly bottles ever streaming from the source of the river in the mountains of information piled up in our pasts and from the seas of future information telling us what the weather is like ahead. These counterstreaming bottles only become real in our hands. When we reach down into that river a past bottle and a future bottle coalesce into one bottle, and like a magical little genie in the bottle, a message instantly appears.
>
> That message explains the situation at the present moment. It also contains an orientation map telling or mapping out what was the past and what will be the future.[7]

But the bottle's message, Wolf further explains, is only a probable truth. Only the present moment, of reading the bottle, is characterized by absolute certainty. It is in the present moment that we concretely lay down our pathway into the future. In terms of the parallel-universe interpretation of quantum theory, we select one of an infinite number of parallel universes coexisting with our own and make it our own reality. Regardless of whether or not this interpretation turns out to be the correct one, it is at least a useful metaphor for our purposes.

We always live at the intersection between past and future, and make our decisions based on the (unconscious) recollection of both. By intensifying our awareness, we can become more sensitive to the future, "remembering" it, and thus making our choices more informed and more intelligent. This is the gist of the philosophical, or spiritual, life of lucid waking. In this way we can move toward greater freedom and abiding happiness.

NOTES

Preface

1. See P. Garfield, *Creative Dreaming* (New York: Simon & Schuster, 1974); C. Green, *Lucid Dreams* (Oxford: Institute of Psychophysical Research, 1968); A. Faraday, *Dream Power: The Use of Dreams in Everyday Life* (London: Pan Books, 1972); S. LaBerge, *Lucid Dreaming* (Los Angeles: J. P. Tarcher, 1985); S. LaBerge and H. Rheingold, *Exploring the World of Lucid Dreaming* (New York: Ballantine Books, 1990).
2. C. Tart, *Waking Up: Overcoming the Obstacles to Human Potential* (Boston: New Science Library, 1987), 106.
3. R. Tarnas, *The Passion of the Western Mind* (New York: Harmony Books, 1991), 434.
4. In the course of brainstorming for a suitable title for the present book, my wife and I ruminated over the dreamlike quality of ordinary life, and she mentioned lucid dreams. This, in turn, led me to respond half jokingly with the phrase "lucid waking." We were both struck by the felicitousness of this coinage, and so it stuck as the book's title. Later that day, I discovered that Charles Tart had used the same phrase in his book *Open Mind, Discriminating Mind* (San Francisco: Harper, 1989), which just goes to show that an original idea need not necessarily be new.
5. Goethe, *Faust*, Part 2, lines 11573–11576.

CHAPTER 1. IN PRAISE OF THE PHILOSOPHICAL LIFE

1. *Great Dialogues of Plato*, trans. by W. H. D. Rouse, ed. by Eric H. Warmington and Philip G. Rouse (New York: Mentor Books, 1960), 443.
2. See A. Soble, *Eros, Agape and Philia: Readings in the Philosophy of Love* (New York: Paragon House, 1989).
3. Aristotle, *Nicomachean Ethics* (VIII:3). My own paraphrase.
4. P. Brunton, *Relativity, Philosophy, and Mind.* Vol. 13: *The Notebooks of Paul Brunton* (Burdett, N.Y.: Larson Publications, 1988), I:25.
5. Ibid., I:61.
6. Ibid., I:65.
7. See H. Skolimowski, *The Participatory Mind: A New Theory of Knowledge and the Universe* (London and New York: Penguin/Arkana Books, 1994), 158.
8. T. McKenna, *The Archaic Revival: Speculations on Psychedelic Mushrooms, the Amazon, Virtual Reality, UFOs, Evolution, Shamanism, the Rebirth of the Goddess, and the End of History* (San Francisco: Harper, 1992), 2.
9. Ibid., 11
10. See my books *The Yoga-Sūtra of Pantañjali: A New Translation and Commentary* (Rochester, Vt.: Inner Traditions International, 1989) and *The Philosophy of Classical Yoga* (Rochester, Vt.: Inner Traditions International, 1996).
11. T. McKenna, *The Archaic Revival*, 45.
12. Ibid., 21.
13. I do not wish to dispute the possible therapeutic value of psychedelic drugs administered in appropriate cases and in an appropriate setting. See, e.g., S. Grof, *LSD Psychotherapy* (Pomona, Calif.: Hunter House, 1980).
14. P. Brunton, *Relativity*, I:160.
15. B. Russell, *The Conquest of Happiness* (New York: Bantam Books, 1968), 167. This book was first published in 1930, when Russell was fifty-eight years old.
16. Ibid., I:167.
17. H. P. Blavatsky, *The Secret Doctrine, Vol. 1: Cosmogenesis*

(Wheaton, Ill.: Theosophical Publishing House, 1993),
Introduction, xx. First published in 1888.

CHAPTER 2. THE SEMINAL QUESTION: WHO AM I?

1. H. Skolimowski, *The Participatory Mind*, 19.
2. See V. Frankl, *The Will to Meaning: Foundations and Applications of Logotherapy* (New York: New American Library, 1970).
3. R. Dawkins, *The Selfish Gene* (Oxford: Oxford University Press, 1976), 206.
4. See the Appendix in H. G. Wells, *Crux Ansata: An Indictment of the Roman Catholic Church* (New York: Free Thought Press, 2d ed., 1953), 155.
5. Gurdjieff, quoted in Henri Tracol, *The Taste for Things That Are True: Essays & Talks by a Pupil of G. I. Gurdjieff* (Shaftesbury, England/Rockport, Mass.: Element Books, 1994), 80–81.
6. See C. T. Tart, *Waking Up*.
7. D. Bohm and M. Edwards, *Changing Consciousness: Exploring the Hidden Source of the Social, Political and Environmental Crises Facing Our World* (San Francisco: Harper, 1991), 210.
8. See S. Langer, *Mind: An Essay on Human Feeling* (Baltimore and London: The Johns Hopkins Press, 1970).
9. F. Franck, *Fingers Pointing Toward the Sacred: A Twentieth Century Pilgrimage on the Eastern and Western Way* (Junction City, Ore.: Beacon Point Press, 1994), 183.

CHAPTER 3. THE CHALLENGE OF EMBODIMENT

1. R. May, *Man's Search for Himself* (New York: Delta Books, 1953), 106–107.
2. K. Dychtwald, *Bodymind* (Los Angeles: J. P. Tarcher, 1986), 8.
3. R. Descartes, *Discourse on Method*, transl. by Arthur Wollaston (Harmondsworth, England: Penguin Classics, 1960), 61.

4. D. Leder, *The Absent Body* (Chicago: University of Chicago Press, 1990), 1.

5. Ibid., 173.

6. Ibid., 166.

7. O. M. Aivanhov, *"Know Thyself"—Jnana Yoga: Part 2* (Fréjus, France: Prosveta, 1992), 13–14.

8. D. Elgin, *Awakening Earth: Exploring the Evolution of Human Culture and Consciousness* (New York: William Morrow, 1993), 302.

9. M. Murphy, *The Future of the Body: Explorations Into the Further Evolution of Human Nature* (Los Angeles: J. P. Tarcher, 1992), 156–158.

CHAPTER 4. THE CHANGING FORTUNES OF THE SOUL

1. M. Berman, *The Reenchantment of the World* (New York: Bantam Books, 1984), 2.

2. See J. Gebser, *The Ever-Present Origin*. Transl. by Noel Barstad with Algis Mickunas (Athens, Ohio: Ohio University Press, 1985). See also G. Feuerstein, *Structures of Consciousness* (Lower Lake, Calif.: Integral Publishing, 1987), which is an introduction to Gebser's evolutionary model of consciousness.

3. See P. Teilhard de Chardin, *The Phenomenon of Man* (New York: Harper Torchbooks, 1965).

4. See L. Dossey, *Recovering the Soul* (New York: Bantam Books, 1989); J. Borysenko, *Fire in the Soul: A New Psychology of Spiritual Optismism* (New York: Warner Books, 1993); G. Zukav, *The Seat of the Soul* (New York: Fireside Books, 1990); J. Singer, *Boundaries of the Soul* (Garden City, N.Y.: Anchor Books, 1972); S. Ingerman, *Soul Retrieval* (New York: HarperCollins, 1991); M. Grosso, *The Frontiers of the Soul* (Wheaton, Ill.: Quest Books, 1992); A. Raheem, *Soul Return* (Lower Lake, Calif.: Aslan, 1991); W. Barrett, *Death of the Soul* (New York: Doubleday, 1986); M. Chapin Massey, *Feminine Soul: The Fate of an Ideal* (Boston: Beacon Press, 1985).

5. See C. G. Jung, *Modern Man in Search of a Soul* (New York: Harcourt, Brace, & Co., 1933).

6. See R. B. Onians, *The Origins of European Thought* (Cambridge: Cambridge University Press, 1954).

7. See E. H. Walker, "Consciousness in the Quantum Theory of Measurement," *Journal for the Study of Consciousness*, Vol. 5 (1972), no. 1, 46; no. 2, 257.

8. See, e.g., B. Rensch, *Biophilosophie auf erkenntnistheoretischer Grundlage* (Stuttgart: Kohlhammer Verlag, 1968).

9. See E. B. Tylor, *Primitive Culture* (London: Murray, 1873).

10. See, e.g., C. Tart, "Out of the Body Experiences," in E. Mitchell, ed., *Psychic Exploration: A Challenge for Science* (New York: Putnam, 1974), and R. Crookall, *The Study and Practice of Astral Projection* (London: Aquarian Press, 1961); see also the references in the massive work by M. Murphy, *The Future of the Body*.

11. C. G. Jung, "Psychological Commentary," in W. Y. Evans-Wentz, *The Tibetan Book of the Dead* (New York: Galaxy Books, 1960), xxxviii. The original edition of this work was published in 1927.

12. K. S. Guthrie, *The Pythagorean Sourcebook and Library*, ed. by D. R. Fiedeler (Grand Rapids: Phanes Press, 1987), 271.

13. See J. J. Poortman, *Vehicles of Consciousness: The Concept of Hylic Pluralism* (Utrecht, The Netherlands: Theosophical Publishing House, 1978). 4 vols.

14. See G. R. S. Mead, *The Doctrine of the Subtle Body in Western Tradition* (Wheaton, Ill.: Quest Books, 1967). First published in 1919.

15. A. A. Brill, ed. and transl., *The Basic Writings of Sigmund Freud* (New York: Modern Library, 1938), 542n.

16. A. Raheem, *Soul Return*, 11–12.

17. C. G. Jung, *On the Nature of the Psyche* (Princeton, N.J.: Princeton University Press, 1969), 127.

CHAPTER 5. WHO OR WHAT IS THE SPIRIT?

1. P. Tillich, *The Courage to Be* (New York: Fontana Library, 1962), 85–86.

2. For an up-to-date appraisal of the age, importance, and spirituality of the Rig-Veda, see G. Feuerstein, S. Kak, and D. Frawley, *In Search of the Cradle of Civilization* (Wheaton, Ill.: Quest Books, 1995).
3. The English rendering of Sanskrit verses from Shantideva's *Bodhicaryavatara* is my own.
4. The Sanskrit term *bodhisattva* is masculine. To be faithful to the text, I have retained "he." However, *bodhisattvas* can be either male or female.
5. W. James, *The Varieties of Religious Experience* (New York: Collier Books, 1961), 283.

CHAPTER 6. THE POWER OF IMAGINATION

1. I. Kant, *Die Drei Kritiken*, ed. by R. Schmidt (Stuttgart: Kröner Verlag, 1960), 131. The translation into English is my own.
2. See P. McKeller, *Experience and Behavior* (Harmondsworth, England: Penguin Books, 1968).
3. W. Harman and H. Rheingold, *Higher Creativity* (Los Angeles: J. P. Tarcher, 1984), 54.
4. Tarthang Tulku, *Openness Mind* (Emeryville, Calif.: Dharma Publishing, 1978), 74.
5. See S. LaBerge, *Lucid Dreaming.*
6. S. LaBerge and H. Rheingold, *Exploring the World of Lucid Dreaming*, 169.
7. Ibid., 169.
8. J. G. Jung, ed., *Man and His Symbols* (New York: Dell Publishing Co., 1968), 81.
9. See O. C. Simonton, S. Matthews-Simonton, and T. F. Sparks, "Psychological Intervention in the Treatment of Cancer," *Psychosomatics*, Vol. 21 (1980), 226–227. See also O. C. Simonton and S. Simonton, *Getting Well Again* (Los Angeles: J. P. Tarcher, 1978).
10. W. Fezler, *Creative Imagery: How to Visualize in All Five Senses* (New York: Fireside Books, 1989), 55.
11. Ibid., 56.

12. See M. L. Rossman, *Healing Yourself* (New York: Pocket Books, 1987).

13. A. Kreinheder, *Body and Soul: The Other Side of Illness* (Toronto: Inner City Books, 1991), 47.

14. Ibid., 61.

15. M. Murphy and R. A. White, *In the Zone: Transcendent Experience in Sports* (New York and London: Penguin Books, 1995).

16. Sermon 42 in J. Quint, *Meister Eckehart: Deutsche Predigten und Traktate* (Munich: Carl Hanser, 1963), 352. The translation from the German is my own.

17. See the excellent article by Hugh Urban, "Imago Magia, Virgin Mother of Eternity: Imagination and Phantasy in the Philosophy of Jacob Boehme," *Alexandria: The Journal of the Western Cosmological Tradition*, ed. by David Fideler (Grand Rapids: Phanes Press, 1993), no. 2, 233–256.

18. G. Epstein, "Healing and Imagination," *Re-Vision*, Vol. 3 (1980), no. 1, 51.

CHAPTER 7. RIGHT VIEW

1. See L. Festinger, *A Theory of Cognitive Dissonance* (Evanston, Ill.: Row, Peterson, 1957).

2. See M. E. Montaigne, *Essays* I:31.

3. Tertullian, *De Carne Christi*, part 2, chapter 5.

4. Caesar, *De Bello Gallico* (III:18).

5. See Seneca, *Hercules Furens* (I:313).

6. B. Russell, *Sceptical Essays* (London and New York: 1927), 28.

7. R. W. Emerson, *Conduct of Life, Nature and Other Essays* (London: Dent/New York: Dutton, 1908), 248.

8. See G. B. Shaw's preface to his satirical play *Androcles and the Lion* (1912).

9. *Samyutta-Nikaya* 56.11.5.

10. *Majjhima-Nikaya* 22.

11. See E. Klinger, *Daydreaming* (Los Angeles: J. P. Tarcher, 1990), 68.

12. D. Elgin, *Awakening Earth*, 238.

13. W. Harman, *Global Mind Change* (Indianapolis: Knowledge Systems, 1988), 168.

CHAPTER 8. INTUITION: THE OTHER WAY OF KNOWING

1. See P. Goldberg, *The Intuitive Edge* (Los Angeles: J. P. Tarcher, 1983).
2. *Intuition* magazine, archives (P.O. Box 460773, San Francisco, CA 94146).
3. K. R. Popper, *The Logic of Scientific Discovery* (New York: Harper Torchbooks, 1965), 317.
4. F. Vaughan, *Awakening Intuition* (New York: Doubleday, 1979), 176.
5. Shakespeare, *The Tempest*, Act 5, scene 1, line 183.
6. See M. Emery, *Intuition Workbook: An Expert's Guide to Unlocking the Wisdom of Your Subconscious Mind* (Upper Saddle River, N.J.: Prentice-Hall, 1995).
7. W. Harman, "Intuition as the Code Word for Global Transformation." This paper is available from the Institute of Noetic Sciences, 475 Gate Five Road #300, Sausalito, CA 94965.
8. Cited in H. R. Pagels, *The Cosmic Code: Quantum Physics As the Language of Nature* (New York: Bantam Books, 1983), 41.
9. Ibid.
10. H. R. Schilling, *The New Consciousness in Science and Religion* (London: SCM Press, 1973), 75.
11. F. A. Wolf, *Star Wave: Mind, Consciousness, and Quantum Physics* (New York: Macmillan, 1984), 6.
12. See K. Pribram, *Languages of the Brain* (Englewood Cliffs, N.J.: Prentice-Hall, 1971).
13. D. Bohm, cited in R. Weber, "The Enfolding-Unfolding Universe: A Conversation with David Bohm," in *The Holographic Paradigm*, ed. by Ken Wilber (Boulder, Colo.: New Science Library, 1982), 72.
14. C. G. Jung, "Definitions," *Collected Works* (Princeton, N.J.: Princeton University Press, 1971), Vol. 6, paragraph 770.

15. D. Rudhyar, *The Astrology of Personality* (Garden City, N.Y.: Doubleday, 1970), 69.
16. H. Bergson, *The Two Sources of Morality and Religion* (Garden City, N.Y.: Doubleday, 1970), 249.
17. Cited in B. Ghiselin, *The Creative Process: A Symposium* (New York: New American Library, 1952), 11.
18. See M. Ullman and C. Limmer, eds., *The Variety of Dream Experience: Expanding Our Ways of Working with Dreams* (New York: Continuum, 1988).
19. See H. Bergson, *The Two Sources of Morality and Religion*, 120.
20. Ibid., 264.
21. Ibid., 258.
22. P. Goldberg, *The Intuitive Edge*, 151.
23. W. Harman and H. Rheingold, *Higher Creativity* (Los Angeles: J. P. Tarcher, 1984), 135.
24. R. W. Emerson, *The Conduct of Life*, 53.

CHAPTER 9. CREATIVITY: SELF-ACTUALIZATION AND TRANSCENDENCE

1. R. May, *The Courage to Create* (New York: Bantam Books, 1976), viii.
2. N. Berdyaev, *The Meaning of the Creative Act* (New York: Collier Books, 1962), 119.
3. H. Skolimowski, *The Participatory Mind*, 5.
4. Ibid., 154.
5. Ibid., 156.
6. R. Sheldrake, *The Rebirth of Nature: The Greening of Science and God* (Rochester, Vt.: Park Street Press, 1991), 139.
7. Ibid., 194.
8. R. May, *The Courage to Create*, 4.
9. J. Gebser, *Verfall und Teilhabe: Über Polarität, Dualität, Identität und den Ursprung* (Salzburg: Otto Müller Verlag, 1974), 133ff.
10. C. G. Jung, *Memories, Dreams, Reflections* (New York: Vintage Books, 1965), 338.
11. O. M. Aivanhov, *Creation: Artistic and Spiritual* (Fréjus, France: Prosveta, 1987), 173.

12. Ibid., 173.
13. R. May, *the Courage to Create*, 27.
14. N. Berdyaev, *The Meaning of the Creative Act*, 93.
15. Ibid., 93.
16. Ibid., 97.
17. C. G. Jung, *Memories, Dreams, Reflections*, 357.
18. W. Fifield, *In Search of Genius* (New York: William Morrow, 1982), 54.
19. Ibid., 119.
20. See K. Wilber, *The Atman Project: A Transpersonal View of Human Development* (Wheaton, Ill.: Quest Books, 1980).
21. N. Berdyaev, *The Meaning of the Creative Act*, 134.
22. Ibid., 150–151.
23. R. May, *The Courage to Create*, 147.
24. See O. Rank, *Art and Artist: Creative Urge and Personality Development* (New York: Agathon Press, 1968).
25. Sermon 48 in J. Quint, *Meister Eckehart*, 381–382.

CHAPTER 10. HIGHER CONSCIOUSNESS

1. See A. Combs, *The Radiance of Being: Complexity, Chaos and the Evolution of Consciousness* (Edinburgh, Scotland: Floris Books, 1995/New York: Paragon House, 1996), 187ff., for a useful discussion of the crucial distinction between *states* and *structures* of consciousness.
2. J. White, ed., *The Highest State of Consciousness* (New York: Anchor Books, 1972), vii.
3. J. White, *The Meeting of Science and Spirit* (New York: Paragon House, 1990), 4.
4. Ibid., 5.
5. See A. Watts, *Psychotherapy East and West* (New York: Mentor Books, 1961).
6. Bubba [Da] Free John, *The Paradox of Instruction* (San Francisco: Dawn Horse Press, 1977), 98.
7. See, e.g., G. I. Gurdjieff, *All and Everything* (New York: Harcourt, Brace, & Co., 1950) and *Meetings with Remarkable Men* (New York: E. P. Dutton, 1963).

Chapter 11. The Art of Self-Understanding and Self-Transformation

1. For an affirmative discussion of self-awareness in nonhuman mammals, see D. R. Griffin, *Animal Minds* (Chicago and London: University of Chicago Press, 1992); J. M. Masson and S. McCarthy, *When Elephants Weep: The Emotional Lives of Animals* (New York: Delacorte Press, 1995); P. Cavalieri and P. Singer, *The Great Ape Project: Equality Beyond Humanity* (New York: St. Martin's Press, 1994); B. Kevles, *Thinking Gorillas: Testing and Teaching the Greatest Ape* (New York: E. P. Dutton, 1980); D. L. Cheney and R. M. Seyfarth, *How Monkeys See the World: Inside the Mind of Another Species* (Chicago and London: University of Chicago Press, 1992); R. J. Schusterman, J. A. Thomas, and F. G. Wood, ed., *Dolphin Cognition and Behavior: A Comparative Approach* (Hillsdale, N.J., and London: Lawrence Erlbaum Associates, 1986).
2. D. Hume, *A Treatise of Human Nature*, I, VI, iv.
3. C. Tart, *States of Consciousness* (El Cerrito, Calif.: Psychological Processes Inc., 1983), 160.
4. M. Csikzsentmihalyi, *Flow: The Psychology of Optimal Experience* (New York: HarperPerennial, 1990), 63.
5. Ibid., 64.
6. K. Wilber, *Sex, Ecology, Spirituality: The Spirit of Evolution* (Boston: Shambhala Publications, 1995), 230.
7. A. Maslow, *The Farther Reaches of Human Nature* (Harmonsworth, England: Penguin Books, 1971), 45–46.
8. Ibid., 49.
9. See S. Keleman, *Your Body Speaks Its Mind* (Berkeley, Calif.: Center Press, 1981).
10. C. T. Tart, *Waking Up*, 197.
11. Ibid., 206–207.
12. *Views from the Real World: Early Talks of Gurdjieff*, ed. anonymously (New York: E. P. Dutton, 1975), 88.

CHAPTER 12. THE SHADOW OF ENLIGHTENMENT

1. See H. V. Guenther, *Tibetan Buddhism in Western Perspective* (Emeryville, Calif.: Dharma Publishing, 1977), 179.
2. Tarthang Tulku, "Bring the Teachings Alive," *Crystal Mirror*, Vol. 4 (1975), 166.
3. G. Feuerstein, *Holy Madness: The Shock Tactics and Radical Teachings of Crazy-Wise Adepts, Holy Fools, and Rascal Gurus* (New York: Paragon House, 1991), 240.
4. Ibid., 204.
5. Ibid., 213.
6. Ibid., 244.
7. Let us recall here Ralph Waldo Emerson's pertinent remarks, "A good deal of our politics is physiological." *The Conduct of Life*, 156.
8. Translated by D. T. Suzuki, as cited in A. W. Watts, *The Meaning of Happiness* (New York: Perennial Library, 1970), 153–154.

CHAPTER 13. FREEDOM, DESTINY, AND THE QUANTUM REALITY

1. Paul Tillich, *The Courage to Be*, 58–59.
2. J. J. Rousseau, *The Social Contract*, I.1.
3. F. Franck, *To Be Human Against All Odds* (Berkeley, Calif.: Asian Humanities Press, 1991), 126.
4. P. Brunton, *Relativity*, 12–13.
5. Ibid., 66.
6. K. Wilber, *The Spectrum of Consciousness* (Wheaton, Ill.: Quest Books, 1993), xvi. First published in 1977.
7. Ibid., xvi.
8. K. Wilber, *Sex, Ecology, and Spirituality*, 268.
9. F. Capra, *The Tao of Physics* (New York: Bantam Books, 1977), 296.
10. C. F. von Weizsäcker, *The Unity of Nature* (New York: Farrar, Straus, Giroux, 1980), 255.
11. Ibid., 391.

CHAPTER 14. THE QUEST FOR WHOLENESS

1. J. Meller, *The Buckminster Fuller Reader* (Harmondsworth, England: Pelican Books, 1972), 358.
2. See J. Gebser, *The Ever-Present Origin*. See also G. Feuerstein, *Structures of Consciousness*.
3. See K. Wilber, *Sex, Ecology, Spirituality*, 50, where he reminds his readers that Arne Naess, "the patron saint of deep ecology," saw hierarchy as a valid and necessary counterpoint to holism on the one side and atomism on the other.
4. See, e.g., the astute and in many respects valid critique of deep ecology by G. Bradford, *How Deep Is Deep Ecology?* (Ojai, Calif.: Times Change Press, 1989).
5. See E. Schur, *The Awareness Trap: Self-Absorption Instead of Social Change* (New York: McGraw Hill, 1977).
6. See W. A. Johnson, *The Search for Transcendence: A Theological Analysis of Nontheological Attempts to Define Transcendence* (New York: Harper Colophon Books, 1974).
7. Ibid., 142.
8. Ibid., 143.
9. Ken Wilber argues against labeling the ultimate Being as "Whole" and prefers to call it "the All." His reason for this is that holarchy is open-ended and that to speak of the ultimate Reality as *the* Whole runs the great risk of projecting totalitarian ideas into it. This makes sense within Wilber's philosophical framework. However, if we understand that "Whole" equals "whole-within-whole-within whole ad infinitum," we will bypass the danger of reductionistic holism. I believe this is how, for the most part, the concept has been understood in the spiritual traditions. See K. Wilber, *Sex, Ecology, Spirituality*, 37.
10. G. B. Leonard, *Education and Ecstasy* (New York: Delta Books, 1968), 215.
11. See O. L. Reiser, *The Integration of Human Knowledge: A Study of the Formal Foundations and the Social Implications of Unified Science* (Boston: Extending Horizons Books, 1958).
12. See J. Gebser, *The Ever-Present Origin*.

13. For a highly readable discussion of symbolist thinking, see R. Grasse, *The Waking Dream* (Wheaton, Ill.: Quest Books, 1996). Grasse rightly calls symbolist thinking the "forgotten language."
14. See G. Feuerstein, S. Kak, and D. Frawley, *In Search of the Cradle of Civilization*.

CHAPTER 15. THE NEW AGE: REGRESSION OR POSSIBILITY?

1. See I. Prigogine and I. Stengers, *Order Out of Chaos: Man's New Dialogue with Nature* (New York: Bantam Books, 1984).
2. R. Walsh, *Staying Alive* (Boston: New Science Library, 1984), 75.
3. R. Heilbroner, *An Inquiry into the Human Prospect* (New York: W. W. Norton, 1974), 142.
4. See R. Sheldrake, *A New Science of Life: The Hypothesis of Formative Causation* (Los Angeles: J. P. Tarcher, 1981).
5. The concept of "New Age" is highly ambiguous, as can readily be gleaned from David Spangler's discussion on "Images of the New Age" in D. Spangler and W. I. Thompson, *Reimagination of the World: A Critique of the New Age, Science, and Popular Culture* (Santa Fe: Bear & Co., 1991), 22–33. Here the New Age is spoken of as "a call to learning," "an image of transformation," "a way of talking about the future," "the effort of people to be midwives of a better future," "a spiritual phenomenon," "a symbol of the spirit of renewal and creativity," "not an event but a process," "a state of mind," "a way of looking at the world," "a specific spiritual force acting upon humanity and the world," "an image of the future." Spangler also observes with regret that "The image of the New Age may well have died as a useful tool of the imagination for anyone seriously attempting to work with civilizational change and betterment"(31).
6. See A. Maslow, *The Farther Reaches of Human Nature* (Harmondsworth, England: Penguin, 1973).
7. B. Lonergan, *Method in Theology* (New York: Herder and Herder, 1972), 104.

8. R. Heinberg, *Memories and Visions of Paradise: Exploring the Universal Myth of a Lost Golden Age* (Wheaton, Ill.: Quest Books, 1995), 277.

9. On the "Yoga of participation," see H. Skolimowski, *The Participatory Mind: A New Theory of Knowledge and of the Universe* (London and New York: Penguin/Arkana Books, 1994).

CHAPTER 16: TOWARD INTEGRAL CONSCIOUSNESS

1. See, e.g., L. deMause, *Foundations of Psychohistory* (New York: Creative Roots Inc., 1982). Lloyd deMause, a trail blazer in the field, is director of the Institute for Psychohistory and publisher of *The Journal of Psychohistory*. See also H. Lawton, *The Psychohistorian's Handbook* (New York: Psychohistory Press, 1988).

2. See J. Gebser, *The Ever-Present Origin*; K. Wilber, *Up From Eden: A Transpersonal View of Human Evolution* (New York: Anchor Press, 1981); D. Elgin, *Awakening Earth*; G. Feuerstein, *Structures of Consciousness* and *Wholeness or Transcendence? Ancient Lessons for the Emerging Global Civilization* (Burdett, N.Y.: Larson Publications, 1992).

3. J. Gebser, *The Ever-Present Origin*, 21.

4. See O. Spengler, *The Decline of the West* (New York: Knopf, 1939).

5. J. Gebser, *In der Bewährung: Zen Hinweise auf das neue Bewusstsein* (Bern and Munich: Francke Verlag, 1969), 7 (my translation).

6. J. Gebser, *The Ever-Present Origin*, 539.

7. See C. Tart, *Waking Up*.

8. C. G. Jung, ed., *Man and His Symbols*, 84.

9. See K. Wilber, *Sex, Ecology, Spirituality*.

10. J. Gebser, *The Ever-Present Origin*, 359.

11. See the excellent account by P. Davis, *About Time: Einstein's Unfinished Revolution* (New York: Simon & Schuster, 1995).

12. See D. Bohm, *Wholeness and the Implicate Order* (London: Routledge & Kegan Paul, 1980).

13. J. Gebser, "In Search of the New Consciousness," transl. by Georg Feuerstein (Lower Lake, Calif.: Integral Publishing, 1992). The essay comprising this broadside was originally published in German in Gebser's book *Verfall und Teilhabe*.

14. See A. Maslow, *The Farther Reaches of Human Nature*.

15. D. Elgin, *Awakening Earth*, 316.

CHAPTER 17. REMEMBERING THE FUTURE

1. See T. McKenna, *The Archaic Revival*.

2. P. Teilhard de Chardin, *The Future of Man* (Glasgow: Fount Paperbacks, 1977), 323.

3. T. McKenna, 113.

4. See R. Erdoes, *AD 1000: Living on the Brink of Apocalypse* (San Francisco: Harper & Row, 1988).

5. A. Toynbee, *Civilization on Trial and The World and the West* (New York: Meridian Books, 1958), 58.

6. See, e.g., T. McKenna, *The Invisible Landscape: Mind, Hallucinogens, and the I Ching* (San Francisco: Harper, 1993); J. Arguelles, *The Mayan Factor: Path Beyond Technology* (Santa Fe: Bear & Co., 1987); B. Marx Hubbard, *The Revelation: A Message of Hope for the New Millennium* (Novato, Calif.: Nataraj, 1995); "Firing the Cosmic Trigger," with R. A. Wilson, in D. J. Brown and R. McClen Novick, *Mavericks of the Mind: Conversations for the New Millennium* (Freedom, Calif.: Crossing Press, 1993); P. Russell, *The White Hole in Time: Our Future Evolution and the Meaning of Now* (San Francisco: Harper, 1992).

7. F. A. Wolf, *Parallel Universe: The Search for Other Worlds* (New York: Simon and Schuster, 1988), 298–299.

SELECT BIBLIOGRAPHY

*Further bibliographic references are given
in the endnotes to each chapter.*

Aivanhov, O. M. *"Know Thyself"—Jnana Yoga*. Part 2. Fréjus, France: Prosveta, 1992.

———. *Creation: Artistic and Spiritual*. Fréjus, France: Prosveta, 1987.

Berdyaev, N. *The Meaning of the Creative Act*. New York: Collier Books, 1962.

Bergson, H. *The Two Sources of Morality and Religion*. Garden City, N.Y.: Doubleday, 1970.

Berman, M. *The Reenchantment of the World*. New York: Bantam Books, 1984.

Bohm, D. *Wholeness and the Implicate Order*. London: Routledge & Kegan Paul, 1980.

———, and M. Edwards, *Changing Consciousness: Exploring the Hidden Source of the Social, Political and Environmental Crises Facing Our World*. San Francisco: Harper, 199ı.

Brunton, P. *Notebooks of Paul Brunton*. Vol. 13: *Relativity, Philosophy, and Mind*. Burdett, N.Y.: Larson Publications, 1988.

Capra, F. *The Tao of Physics*. New York: Bantam Books, 1977.

Combs, A. *The Radiance of Being: Complexity, Chaos and the Evolution of Consciousness*. New York: Paragon House, 1996.

Csikzsentmihalyi, M. *Flow: The Psychology of Optimal Experience*. New York: HarperPerennial, 1990.

deMause, L. *Foundations of Psychohistory*. New York: Creative Roots Inc., 1982.

Dossey, L. *Recovering the Soul*. New York: Bantam Books, 1989.

———. *Healing Words: The Power of Prayer and the Practice of Medicine*. New York: HarperCollins, 1993.

Dychtwald, K. *Bodymind*. Los Angeles: J. P. Tarcher, 1986.

Elgin, D. *Awakening Earth: Exploring the Evolution of Human Culture and Consciousness*. New York: William Morrow, 1993.

Emerson, R. W. *Conduct of Life, Nature and Other Essays*. London: Dent; New York: Dutton, 1908.

Feuerstein, G. *Structures of Consciousness: The Genius of Jean Gebser*. Lower Lake, Calif.: Integral Publishing, 1987.

———. *Wholeness or Transcendence? Ancient Lessons for the Emerging Global Civilization*. Burdett, N.Y.: Larson Publications, 1992.

———, S. Kak, and D. Frawley. *In Search of the Cradle of Civilization: New Light on Ancient India*. Wheaton, Ill.: Quest Books, 1995.

Franck, F. *Fingers Pointing Toward the Sacred: A Twentieth Century Pilgrimage on the Eastern and Western Way*. Junction City, Ore.: Beacon Point Press, 1994.

———. *To Be Human Against All Odds*. Berkeley, Calif.: Asian Humanities Press, 1991.

Frankl, V. *The Will to Meaning: Foundations and Applications of Logotherapy*. New York: New American Library, 1970.

Gebser, J. *The Ever-Present Origin*. Transl. by N. Barstad with A. Mickunas. Athens, Ohio: Ohio University Press, 1985.

Ghiselin, B. *The Creative Process: A Symposium*. New York: New American Library, 1952.

Goldberg, P. *The Intuitive Mind*. Los Angeles: J. P. Tarcher, 1983.

Grasse, R. *The Waking Dream: Unlocking the Symbolic Language of Our Lives*. Wheaton, Ill.: Quest Books, 1996.

Grosso, M. *The Frontiers of the Soul*. Wheaton, Ill.: Quest Books, 1992.

Guenther, H. V. *Tibetan Buddhism in Western Perspective*. Emeryville, Calif.: Dharma Publishing, 1977.

Gurdjieff, G. I. *All and Everything*. New York: Harcourt, Brace, & Co., 1950.

————. *Meetings with Remarkable Men.* New York: E. P. Dutton, 1963.

Harman, W. *Global Mind Change.* Indianapolis: Knowledge Systems, 1988.

————, and H. Rheingold. *Higher Creativity.* Los Angeles: J. P. Tarcher, 1984.

Heilbroner, R. *An Inquiry Into the Human Prospect.* New York: W. W. Norton, 1974.

Heinberg, R. *Memories and Visions of Paradise: Exploring the Universal Myth of a Lost Golden Age.* Wheaton, Ill.: Quest Books, 1995.

Huxley, A. *The Perennial Philosophy.* New York: Harper & Row, 1970.

Integrative Explorations: Journal of Culture and Consciousness. Edited by M. Purdy. University Park, Ill.: Governors State University, 1993–present.

James, W. *The Varieties of Religious Experience.* New York: Collier Books, 1961.

Johnson, W. A. *The Search for Transcendence: A Theological Analysis of Nontheological Attempts to Define Transcendence.* New York: Harper Colophon Books, 1974.

Jung, C. G. *Modern Man in Search of a Soul.* New York: Harcourt, Brace, & Co., 1933.

————. *On the Nature of the Psyche.* Princeton, N.J.: Princeton University Press, 1969.

————. *Man and His Symbols.* New York: Dell Publishing, 1968.

————. *Memories, Dreams, Reflections.* New York: Vintage Books, 1965.

Keleman, S. *Your Body Speaks Its Mind.* Berkeley, Calif.: Center Press, 1981.

La Berge, S. *Lucid Dreaming.* Los Angeles: J. P. Tarcher, 1985.

————, and H. Rheingold, *Exploring the World of Lucid Dreaming.* New York: Ballantine Books, 1990.

Lawton, H. *The Psychohistorian's Handbook.* New York: Psychohistory Press, 1988.

Leder, D. *The Absent Body.* Chicago: University of Chicago Press, 1990.

Leonard, G. B. *Education and Ecstasy.* New York: Delta Books, 1968.

Maslow, A. *The Farther Reaches of Human Nature.* Harmonsworth, England: Penguin Books, 1971.

May, R. *Man's Search for Himself.* New York: Delta Books, 1953.

———. *The Courage to Create.* New York: Bantam Books, 1976.

McKenna, T. *The Archaic Revival.* San Francisco: Harper, 1992.

———. *The Invisible Landscape: Mind, Hallucinogens, and the I Ching.* San Francisco: Harper, 1993.

Murphy, M. *The Future of the Body: Explorations Into the Further Evolution of Human Nature.* Los Angeles: J. P. Tarcher, 1992.

———, and R. A. White. *In the Zone: Transcendent Experience in Sports.* New York and London: Penguin Books, 1995.

MuseLetter. Published and edited by R. Heinberg, 1433 Olivet Road, Santa Rosa, CA 95401, 1992–present.

Needleman, J. *A Sense of the Cosmos: The Encounter of Modern Science and Ancient Truth.* New York: E. P. Dutton, 1977.

Nelson, J. *Healing the Split: Integrating Spirit Into Our Under-standing of the Mentally Ill.* Albany, N.Y.: SUNY Press, rev. ed. 1994.

Pagels, H. R. *The Cosmic Code: Quantum Physics as the Language of Nature.* New York: Bantam Books, 1983.

Penfield, W. *The Mystery of the Mind.* Princeton, N.J.: Princeton University Press, 1975.

Plotinus. *The Enneads.* Transl. by S. MacKenna. Burdett, N.Y.: Larson Publications, 1992.

Poortman, J. J. *Vehicles of Consciousness: The Concept of Hylic Pluralism,* 4 vols. Utrecht, The Netherlands: Theosophical Publishing House, 1978.

Pribram, K. *Languages of the Brain.* Englewood Cliffs, N.J.: Prentice-Hall, 1971.

Prigogine, I., and I. Stengers. *Order Out of Chaos: Man's New Dialogue with Nature.* New York: Bantam Books, 1984.

Quint, J. *Meister Eckehart: Deutsche Predigten und Traktate.* Munich: Carl Hanser, 1963.

Ring, K. *Heading Toward Omega.* New York: Morrow, 1985.

Roszak, T. *The Voice of the Earth.* New York: Simon & Schuster, 1992.

Russell, P. *The White Hole in Time: Our Future Evolution and the Meaning of Now.* San Francisco: Harper, 1992.

Schilling, H. R. *The New Consciousness in Science and Religion.* London: SCM Press, 1973.

Schur, E. *The Awareness Trap: Self-Absorption Instead of Social Change.* New York: McGraw-Hill, 1977.

Sheldrake, R. *A New Science of Life: The Hypothesis of Formative Causation.* Los Angeles: J. P. Tarcher, 1981.

————. *The Rebirth of Nature: The Greening of Science and God.* Rochester, Vt.: Park Street Press, 1991.

Smith, H. *Forgotten Truth.* New York: Harper & Row, 1976.

Spangler, D. and W. I. Thompson. *Reimagination of the World: A Critique of the New Age, Science, and Popular Culture.* Santa Fe: Bear & Co., 1991.

Spengler, O. *The Decline of the West.* New York: Knopf, 1939.

Talbot, M. *The Holographic Universe.* New York: HarperCollins, 1991.

Tarnas, R. *The Passion of the Western Mind.* New York: Ballantine Books, 1991.

Tart, C. *Waking Up: Overcoming the Obstacles to Human Potential.* Boston: New Science Library, 1987.

————. *Open Mind, Discriminating Mind.* San Francisco: Harper, 1989.

————. *States of Consciousness.* El Cerrito, Calif.: Psychological Processes, Inc., 1983.

Tarthang Tulku. *Openness Mind.* Emeryville, Calif.: Dharma Publishing, 1978.

Teilhard de Chardin, P. *The Phenomenon of Man.* New York: Harper Torchbooks, 1965.

————. *The Future of Man.* Glasgow: Fount Paperbacks, 1977.

Tillich, P. *The Courage to Be.* New York: Fontana Library, 1962.

Toynbee, A. *Civilization on Trial and The World and the West.* New York: Meridian Books, 1958.

Ullman, M., and C. Limmer, eds. *The Variety of Dream Experience: Expanding Our Ways of Working with Dreams.* New York: Continuum, 1988.

Vaughan, F. *Awakening Intuition.* New York: Doubleday, 1979.

Walsh, R. *Staying Alive.* Boston: New Science Library, 1984.

Watts, A. *Psychotherapy East and West.* New York: Mentor Books, 1961.

———. *The Meaning of Happiness.* New York: Perennial Library, 1970.

Weizsäcker, C. F. von. *The Unity of Nature.* New York: Farrar, Straus, Giroux, 1980.

White, J. *The Meeting of Science and Spirit.* New York: Paragon House, 1990.

———, ed. *The Highest State of Consciousness.* New York: Anchor Books, 1972.

———, ed. *Frontiers of Consciousness.* New York: Avon, 1974.

Wilber, K. *The Spectrum of Consciousness.* Wheaton, Ill.: Quest Books, 1993.

———. *Sex, Ecology, Spirituality: The Spirit of Evolution.* Boston: Shambhala Publications, 1995.

———. *The Atman Project: A Transpersonal View of Human Development.* Wheaton, Ill.: Quest Books, 1980.

———, ed. *The Holographic Paradigm.* Boulder, Colo.: New Science Library, 1982.

Wolf, F. A. *Parallel Universes: The Search for Other Worlds.* New York: Simon and Schuster, 1988.

INDEX